FACULTY
DEVELOPMENT
COLLECTION

COOPERATIVE LEARNING FOR HIGHER EDUCATION FACULTY

COOPERATIVE LEARNING FOR HIGHER EDUCATION FACULTY

Barbara J. Millis
and
Philip G. Cottell, Jr.

AMERICAN COUNCIL ON EDUCATION ★
ORYX PRESS ★
Series on Higher Education
1998

© 1998 by American Council on Education and The Oryx Press
Published by The Oryx Press
4041 North Central at Indian School Road
Phoenix, Arizona 85012-3397

Published simultaneously in Canada
Printed and bound in the United States of America

∞ The paper used in this publication meets the minimum requirements of the American National Standard for Information Sciences—Permanence of Paper for Printed Library Materials, ANSI Z39.48-1984.

Portions of this book have been adapted from Cooperative Learning Techniques and Instructors Guide: *Managerial Accounting*, by Cottell, Millis, et. al. Copyright 1997. By permission of South-Western College Publishing, a division of International Thompson Publishing Inc., Cincinnati, Ohio 45227.

Library of Congress Cataloging-in-Publication Data

Millis, Barbara J.
    Cooperative learning for higher education faculty / Barbara J.
Millis & Philip G. Cottell.
        p. cm.—(American Council on Education/Oryx Press series on higher
education)
    Includes bibliographical references (p.) and index.
    ISBN 0-89774-990-1 (alk. paper)
    1. College teaching—United States.   2. Group work in education—
United States.   3. Team learning approach in education—United
States.   4. Teaching teams—United States.   I. Cottell, Philip G.
II. Title.   III. Series.
LB2331.M4816   1998
378.1'2—dc21   97-34256
                                                              CIP

We dedicate this book:

To my family, including my beloved in-laws, Jack and Jean Millis, and in particular to Jeanne Millis, age 11, whose imitations of my cooperative-learning workshops have kept me joyful and humble. She brings love and meaning to my life.

Barbara Millis

To Lin, who has faithfully shared life with me, and to Pippin, who sat by me as I worked on the book.

Phil Cottell

CONTENTS

PREFACE

W hen Neil Davidson, president, gave a keynote address at the 1990 Conference of the International Society for the Study of Cooperation in Education, he emphasized that cooperative learning—because of its fulfillment of basic human needs, its growth as a grassroots movement, its solid research base, its endorsement by numerous state and national educational commissions, and its compatibility with virtually every sound pedagogical practice in education—was far from a passing fad.

While we were in agreement with Neil's viewpoint, we certainly did not anticipate the staggering growth of interest in cooperative learning at the postsecondary level within the past seven years. Our first attempt at collaboration, a paper on cooperative learning and accounting that was later published in the *Journal of Accounting Education*, also began at that conference. With Barbara's Ph.D. in English literature and background in faculty development, and Phil's Ph.D. in accounting and background in college teaching and research, we made an unlikely pair. On the patio of the Baltimore Convention Center, Barbara painstakingly reshaped Phil's often cumbersome prose and jokingly told him that, as a writer, he was a great accountant. Phil, on the other hand, patiently explained terms such as "fixed assets" and "accrual accounting," and dazzled Barbara with his creative accounting applications for cooperative learning. Just as we could not have predicted the surge of interest in cooperative learning, we likewise did not anticipate that our initial collaboration would lead to more co-authored articles, joint workshop presentations, an ongoing friendship between our two families, and, finally, this book.

This book has been a genuine labor of love as the two of us, in our respective disciplines, have explored the efficacy and the enjoyment of using cooperative-learning approaches. We are thrilled at the opportunity to share with readers what we and our cooperative friends and colleagues have discovered. We are putting into this book all the things we wish someone would have told us earlier. We are trying to address all the questions, issues, and concerns that faculty have raised at workshops, in e-mail messages, or even on airplanes. Since we find faculty both curious and hesitant, we go into detail about essential matters, such as classroom management. We also carefully provide examples of many cooperative structures in a variety of disciplines, so that faculty can "connect" with the abstractions. Chapters cover the theory and research base of cooperative learning; assessment and faculty development issues; technology compatibility; and the use of cooperative learning with teaching approaches such as the case method, problem-based learning, and cooperative games.

There is also much more.

Perhaps the greatest strength of this book lies in its thorough grounding in what is known about student learning. Too often, cooperative learning is viewed as a series of quick gimmicks, or, worse, it is simply equated with other less-structured approaches to group work. It has been confused, for example, with the ubiquitous group project, where students struggle to find mutual meeting times outside of class to produce a product, unified only by the click of a stapler, for which they all receive the same grade, regardless of effort or merit.

This book emphasizes the two key characteristics of cooperative learning. The first is its ability to create genuine communities within classrooms. Both research and practice converge on this point: when students, however diverse, work together on cooperative tasks in an atmosphere of cooperative civility where they contribute their fair share, they grow to like and respect one another.

The second characteristic is equally compelling. Deep learning is promoted by well-structured, sequenced assignments where students learn independently outside of class and then "process" the material cooperatively, in meaningful ways, to receive feedback on learning. Cooperative-learning activities allow students to internalize information, linking it in personal ways to what they already know. Thus, cooperative learning promotes both positive affective outcomes and academic achievement. Students connected to each other and to the topics they study are more motivated to learn.

Phil and I have witnessed, firsthand, the power cooperative learning has to transform students. Between us, we have taught both traditional and nontraditional students in a variety of settings, including a liberal arts college, a state research institution, a community college, an international school, a continuing education program, and a U.S. service academy. In our community service efforts, we have also seen cooperative-learning approaches have an impact on

Sunday school students, Slim for Life teachers, sheriff's deputies, and Girl Scouts. We have also seen the rejuvenating influence cooperative learning has had on us. It has prompted reflection, creativity, and laughter, and has created touching memories, such as the poignant end-of-course comment by a young Vietnamese daycare worker in Barbara's literature course: "In this class, I have found true friends."

We sincerely hope that, as it moves you toward cooperative classrooms, this book will have an impact on you as well. We wish you joyful success.

PART ONE

· · · · · · · · ·

Overviews of Cooperative Learning and Teaching and Learning

CHAPTER 1

An Overview of Cooperative Learning in Higher Education

"Tell me and I'll listen. Show me and I'll understand. Involve me and I'll learn."

Teton Lakota Indians

This book is about innovation, change, and renewal. It offers faculty members the rationale for such changes, including theory and research, and also provides a commonsense, one-step-at-a-time approach. It invites faculty to engage in what might be called "reflective action" and encourages them to deliberately bridge the gap between theory and practice, becoming what Schon (1987) calls "reflective practitioners." Reflective practice is inevitably context-specific. It asks key questions such as what is being taught to whom, and how and why? Perhaps most important, it initiates a call for action through a final question, "What might I do differently?"

This question of action is critically important because much of the well-intentioned literature on higher education reform tends to be theoretical and exhortative: Use active learning techniques; Be responsive in the classroom; Respect diversity. Well-intentioned faculty are often at a loss for practical ways to operationalize these new challenges. Such challenges have come from many professions, including accounting, mathematics, and the sciences. The Accounting Education Change Commission (1990), for example, has alerted faculty to the need for new approaches to teaching and learning. Specifically, the commission endorses active learning, complex problem solving, experiential approaches, group work, and innovative uses of technology.

Too often, such challenges leave faculty with a sense of schizophrenic overload. How can they respond simultaneously and responsibly to demands to internationalize the curriculum, help students from various ethnic and educational backgrounds become information literate, and introduce meaningful writing and critical-thinking activities? Inserting new elements into existing courses—without a clear sense of purpose, commitment, or competence—can result in a half-hearted "Band-Aid" approach. Worse still, faculty, feeling under siege, may simply reject calls for innovation entirely and retreat to the well-known, comfortable techniques they have always used.

Neither of these responses need occur. Faculty can thoughtfully and deliberately transform their classes through a time-tested, increasingly well-known pedagogy called cooperative learning. They can do so initially without altering their evaluation criteria, radically changing course content, or eschewing creative lecturing or other effective teaching methods. Too good to be true? Not necessarily. Cooperative learning offers faculty members and students a clear philosophical basis for change, one solidly grounded in theory and research. Furthermore, because cooperative learning offers specific implementation tools called *structures*, which are discussed and illustrated in later chapters, faculty can move directly from theory and research toward successful classroom applications.

THE THEORETICAL BASE FOR COOPERATIVE LEARNING

The idea of collaboration and cooperation in education is far from new. Early humans functioned in groups, training their young to be hunters and gatherers. The Talmud ties learning to a text, a teacher, and a learning partner. The early Greeks valued—if not Socrates—the Socratic method, and apprenticeship/mentoring practices have a long and viable history. Both the United States and Canada share the tradition of the "little red schoolhouse," where older scholars coached younger ones over well-worn pages of McGuffey Readers. Bruffee (1993) points out that interdependence is well-known to current college and university students who participate in sports activities or community projects, plan parties or protest marches, and recognize that their future lies in arenas such as government, industry, science, and the professions, where teamwork and cooperation are increasingly important (p. 2). Thus, although faculty may be skeptical about the aura of newness surrounding cooperative learning in higher education, its concepts and approaches have been known and used for decades.

Cooperative learning can be regarded as a more-structured, hence more-focused, form of collaborative learning. Cuseo (1992), for example, has developed an elaborate taxonomy that places cooperative learning as a collaborative learning subtype under "Collaboration between Students."

Smith and MacGregor (1992) agree with Cuseo that collaborative learning is the broader term, one encompassing

> A variety of educational approaches involving joint intellectual effort by students, or students and teachers together. In most collaborative-learning situations, students are working in groups of two or more, mutually searching for understanding, solutions, or meanings, or creating a product. There is wide variability in collaborative-learning activities, but most center on the students' exploration or application of the course material, not simply the teacher's presentation or explication of it. Everyone in the class is participating, working as partners or in small groups. Questions, problems, or the challenge to create something drive the group activity. Learning unfolds in the most public of ways (p. 10).

As a highly structured subset of collaborative learning, Cuseo (1992) finds cooperative learning to be "the most operationally well-defined and procedurally structured form of collaboration among students . . . [and it] has been the most researched and empirically well-documented form of collaborative learning in terms of its positive impact on multiple outcome measures" (p. 3).

As might be expected, cooperative learning and collaborative learning share a common philosophical framework. Underlying both approaches are a respect for students of all backgrounds and a belief in their potential for academic success. Thus, as Sapon-Shevin, Ayres, and Duncan (1994) suggest: "Cooperative learning . . . builds upon heterogeneity and formalizes and encourages peer support and connection. . . . **All** students need to learn and work in environments where their individual strengths are recognized and individual needs are addressed. **All** students need to learn within a supportive community in order to feel safe enough to take risks" (p. 46).

Both cooperative learning and collaborative learning share a sense of community; learning is inherently social. This socioinstructional approach helps students become cognitively involved with content through systematic classroom interactions, and an intellectual synergy develops. Furthermore, positive peer relationships typically emerge. Cooper and Mueck (1990) note: "The most consistent positive findings for cooperative learning . . . have centered on affective or attitudinal change. Outcome measures such as racial/ ethnic relations, sex difference relations, self-esteem, and other prosocial outcomes have all been documented in the cooperative learning research" (p. 71).

This belief in constructive social interaction leads to a third commonality. Both cooperative and collaborative learning share a belief that learning is an active, constructive process. Myers and Jones (1993) find that such learning "provides opportunities for students to **talk and listen, read, write,** and **reflect** as they approach course content through problem-solving exercises, informal small groups, simulations, case studies, role playing, and other activities—all of which require students to **apply** what they are learning" (p. xi). As a result, learning is not passively absorbed, nor are facts simply added systematically to existing schemata. Students often take new material and integrate, reinterpret, and transform it until new knowledge is forged. In this way, learning is produced, not reproduced, and the role of the instructor changes from a deliverer of information to a facilitator of learning. This does not mean that faculty members, who will always remain authorities in the definitive sense, abdicate their responsibility to students; rather, it means that they assume different roles, such as that of midwife professors who "assist . . . students in giving birth to their own ideas, in making tacit knowledge explicit and elaborating on it" (Belenky, Clinchy, Goldberger, and Tarule, 1986, p. 217).

Several recent articles have explored more fully the commonalities and distinctions between collaborative and cooperative learning. Kenneth Bruffee (1995), for example, sees cooperative learning, because it was developed at the pre-collegiate level, as a more "repressive" form of pedagogy with teacher-developed goals and assessments, constant supervision, and the discouragement of dissent. Collaborative learning, he feels, is more adult-centered because it assumes student responsibility for governance and evaluation and encourages disagreement. Bruffee's position fails to recognize the major concerns of virtually all faculty committed to group work: time and content coverage. In an ideal learning environment, students would be free to explore topics as a "shared conversation," reach their own conclusions, and clarify, and sometimes resolve, any academic or interpersonal disagreements. The reality is that the typical classroom is still bounded by traditional "seat time" constraints and the enormous pressure on disciplines, in an expanding "information age," to introduce students to important concepts and core knowledge. Furthermore, in classrooms filled with diverse learners at all levels of academic preparation and social enculturation, there are compelling reasons why faculty and students should deliberately create an environment where learning can be both efficient and effective. Bruffee also neglects to emphasize the wide range of shared assumptions between the two approaches. These shared assumptions are clearly articulated in a later article by Matthews, Cooper, Davidson, and Hawks (1995):

- learning in an active mode is more effective than passively receiving information;
- the teacher is a facilitator, coach, or midwife rather than a "sage on the stage";
- teaching and learning are shared experiences between teacher and students;
- balancing lecture and small-group activities is an important part of a teacher's role;

- participating in small-group activities develops higher-order thinking skills and enhances individual abilities to use knowledge;
- accepting responsibility for learning as an individual and as a member of a group enhances intellectual development;
- articulating one's ideas in a small-group setting enhances a student's ability to reflect on his or her own assumptions and thought processes;
- developing social and team skills through the give-and-take of consensus building is a fundamental part of a liberal education;
- belonging to a small and supportive academic community increases student success and retention; and
- appreciating (or at least acknowledging the value of) diversity is essential for the survival of a multicultural democracy (p. 37).

Perhaps a sensible approach is one advocated by Macaulay and Gonzales (1996). They view collaborative and cooperative learning as lying on a continuum, with collaborative learning being the least structured and cooperative learning the most structured. In practice, most faculty will cruise from one end of this theoretically constructed Likert scale to the other, varying their approaches from course to course or class to class. In fact, when the planning areas are taken into account (instructional activity; instructor's role; students' roles; introduction of group dynamics; group formation; rules for instruction; and assessment/evaluation), faculty may vary their approaches within an activity. During a peer-editing session, for example, the students' roles within deliberately teacher-formed teams might be carefully and fully designated by the instructor (a cooperative approach) who then leaves the room (a collaborative approach).

Most faculty find that students, even adults, welcome the structure provided by a cooperative approach. In fact, practitioners find that the structured nature of cooperative learning results in both efficiency and accountability in the classroom. Cooper (1990) regards the key to successful cooperative learning as "Structure! Structure! Structure!" (p. 1). The end goal should be a smoothly operating classroom, but not one that runs with clockwork-like precision. Palmer (1996) eloquently reminds us that

> It seems to me terribly important that when we look at a model . . ., we not ask ourselves what I think is a dead-end question, which is, "How can we replicate this exact approach in our situation?" I don't think that's the issue here. I think the issue here is to understand the underpinnings of the model itself. How it is that knowing, teaching, and learning are enhanced, not just by a particular form of community, but by engendering a "capacity for connectedness?" Our challenge is not to reduce good teaching to a particular form, model, methodology, or technique, but to understand its dynamics at the deeper levels, the underpinnings, to understand the dynamics that make connectedness a powerful force for learning in whatever form it takes (p. 12).

It is difficult to dissect learning. It cannot be, to quote T. S. Eliot in another context, "spread out like a patient etherized upon a table." Nonetheless, over the years a great deal of research has looked at the efficacy of cooperative learning, often based on outcome measures, and more recently at the "conditions under which the use of small groups in classrooms can be productive" (Cohen, 1994, p. 1). The theoretical underpinnings of cooperative learning are, in fact, solidly grounded in research—a comfort to faculty members who need reassurance that cooperative learning is not merely an educational fad.

THE RESEARCH BASE

Faculty reluctant to consider cooperative learning can be reassured by the fact that the research base for cooperative learning is longstanding and solid. Both the learning outcomes and the social dynamics of cooperative learning have been studied under a number of conditions. Slavin (1989-1990) regards it as "one of the most thoroughly researched of all instructional methods" (p. 52). Similarly, Johnson, Johnson, and Smith (1991) describe the amount of research conducted as "staggering" and conclude that:

> During the past 90 years, more than 600 studies have been conducted by a wide variety of researchers in different decades with different age subjects, in different subject areas, and in different environments. We know far more about the efficacy of cooperative learning than we know about lecturing . . . or almost any other facet of education" (p. 28).

In addition to cooperative learning's positive effect on student achievement, Johnson, Johnson, and Smith (1991) also find that it significantly affects interpersonal relations:

> As relationships within the class or college become more positive, absenteeism decreases and students' commitment to learning, feeling of personal responsibility to complete the assigned work, willingness to take on difficult tasks, motivation and persistence in working on tasks, satisfaction and morale, willingness to endure pain and frustration to succeed, willingness to defend the college against external criticism or attack, willingness to listen to and be influenced by peers, commitment to peer's success and growth, and productivity and achievement can be expected to increase (p. 44).

Faculty in higher education can feel assured, also, that, although much of the research in the last decades has been conducted at the kindergarten through twelfth grade level, its benefits, according to Natasi and Clements (1991), seem to be universal:

> Cognitive-academic and social-emotional benefits have been reported for students from early elementary through college level, from diverse ethnic and cultural backgrounds, and having a wide range of ability levels. . . .

> Furthermore, cooperative learning has been used effectively across a wide range of content areas, including mathematics, reading, language arts, social studies, and science (p. 111).

Similarly, Bossert (1988), after a meta-analysis on the now-substantial body of research, concludes that its benefits affect students of all ages, in all content areas, for a wide variety of tasks, including problem solving. Cooper and Mueck (1990) cite some important earlier studies in higher education, conducted by Dansereau (1983), Treisman (1985), and Freirson (1986), that show positive achievement gains using cooperative-learning approaches. On-going research at their campus, California State University, Dominguez Hills, suggests that "the overwhelming majority of the students prefer cooperative learning. Outcome measures such as higher-level thinking skills, interest in subject matter, general class morale, and frequency/quality of interactions with classmates receive particularly favorable ratings" (p. 71).

Johnson and Johnson (1993), after having completed a meta-analysis of the studies of cooperative learning, using college students, offer five reasons to take this research seriously:

1. CL has a rich history of theory, research, and practice. . . .
2. The research on CL has a validity and generalizability rarely found in the education literature. . . .
3. CL affects many different instructional outcomes simultaneously. . . .
4. Quite a bit is known about the essential components that make it work. . . .
5. Finally, CL creates learning opportunities that do not exist when students work competitively or individually . . . (p. 17–18).

Thus, the research from a variety of grade levels, including the college level, consistently shows positive results.

Perhaps the most compelling endorsement of cooperative learning in higher education has come from Astin's (1993) comprehensive longitudinal study of the impact of college on undergraduate students. Using samples from 159 baccalaureate-granting institutions, Astin investigated 22 outcomes affected by 88 environmental factors to determine influences on students' academic achievement, personal development, and satisfaction with college. He determined that two factors in particular, student-student interaction and student-faculty interaction, carried the largest weights and affected the greatest number of general education outcomes. Because of the influence of peers and faculty, he concludes that "how students **approach** general education (and how the faculty actually **deliver** the curriculum) is far more important than the formal curricular content and structure" (p. 425). He unequivocally endorses cooperative learning as a valid and effective pedagogical approach:

Under what we have come to call cooperative-learning methods, where students work together in small groups, students basically teach each other, and our pedagogical resources are multiplied. Classroom research has consistently shown that cooperative-learning approaches produce outcomes that are superior to those obtained through traditional competitive approaches, and it may well be that our findings concerning the power of the peer group offer a possible explanation: cooperative learning may be more potent than traditional methods of pedagogy because it motivates students to become more active and more involved participants in the learning process. This greater involvement could come in at least two different ways. First, students may be motivated to expend more effort if they know their work is going to be scrutinized by peers; and second, students may learn course material in greater depth if they are involved in helping teach it to fellow students (p. 427).

Light (1990; 1992) supports Astin's findings, particularly in the preface to the *Harvard Assessment Seminars: Second Report*, when he concludes, "All the specific findings point to, and illustrate, one main idea. It is that students who get the most out of college, who grow the most academically, and who are the happiest, organize their time to include interpersonal activities with faculty members, or with fellow students, built around substantive, academic work" (p. 6). As Cooper (1993) points out in a review, the efficacy of small groups is the overriding finding that dominates both Harvard reports.

Faculty interested in an overview of the cooperative learning research base should consult Johnson and Johnson (1994); Johnson, Johnson, and Smith (1991), particularly chapter 3; Cooper, Prescott, Cook, Smith, Mueck, and Cuseo (1990); and the cooperative learning special interest group (SIG) of the American Educational Research Association (AERA).

SOME SPECIFIC COMPONENTS OF COOPERATIVE LEARNING

Cooperative learning tends to be more carefully structured and delineated than most other forms of small-group learning. Cooper and Mueck (1990) describe it as "a structured, systematic instructional strategy in which small groups work together toward a common goal" (p. 1). Macaulay and Gonzalez (1996) characterize it as:

The instructional use of small groups so that learners are able to work together in a manner which enhances both group and individual learning. The key to cooperative learning is the careful structuring of learning groups. There are many ways to structure such groups, but some of the key elements are the building of interdependence, the designing of interactive processes, and accountability. The building of social skills around such areas as decision making, communication, and conflict management is also fundamental to cooperative learning.

An exact definition of cooperative learning is impossible because, as Davidson (1994) points out, the field offers diverse viewpoints with few points in common. He finds only five common attributes in the six major approaches. "These attributes are: (1) a common task or learning activity suitable for group work; (2) small-group learning; (3) cooperative behavior; (4) interdependence; and (5) individual accountability and responsibility" (p. 25).

Most experts, including Cooper (1990), agree that the most important of these cooperative-learning elements are positive interdependence and individual accountability. Three other components important to the authors' teaching approaches are appropriate grouping (which usually means heterogeneous grouping), group processing, and cooperative social skills.

TWO KEY COMPONENTS

Positive interdependence occurs, according to Kagan (1992), "when gains of individuals or teams are positively correlated" (p. 4:7). Johnson, Johnson, and Smith (1991) describe positive interdependence in these words:

> Cooperation results in participants' striving for mutual benefit so that all members of the group benefit from each other's efforts (your success benefits me and my success benefits you), their recognizing that all group members share a common fate (we sink or swim together) and that one's performance depends mutually on oneself and one's colleagues (we cannot do it without you), and their feeling proud and jointly celebrating when a group member is recognized for achievement (you got an A! that's terrific!) (p. 3).

In a traditional educational setting, students tend to work either on their own or in competition with one another. In a cooperative setting, all class members contribute to each other's learning. Through careful planning, positive interdependence can be established by having students achieve: (1) mutual goals, such as solving specific problems or creating a team project; (2) mutual rewards, such as individually assigned cooperative-learning points that count toward a criterion-referenced final grade (points that only help, but never handicap); (3) structured tasks, such as a report or complex problem with sections contributed by each team member; and (4) interdependent roles, such as group members serving as discussion leaders, organizers, recorders, and spokespersons. Contrary to popular opinion, cooperative learning does not entail undifferentiated group grades.

Positive interdependence empowers students who might lose their voices in traditional learning situations where the teacher and high-achieving or more vocal students tend to dominate whole-class discussions. Everyone in a well-conducted cooperative-learning classroom has an opportunity for equal participation and equal validation.

In cooperative learning, faculty members build into their syllabus and class norms the expectation that students will work together. Positive interdependence can be developed in many different ways; many would argue that it can be established most effectively through the design of the assigned activity.

A second component, individual accountability, indicates to students who might be "hitchhikers" (students who do not typically do a fair share of assigned group work) or "overachievers" or "workhorses" (students who assume a disproportionate amount of the workload), that these roles are unacceptable in a cooperative setting. Such practices are counterproductive in an environment where students, no matter how much mutual support, coaching, and encouragement they receive, are individually responsible for their own academic achievements. Because most American students, accustomed to traditional education, have been acclimated to an academic setting in which they compete against fellow classmates, this aspect of cooperative learning is somehow reassuring: their final course grades will be based on their own efforts, uncompromised and uncomplicated by the achievements of others. Faculty also generally applaud this important aspect of cooperative learning. In fact, when grading systems are formulated, students find that their efforts to help others never hurt their own achievements and can, in some cases, actually increase their course grades, either directly or indirectly. Research by Webb (1983, 1991), for example, indicates that student achievement is directly correlated to the level of elaboration of help that students provide to other group members. This finding should come as no surprise to faculty, who already know that those who teach learn the most, establishing a "win-win" situation for students.

Evaluation of students, an area of teaching often disparaged by faculty, consumes enormous energy that could be channeled more productively into teaching/learning activities. The question of how to evaluate students engaged in cooperative activities can produce anxiety and uncertainty. Unfortunately, no easy solution exists. Much of the debate centers on the question of whether students are intrinsically or extrinsically motivated. Will they work together, helping one another, when they perceive no direct "payoff"? The debate is not resolved, but a lot of good arguments on both sides have arisen. Kohn (1986; 1993) for example, argues that rewarding students by putting a price tag on efforts undermines their natural altruistic desire to help others.

There is a common misconception that group work automatically entails group grades. Nothing could be further from the truth. Individual accountability precludes this practice. Undifferentiated group grades for a single project, particularly if the majority of the work is expected out-of-class, invite equity problems. Too often, one student ends up doing the majority of the work. That student often relishes the power associated with this role, but resents the lack of input from students who will benefit from the same grade. The students who contribute little receive signals that their efforts are unappreciated or un-wanted, and they learn that there is such a thing as a "free lunch": they receive a grade they did not earn. More emphatically, Kagan suggests that basing even part of student grades on the efforts and achievements of others may be both ethically and legally unwise (private conversation, December 11, 1992).

Some professors, including those in preprofessional disciplines, may argue that "real world" preparation should put students in situations where they must negotiate each team member's input and be prepared to accept less-than optimum results. This would include situations where one team member's lack of performance drags down the team grade for all members. Decisions about grading criteria established this way obviously lie with the individual faculty member, but most cooperative-learning researchers and practitioners do not advocate undifferentiated group grades. Ethical, legal, and moral issues may be involved. Arguably, the norms, expectations, and rewards in a university setting do not equate to workplace realities, although other practices, such as teamwork itself, may have direct applications. These evaluation issues will be discussed in more detail in chapter 11.

SOME FURTHER ATTRIBUTES OF A COOPERATIVE CLASSROOM

Appropriate grouping is also essential. Researchers such as Kagan (1992) and Johnson, Johnson, and Smith (1991) recommend heterogeneous teams, re-flecting varied learning abilities, ethnic and linguistic diversity, and gender mixes. In a semester-length academic course, most practitioners recommend teacher-selected learning teams of four. Teams composed of four students work effectively because they are small enough to promote interaction, large enough to tolerate an occasional absence, and balanced enough to permit focused activities in pairs. The teams can be kept in place throughout the semester or, more typically, rearranged at the midsemester point. In briefer situations, a short-term mix of students focusing on specific learning goals is appropriate; depending on the task and the group members, these teams can be homogenous. Because most employers value cooperation and teamwork, heterogeneous teams provide opportunities to prepare for or to reinforce practices that will be needed in the workplace. Teacher-selected teams ensure heterogeneity along a number of lines, including age, ethnicity, and ability. If students are allowed to select their teammates, they tend to seek out friends or students who share similar educational, economic, or ethnic backgrounds. These homogeneous groupings tend to undermine the heterogeneity that promotes creative problem solving. When teams are formed randomly, they may be unbalanced. It could be counterproductive, for example, if all the less academically prepared students found themselves on one team.

A fourth component, group processing, helps build team skills, allows students to reflect on the learning process and outcomes, and provides teachers with continuous feedback. Teachers and students monitor group and individual progress. After an assignment or activity, for instance, students could respond to questions such as: Did all members of the group contribute? What could be done next time to make the group function better? or What were the most important things I learned today?

Social skills are also important in cooperative learning. These go beyond mere politeness. Students must recognize the importance of cooperative interaction and mutual respect. Teachers should model appropriate social skills, including ways of providing constructive feedback or eliciting more in-depth responses through probing questions. They should also reinforce these social skills by publicly commenting on ways students use them effectively.

A recent cartoon by Mel Lazarus depicts a swimming coach urging his charges to follow the "buddy system" before leaping into a lake. "Are we here to learn swimming or interpersonal relationships?" demands Ira. The answer, of course, is that collaboration in this situation provides a safe environment where learning can occur. In the college classroom a safe, supportive environment is also important. No one suggests that any students should be "coddled" or that standards should be lowered or altered; however, a positive classroom climate that encourages all students to support one another as they strive for excellence is a worthy goal. Mixing cooperative learning with traditional delivery methods allows instructors to accommodate special needs or learning styles. Developmental growth is enhanced by a climate of challenge and support. Too much challenge can discourage students, causing dropouts; too much support may result in loss of interest. Faculty members have traditionally focused on covering content, not on uncovering material, with students. Those committed to student learning will use a variety of approaches, including cooperative learning, to foster student achievement.

Would-be practitioners are reassured by the fact that cooperative-learning techniques rarely replace, in toto, such traditional approaches to learning as the lecture or teacher-directed discussion. Cooper (1990) notes that most college and university faculty use cooperative-learning techniques only about 15% to 40% of the total class time available (p. 2). As Slavin (1989-1990) cautions, "Successful [cooperative-learning] models always include plain old good instruction; the cooperative activities *supplement*, but do not replace, direct instruction" (p. 3).

The integration of cooperative-learning techniques into traditional delivery methods does emphasize a facilitative approach most students welcome. Power is shifted from the authority figure of the instructor to the students, who then become actively involved in their own learning and in the learning processes of their peers. In informal terms, the teacher becomes not the "sage on the stage," but the "guide on the side." Too often, faculty, hoping to improve their teaching, focus on How am I doing? Is my delivery well-paced? Am I covering the content? Do my students like me? A cooperative-learning approach reformulates those questions and asks such things as: How are my students doing? How can I discover if they are learning the material? Are they relating to me, the other students in class, and the learning experience? Thus, the cooperative-learning approach complements and enhances the movement fostered by Angelo and Cross (1993) toward classroom research. Such research is directed not toward traditional "publish or perish" projects, but to the assessment of what students are learning in an individual classroom. In fact, Cross postulates that this type of "pedagogical assessment" differs from traditional assessment in that it is tied directly to the teaching and learning process, looking not at "what is," but "what might be." In other words, faculty members who introduce activities such as the one-minute-paper into their classroom—an activity that asks students to answer two questions: (1) What was the most useful/meaningful thing you learned during this session? and (2) What question(s) remain uppermost in your mind as we end this session?—can use the data they collect to stimulate informed adjustments in their teaching. They can also share this feedback with students to help them improve their learning strategies and study habits. The research on what we already know about student learning provides a strong incentive for innovative changes in the way faculty teach.

For this reason, cooperative learning is also one of the most versatile educational strategies available. It complements and enhances virtually every pedagogy or approach that promotes effective teaching and learning, including classroom research; case studies; "The Seven Principles for Good Practice in Undergraduate Education" (Chickering and Gamson, 1987); and problem-based curriculum. Many of these connections will be explored in later chapters.

ACCEPTANCE OF COOPERATIVE LEARNING

Given the solid research base upon which cooperative learning rests and the testimonials of committed practitioners in all disciplines, faculty members can be confident that they are embracing a pedagogy that will pay enormous dividends, not just in student achievement, but also in affective ways. It should come as no surprise that cooperative-learning practices are becoming more and more accepted on college and university campuses. For example, Smith, Johnson, and Johnson (1992), after a review of the research, note these four trends:

1. Interest in cooperative learning in colleges and universities is growing at an incredible rate.
2. Cooperative learning is equally or more effective than lecturing in helping student[s] master conceptual material and in helping them develop cooperative skills.
3. Cooperative learning is being implemented in a wide range of courses and programs including health sciences, law, engineering, math and science, writing, communication, study skills, professional development, and teacher preparation.
4. Instructors are applying cooperative learning in a variety of ways— cooperative lecture, base groups, formal task groups, structured controversy discussion groups, jigsaw groups, and computer enhanced courses (pp. 34–35).

Similarly, another researcher in cooperative learning, Slavin (1993), announced that "After many years in elementary and secondary schools, cooperative learning (CL) is finally going to college. Of course, CL has long existed in postsecondary education; study groups, discussion groups, and work groups of various kinds are hardly new. . . . What is new in recent years is that postsecondary professors are beginning to use CL as a major focus of their teaching, and research on such applications in higher education is growing. This is an important and fundamental change" (p. 2). Practical corroboration from faculty came at the 1994 meeting of the Lilly-West Conference on College Teaching when participants were asked by Milton Cox to "list some teaching approaches that you think are emerging trends in college teaching." The ones most frequently mentioned were "collaborative and cooperative learning" (cited in Rhem, 1994, p. 12).

The latest version of a survey conducted by the Higher Education Research Institute at the University of California at Los Angeles offers even more compelling evidence that cooperative learning is becoming widely accepted in higher education. The survey, published as *The American College Teacher*, and summarized in *The Chronicle of Higher Education*, suggests that faculty are more sensitive to diversity issues, more aware of the need for varied teaching methods, and more committed to change. It indicates that faculty "are relying less on extensive lecturing—although 49% still give a lot of lectures—and more on small-group learning, group projects, and computer-aided instruction." Topping the list of teaching methods used in all or most courses is "cooperative learning," showing a 9% increase from 1989 to 1995, followed by "group projects" with a 7% increase (Magner, 1996). This finding is particularly significant because few faculty before 1988 were aware of the rapid growth of cooperative learning at the elementary and secondary levels and far fewer would have claimed to be practitioners on the university level. In fact, noneducation faculty attending the International Association for the Study of

Cooperation in Education's annual conference in Baltimore in 1990 numbered less than 30.

SUMMARY

Faculty wishing to respond to the external cries for educational reform (including those initiated within their own disciplines) and their own intrinsic desire to excel will find cooperative learning to be a practical, research-based pedagogy that will improve teaching and learning in higher education classrooms. The critical attributes of cooperative learning, a more structured form of collaborative learning, are: positive interdependence, individual accountability, appropriate grouping, group processing, and social skills. The teacher serves as a facilitator rather than as an authority figure. Cooperative-learning techniques supplement, rather than replace, traditional approaches in the classroom, but their adoption requires a student-centered, noncompetitive approach to learning.

REFERENCES

Accounting Education Change Commission. (1990, August). *AECC Urges Priority for Teaching in Higher Education*. Issues Statement No. 1, Torrance, CA: Accounting Education Change Commission.

Angelo, T.A. and Cross, K.P. (1993). *Classroom Assessment Techniques: A Handbook for College Teachers* 2d Ed. San Francisco: Jossey-Bass.

Astin, A.W. (1993). *What Matters in College: Four Critical Years Revisited*. San Francisco: Jossey-Bass.

Belenky, M.F., Clinchy, B.M., Goldberger, N.R., and Tarule, J.M. (1986). *Women's Ways of Knowing: The Development of Self, Voice, and Mind*. New York: Basic Books, Inc.

Bossert, S.T. (1988). "Cooperative Activities in the Classroom." *Review of Educational Research*, 15, 225–50.

Bruffee, K.A. (1993). *Collaborative Learning: Higher Education, Interdependence, and the Authority of Knowledge*. Baltimore, MD: The Johns Hopkins University Press.

Bruffee, K.A. (1995, Jan./Feb.). "Sharing Our Toys: Cooperative versus Collaborative Learning." *Change: The Magazine of Higher Learning*, 27(1), 12–18.

Chickering, A.W. and Gamson, A.F., (1987). *Seven Principles for Good Practice in Undergraduate Education*. Racine, WI: The Johnson Foundation, Inc./Wingspread. [Available by contacting the Seven Principles Resources Center, P.O. Box 5838, Winona State University, Winona, MN 55987-5838; (507) 457-5020].

Cohen, E.G. (1994). "Restructuring the Classroom: Conditions for Productive Small Groups." *Review of Educational Research*, 64, 1–35.

Cooper, J. (1990, May). "Cooperative Learning and College Teaching: Tips from the Trenches." *The Teaching Professor*, 4(5), 1–2.

Cooper, J. (1993). "Review of the Harvard Assessment Seminars." *Cooperative Learning: The Magazine for Cooperation in Higher Education*, 13(30), 46–47.

Cooper, J. and Mueck, R. (1990). "Student Involvement in Learning: Cooperative Learning and College Instruction." *Journal on Excellence in College Teaching*, 1, 68–76. [Article is reprinted in A. Goodsell, M. Mahler, V. Tinto, B.L. Smith, and J. MacGregor (Eds.), (1992). *Collaborative Learning: A Sourcebook for Higher Education* (pp. 68–74). University Park, PA: National Center on Postsecondary Teaching, Learning, & Assessment].

Cooper, J., Prescott, S., Cook, L., Smith, L., Mueck, R., and Cuseo, J. (1990). *Cooperative Learning and College Instruction: Effective Use of Student Learning Teams*. Long Beach, CA: The California State University Foundation.

Cuseo, J. (1992, Winter). "Collaborative & Cooperative Learning in Higher Education: A Proposed Taxonomy." *Cooperative Learning and College Teaching*, 2(2), 2–4.

Dansereau, D.F. (1983). *Cooperative Learning: Impact on Acquisition of Knowledge and Skills*. [Report No. 341]. Abilene, TX: U.S. Army Research Institute for the Behavioral and Social Sciences. [ERIC Document Reproduction Service No. ED 243 088].

Davidson, N. (1994). "Cooperative and Collaborative Learning: An Integrative Perspective." In S. S. Thousand, R.A. Villa, and A.I. Nevin (Eds.), *Creativity and Collaborative Learning: A Practical Guide to Empowering Students and Teachers*. Baltimore, MD: Paul H. Brookes Publishing Co.

Frierson, H. (1986). "Two Intervention Methods: Effects on Groups of Predominantly Black Nursing Students' Board Scores." *Journal of Research and Development in Education*, 19, 18–23.

Johnson, D.W. and Johnson, R.T. (1993, Spring). "What We Know about Cooperative Learning at the College Level." *Cooperative Learning: The Magazine for Cooperation in Higher Education*, 13(3), 17–18.

Johnson, D.W., Johnson, R.T., and Smith, K.A. (1991). *Cooperative Learning: Increasing College Faculty Instructional Productivity*. ASHE-ERIC Higher Education Report No. 4. Washington, DC: The George Washington University School of Education and Human Development.

Johnson, R.T. and Johnson, D.W. (1994). "An Overview of Cooperative Learning." In J.S. Thousand, R.A. Villa, and A.I. Nevin (Eds.), *Creativity and Collaborative Learning: A Practical Guide to Empowering Students and Teachers* (pp. 31–44). Baltimore, MD: Paul H. Brookes Publishing Co.

Kagan, S. (1992). *Cooperative Learning*. San Juan Capistrano, CA: Resources for Teachers.

Kohn, A. (1986). *No Contest: The Case Against Competition*. Boston: Houghton Mifflin.

Kohn, A. (1993). *Punished by Rewards: The Trouble with Gold Stars, Incentive Plans, A's, Praise, and other Bribes*. Boston: Houghton Mifflin.

Light, R.J. (1990). *The Harvard Assessment Seminars: First Report*. Cambridge, MA: Harvard University Press.

Light, R.J. (1992). *The Harvard Assessment Seminars: Second Report*. Cambridge, MA: Harvard University Press.

Macaulay, B. A. and Gonzales, V.G. (1996, Mar.). *Enhancing the Collaborative/Cooperative Learning Experience: A Guide for Faculty Development*. Workshop presented at the AAHE National Conference on Higher Education.

Magner, D.K. (1996, Sept.). "Fewer Professors Believe Western Culture should be the Cornerstone of the College Curriculum: A Survey Finds Growing Commitment to Diversity and Multiculturalism." *The Chronicle of Higher Education*, 43(3), A12–A15.

Matthews, R. S. , Cooper, J. L., Davidson, N., and Hawkes, P. (1995, Jul./Aug.). "Building Bridges between Cooperative and Collaborative Learning." *Change: The Magazine of Higher Learning*, 35–39.

Myers, C. & Jones, T.B. (1993). *Promoting Active Learning: Strategies for the College Classroom.* San Francisco: Jossey-Bass.

Natasi, B.K. and Clements, D.H. (1991). "Research on Cooperative Learning: Implications for Practice." *School Psychology Review, 20*(1), 110–31.

Palmer, P. J. (1996). "The Renewal of Community in Higher Education." In W. E. Campbell and K. A. Smith (Eds.), *New Paradigms for College Teaching* (pp. 1–18). Edina, MN: Interaction Book Company.

Rhem, J. (1994). "Conference Report: Emerging Trends in College Teaching for the 21st Century." *The National Teaching and Learning Forum, 3*(4), 12.

Sapon-Shevin, M., Ayres, B.J., and Duncan, J. (1994). "Cooperative Learning and Inclusion." In J.S. Thousand, R.A. Villa, and A.I. Nevin, (Eds.), *Creativity and Collaborative Learning: A Practical Guide to Empowering Students and Teachers* (pp. 45–58). Baltimore, MD: Paul H. Brookes Publishing Co.

Schon, D. A. (1987). *Educating the Reflective Practitioner: Toward a New Design for Teaching and Learning in the Professions.* San Francisco: Jossey-Bass.

Slavin, R.E. (1989-1990). "Research in Cooperative Learning: Consensus and Controversy." *Educational Leadership, 47*(4), 52–55.

Slavin, R.E. (1993). "What Can Postsecondary Cooperative Learning Learn from Elementary and Secondary Research?" *Cooperative Learning and College Teaching, 4*(1), 2–3.

Smith, B.L. and MacGregor, J.T. (1992). "What is Collaborative Learning?" In A. Goodsell, M. Mahler, V. Tinto, B.L. Smith, and J. MacGregor, (Eds.), *Collaborative Learning: A Sourcebook for Higher Education* (pp. 9–22). University Park, PA: National Center on Postsecondary Teaching, Learning, and Assessment.

Smith, K.A., Johnson, D.W., and Johnson, R.T. (1992). "Cooperative Learning and Positive Change in Higher Education." In A. Goodsell, M. Mahler, V. Tinto, B.L. Smith, and J. MacGregor, (Eds.), *Collaborative Learning: A Sourcebook for Higher Education.* (pp. 34–36). University Park, PA: National Center on Postsecondary Teaching, Learning, and Assessment.

Treisman, U. (1985). "A Study of the Mathematics Performance of Black Students at the University of California, Berkeley [Doctoral Dissertation, University of California, Berkeley, 1986]." *Dissertation Abstracts International, 47,* 1641A.

Webb, N. (1983). "Predicting Learning from Student Interaction: Defining the Interaction Variable." *Educational Psychologist, 18,* 33–41.

Webb, N. (1991). "Task-related Verbal Interaction and Mathematics Learning in Small Groups." *Journal of Research in Mathematics Education, 22,* 366–389.

CHAPTER 2

Why Change?

"Nothing ventured, nothing gained."

A Proverb

nnovative teaching methods in college courses should be considered within the larger context of teaching in higher education. Issues of quality and accountability have fueled a general movement for educational reform, including a more enlightened view of the research/teaching imbalance in the faculty reward structure (Boyer, 1990). These changing expectations about the need for effective undergraduate education are reinforced by broader societal needs, including the increased use of technology and the short half-life of knowledge in most discipline areas. Lifelong learning, which includes interpersonal and team building skills, is a virtual necessity for all members of the workforce today. The nature of the workforce and the diverse student populations that feed it also call for new innovations in the classroom.

THE CHANGING WORKPLACE

In today's business sector, there is a new emphasis on cooperation and teamwork. The pioneering metaphors of the lone gunslinger blazing away at clearly defined enemies, or the business tycoon rising to the top of the entrepreneurial heap, have been replaced by new metaphors of interdependence and cooperation. Many of the leading corporations are moving toward the use of facilitative management practices involving cooperation and teamwork. The movement toward total quality management, for example, incorporates development of cross-functional work teams, quality circles, and a host of other small-group techniques as a means of fostering continuous improvement in quality and timeliness of work. Covey (1989) notes that "cooperation in the workplace is as important to free enterprise as competition in the market-place" (p. 230). Many factors have fueled this redirection: the increasing turbulence and complexity of the international scene; fast-paced technological change; opening markets accompanied by intense competition; and recessionary trends necessitating quality products at competitive prices.

In recent years, many authors such as Kinlaw (1990) or Wellins, Byham, and Wilson (1991), have written about cooperation and teamwork in the business world. The emphasis on teamwork in business and industry parallels the emphasis on cooperative learning in schools, colleges, and continuing education. Students who are learning skills in interpersonal communication, conflict resolution, group problem solving, and group decision making are being appropriately prepared to function in the contemporary business world. Strong arguments can be made for the fact that faculty who neglect these aspects of undergraduate education are doing their students and the profession a disservice.

The workforce will also have to address the population shifts occurring throughout the 1990s. John Roueche notes that the workforce of 2000 is already in place, but 75% of these workers will need significant retraining in the next decade. (cited in Culross, 1996). Workers will need lifelong learning skills and the ability to work cooperatively and productively with diverse colleagues. This diversity is also evident in our colleges and universities.

THE CHANGING STUDENT POPULATIONS

Most faculty are aware of the federal Census Bureau's prediction that by the year 2005, 52% of the United States' population will be "minority" and one in three students will be of color. College and university faculty on most campuses are already seeing an influx of part-time and minority students, many of whom have educational needs and approaches to learning that differ from those of more traditional students.

Moreover, even the traditional student is a vanishing species: the myth of the well-prepared 18-year-old enrolling in college to complete a degree within four years died many years ago. Carol Aslanian of the College Board has spoken widely about the new populations. Less than a quarter of enrolled students could be labeled "traditional." Almost half of all college and university students are over 25. In fact, a Census Bureau survey showed that approximately 41% of all students enrolled in colleges and universities in the fall of 1993 fell into the 17–21 year age range (cited in *The Chronicle of Higher Education Almanac*, 1996). Furthermore, an increasing number of students are part-timers balancing academic demands with vocational commitments. Ryan

(1993) reports that, from 1960 to 1990, college enrollments climbed from 3.6 million students to 12.8 million; over 5 million were part-time: "By 1988, mature students accounted for over 40% of all enrolled students, and the proportion of minority students had risen to 18%. The proportion of women grew from 37% of the undergraduate population in 1960 to 54% in 1988" (p. 13). Many of these part-timers are working students.

With this diverse student population, Gaff (1992) emphasizes that "Pedagogical 'business-as-usual' in any program—listening to lectures, reading a pre-digested textbook, memorization, and multiple-choice tests—will not allow students to learn what even the most fervently argued courses have to teach" (p. 35). The secret to successful teaching in all disciplines is a broad, flexible, well-adapted teaching repertoire.

With this new influx of diverse students, learning cannot occur through traditional delivery methods, with "authority figures" lecturing to passive adults. In fact, as Giezkowski (1992) points out, the large influx into colleges and universities of adult students who are focused, pragmatic, and bring with them a wealth of life experiences has revitalized the learning environment. Faculty are challenged to juggle the conflicting expectations these adult students may have. As emphasized earlier, versatility is the key. Successful teaching depends on "the flexibility of a college instructor's teaching repertoire and his or her readiness to draw on a range of teaching styles for a variety of ends" (Adams, 1992, p. 15). Varied learning approaches are critically important, Cross (1991) argues, because of what we know of learning:

> What do students already know, and how can new learning be framed to make meaningful connections? The more teachers can develop analogies and metaphors to relate to the backgrounds of students, the more likely new knowledge will become integrated into the schemata or knowledge structure that represents the student's understanding (p. 28).

Dentler (1994), a community college history teacher, observes that many teachers have radically different backgrounds than the students they teach:

> Our students, shaped by far different academic, economic, personal, and political experiences, typically do not feel empowered in the classroom. They are alienated from institutions, including colleges, that too often serve to heighten their sense of exclusion from positions of power and privilege in society. Most importantly, our students do not have the self-esteem required to confidently participate in competition-based class discussion that follows the traditional passive-learning lecture methods (p. 12).

Dentler finds that cooperative-learning approaches empower her students, bolstering their self-esteem and confidence. She concludes:

> When we ask our urban community college students to find answers on their own and share them, non-competitively, with their classmates, we

empower them in a way that wasn't even necessary for my generation of college students. When our students work with their peers on research projects . . . we are literally inviting them to participate in the system. For many, this is the first time the system has welcomed them at the table (p. 12).

A scientist, Nelson (1996), from a traditional research institution, initially thought that diversity issues did not affect his teaching. He now takes a radically different stance:

Subsequently, I have come to understand that much of what I took as neutral teaching practice actually functions to keep our courses less accessible to students from nontraditional backgrounds. If my current understandings are a reasonable reflection of reality, then (almost) all traditionally taught courses are unintentionally, but nevertheless deeply, biased in ways that make substantial differences in performance for many students. (p. 165)

Among other approaches, Nelson advocates "a shift to structured, student-student group work" with the caveats that "the teacher must make sure that the students are prepared for the discussion, that the students participate constructively and fairly evenly, and that the students are addressing questions that are sufficiently challenging" (p. 167). He, like others, sees a shift in teaching/learning paradigms.

THE CHANGING TEACHING PARADIGM

As Kuhn (1962) emphasized, breakthroughs in science tend to follow altered ways of thinking or viewing the world. Paradigms frame the way individuals and societies perceive and understand the universe. There is considerable evidence, as several researchers point out (Johnson, Johnson, and Smith, 1991; Boehm, 1992), that a paradigm shift is occurring in teaching. The shift results in a new emphasis on delivery and the role of the teacher. As Boehm states, "We are beginning to understand that how we teach is central; it is, in fact, the second content of every course" (p. 37).

The concept of a paradigm shift has been invigorated by Barr and Tagg's (1995) influential article, "From Teaching To Learning—a New Paradigm for Undergraduate Education." They contrast the Instructional Paradigm, which focuses on the means (teaching) and is based on ineffective teaching practices, with the Learning Paradigm, where student learning and success are the ends. In the latter:

A college's purpose is not to transfer knowledge but to create environments and experiences that bring students to discover and construct knowledge for themselves, to make students members of communities of learners that make discoveries and solve problems (p. 15).

The end goal is to maximize learning for individual students and for students in the aggregate, an outcome that requires continuous refinement of effective structures and approaches. The Learning Paradigm, which often involves teamwork, recognizes the student as the chief agent in the learning process. All members of an institution are committed to the success of each student.

Paradigm shifts do not come easily, however, because the beliefs are both deeply ingrained and often unconscious. Thus, faculty moving toward cooperative, structured-group work may find themselves challenged on many levels.

RESISTANCE TO CHANGE

Any change involves risk-taking. Faculty must be convinced and confident that the cooperative-learning activities they introduce are worthwhile. This conviction and confidence will go a long way toward persuading students of the value and efficacy of the new approaches.

Because of the risks involved, however, it is easier for faculty to maintain the status quo, which in most cases means a lecture-centered, faculty-directed classroom. Ekroth (1990) has identified six barriers to faculty change, which have been amplified by Bonwell and Eison (1991, pp. 53–59). One of these barriers is what Ekroth calls "the stability of the situation": on a mundane level, physical settings, seating arrangements, and time schedules rarely vary; more significantly, institutional procedures, the reward system, and the fact that many faculty teach as they were taught argue against innovation. Students, too, reinforce expectations about traditional behaviors: faculty (who contain the knowledge) lecture, and students (who are empty vessels) listen. Furthermore, departures from these traditional roles cause anxiety: Will this work? What if students rebel? How will my colleagues or chair react?

College and university faculty considering adoption of cooperative learning have usually overcome these barriers. They should be reassured by the answers to the following concerns:

1. Group work is "soft." By using it, I will lower my standards and make less rigorous demands on my students.

As Cross (1986) and many others have emphasized, if we set high expectations for our students, they will rise to meet them. Faculty have an obligation to society to produce graduates who are competent. Thus, group work must not reduce actual mastery. The good news is that the research consistently shows that structured small-group work that builds in positive interdependence and individual accountability also raises student achievement. In the few studies where cooperative-learning student achievement does not exceed those in control groups taught by traditional methods, the students learned at least equally well (Davidson, 1990).

When college students are placed in heterogeneous teams and given structured tasks, the teams usually strive for a quality product. Faculty using cooperative-learning approaches find that students have three reasons to aspire for quality: (1) their own intrinsic motivation, whether it is stimulated by personal fulfillment/learning or for a targeted grade; (2) their wish to please the instructor, whether it is for affiliative approval or again for a specific grade; and (3) their team commitment, whether their actions are predicated on a desire to "come through" for the team or to avoid the censure of their fellow learners. In a traditional competitive classroom, usually only the first two stimuli are operative; peer pressure, a strong motivating force in structured groups, is not a factor.

Furthermore, in cooperative classrooms, the faculty members remain attentive and involved. As groups work on specific tasks, they constantly monitor quality by actively moving among them. Faculty, therefore, are able to determine and influence the level of learning and eliminate potential pitfalls, including dysfunctional group interactions that might interfere with mastery of the course content. By listening to the student interactions, they can also identify problem areas in the instruction and sometimes benefit from hearing students "translate" their lecture material into meaningful language for fellow classmates. Students appreciate their interest and involvement and the opportunity to sit with them, face-to-face, without an intervening podium.

Quality is also reinforced by the insistence in cooperative-learning classrooms on individual accountability. Group members, although they coach one another and cooperate on projects, are no less responsible for their own learning and are usually tested individually. No one is allowed to coast on the achievements of others, as sometimes happens in less-structured group settings, where one or two team members do most of the work on a joint project but all members receive the same grade.

2. I can't possibly cover all the content using group work. Lectures are efficient ways to deliver the curriculum needed by students who must take further courses for which mine is a prerequisite.

The question of coverage really falls back on the key distinction between teaching and learning. A widely circulated cartoon by Bud Blake shows a young boy declaring of his dog, "I taught Stripe how to whistle." A skeptical friend notes, "But I don't hear him whistling." The boy retorts, "I said I taught him to whistle, I didn't say he learned it." This distinction is critically important. It underscores the need to look beyond content coverage to what students are actually learning.

During course planning, many difficult decisions must be made in terms of curriculum, course requirements, classroom activities, and so forth. It is never possible to include everything. Thus, when incorporating group work into a syllabus, it may become necessary to cover less, but to cover it in depth, so that students are actually learning the material. Longtime cooperative-learning practitioners suggest, however, that through careful structuring, they can actually cover more material than under the traditional lecture-recitation model. The secret lies in developing strategies that encourage out-of-class learning, which is then reinforced and validated through in-class activities. Such activities offer feedback on the amount of learning that has occurred, or faculty can offer the "expert" viewpoint (a lecture, a handout, etc.) against which students measure their own efforts. We call this approach, which will be discussed in more detail later, "sequenced learning."

Cooperative classrooms emphasize "learning by doing." In traditional classrooms, many faculty routinely prepare oral presentations to augment each assigned chapter. Too often for too many students, these lectures, however carefully crafted, become rehashes of the textbook material, thus robbing even well-motivated students of any incentive to prepare for class in advance. Carefully structured homework assignments can eliminate the need to lecture in detail on the assigned chapters. For example, instructors might use the Dyadic Essay Confrontation (DEC) model, described in chapter 8, where students work in pairs on essays covering the chapter material. Much time can be saved, also, by focusing homework reviews within groups rather than covering problems with the entire class. Michaelson (1992) describes a variation of cooperative learning called Team Learning (chapter 9), which uses a series of minitests, administered five to seven times a semester, that are given at the beginning of each major unit of instruction. The tests are taken individually and retaken as a group; a group appeals process provides opportunities for immediate, focused feedback and builds group cohesiveness. These mini-tests enable faculty members to "cover" content without lectures, particularly theoretical material, freeing time in class for applied activities such as problem solving. Even though lectures are not as extensive as they might be under a traditional approach, faculty can increase the overall achievement level of students by allowing them time to work directly on content-related problem solving, to explore direct applications, and to undertake guided practice.

3. If I turn the class over to small groups, I will lose control.

Professors who assume they are in control of a class simply because they have possession of a lectern will do well to review Boyer's (1987) description of a scene repeated on many campuses where large classes are the norm:

> At a freshman psychology lecture we attended, 300 students were still finding seats when the professor started talking. "Today," he said into the microphone, "we will continue our discussion of learning." He might as well have been addressing a crowd in a Greyhound bus terminal. Like commuters marking time until their next departure, students in this class alternatively read the newspaper, flipped through a paperback novel, or propped their feet on the chairs ahead of them, staring into space. Only

when the professor defined a term [that] he said "might appear on an exam" did they look up and start taking notes (p. 140).

Despite the elevated noise level, students in a well-conducted cooperative classroom are focused on course content. Through systematic group monitoring, instructors can assess student progress on clearly defined tasks. Furthermore, each group typically has one student whose specific assignment is to ensure that the group stays focused on the learning objectives. Thus, students routinely complete their work within a specified time frame. Unlike a typical lecture hall, where even seemingly attentive students may be daydreaming, virtually all students are actively involved in their own learning.

4. My students will reject classroom activities they regard as frivolous or irrelevant. Students want to learn from an authority figure—me!

Instructors who convey a lack of confidence in the cooperative-learning structures they initiate, or fail to prepare adequately, are courting disaster. But thousands of higher education practitioners can testify that well-designed, well-directed cooperative activities tied to course objectives consistently receive "rave" reviews from students. Johnson, Johnson, and Smith (1991) summarize a wide variety of research findings on cooperative learning. They find that its positive effects on interpersonal relationships have far-reaching results:

> As relationships within the class or college become more positive, absenteeism decreases and students' commitment to learning, feeling of personal responsibility to complete the assigned work, willingness to take on difficult tasks, motivation and persistence in working on tasks, satisfaction and morale, willingness to endure pain and frustration to succeed, willingness to defend the college against external criticism or attack, willingness to listen to and be influenced by peers, commitment to peers' success and growth, and productivity and achievement can be expected to increase (p. 44).

Instructors should explain to students exactly what they are doing and why. Dualistic thinkers who assume there are absolute answers to questions [i.e, those in stages one through three in Perry's (1970) scheme or in the early stages of the hierarchy described by Belenky, Clinchy, Goldberger, and Taruk (1986)] may initially reject processes and procedures that cause them to question their entrenched value systems. Talking with students about different learning styles and the desirability of moving toward more sophisticated modes of thinking can help put cooperative learning in a positive perspective. Cooper, Prescott, Cook, Smith, Mueck, and Cuseo (1990) suggest that the cognitive development of beginning college students can be stimulated by exposure to the differing viewpoints of group members.

More important, through the structure of the assignments and the group processes, faculty can provide the combination of challenge and support essential for student success (Widick, Knelfelkamp, and Parker, 1975). Challenges often take the form of concepts or tasks designed to increase higher-order thinking skills and move students beyond dualistic thinking. Such challenges often force students to confront alternate viewpoints and to take demanding intellectual and sometimes personal risks. Supports to counter these challenges include a learning environment that minimizes the risks and maximizes students' likelihood of success.

Cooperative learning, for many reasons, provides both challenge and support. The carefully structured tasks challenge students to move beyond memorization and single-minded viewpoints. The heterogeneity of the groups prompts the exchange of diverse opinions and intellectual stances, plus a thoughtful probing of the team members' reasons for adopting such viewpoints. The groups, through careful selection, monitoring, and reinforcement of positive interactions, provide a great deal of support for the individual members. In these groups, students can immerse themselves in hands-on, practical applications and concrete problems where they can begin to understand the more challenging abstractions. Groups also provide a safe environment where students can speak freely about their own fears of mastery or their misgivings about alternate viewpoints that challenge their preconceived notions of reality. This opportunity to verbalize is particularly important for the many dualistic college students who enter classrooms looking for the "answers." Discussing issues with students who have moved beyond these "black and white" stances can enlarge their understanding.

5. If I learned my discipline the traditional way, then everyone must learn it the traditional way. Furthermore, I have no role models. How can I change?

As mentioned earlier, a paradigm shift has occurred in college teaching. Refusing to consider other delivery options simply because of past experiences is a shortsighted, counterproductive stance. Certainly, as academics we should be willing to espouse an open viewpoint and approach cooperative-learning opportunities with a critical-thinking stance. At the very least, a review of some of the cogent literature and discussions with practitioners in various fields will help us make informed choices. Because there is now such widespread interest in cooperative learning, role models are more accessible than they were a few years ago. Interested faculty should subscribed to the *Cooperative Learning in Higher Education* newsletter edited by Dr. James Cooper of California State University, Dominguez Hills. Workshops on cooperative learning are increasingly common on many campuses and at national conferences sponsored by organizations such as the American Association of Higher Education or the Lilly Teaching Conference at Miami of Ohio.

6. Colleagues, as well as students, will think I'm not fulfilling my professional obligations if my classroom seems noisy and out-of-control.

They won't understand or appreciate these departures from traditional teaching.

The solution here is simple communication. Faculty should openly discuss their efforts to integrate structured small-group work into their courses. They can share with colleagues some of the voluminous literature on cooperative learning and college teaching, preferably material in their disciplines such as Cottell & Millis (1992; 1993) in accounting, Nurrenbern (1995) in chemistry, and Felder in engineering (Felder's Website—http://www.coe.ncsu.edu/departments/che/faculty/rmf.html). Support from department chairs, discussions at department meetings, and "success stories" will go a long way toward convincing skeptical colleagues that these innovations have merit. Even if a department seems hostile to innovation, Combs (1979) reminds us that "teachers have far more freedom to innovate than they ever use. When the classroom door is closed, nobody, but nobody, knows what is going on in there except the teacher and the students. . . . Teachers may not be able to change the educational system, or their administrator, but the variations possible within an ordinary classroom are almost limitless" (p. 212).

7. I don't know how to evaluate students who spend so much time focused on group work.

When faculty members are perplexed about whether to assign grades for group activities, they need to put the entire classroom experience into perspective. Do they, for example, assign specific grades to students for their attentiveness during lectures? Similarly, group activities do not have to be graded per se. Students will recognize the value of these activities once they see how they relate to their increased learning.

In-class cooperative-learning activities offer a concrete, ongoing way to assess student learning and commitment. Even though teachers do not typically grade assignments, in most classes they can review them and write brief comments without seriously compromising their workload. Larger classes obviously are a different story, but, often, graduate teaching assistants can be trained to quickly review and respond to student in-class work.

As emphasized in chapter 1, a key component of cooperative learning is individual accountability. Students should take quizzes and examinations individually after they have coached one another through the group activities. To insure cooperation, however, it is essential that the grading scheme be criterion-referenced, a practice strongly recommended by educational researchers and faculty development experts in any case. Grading on the curve, where students are pitted against one another for a finite number of A's, will destroy classroom cohesiveness. Many suggest, also, that such practices are inherently unfair because the ability levels of competing students will vary from class to class. Furthermore, the concept of a bell-shaped curve was never intended to apply to atypical populations, such as the segment of the population which attends college. Chapter 11 explores grading issues in more detail.

8. Introducing cooperative-learning activities will take too much time. I already suffer from too many demands; I cannot possibly revise my course syllabus and rework my course content.

The time factor is a valid concern. Any course revisions take careful preparation and thought. As Cooper (1990) cautions: "The three most important things in setting up a cooperative learning classroom are Structure, Structure, and Structure" (p.1). But, as we will emphasize, cooperative-learning activities complement, rather than replace entirely, more traditional approaches, such as the lecture. It is important to begin slowly with some of the more basic structures such as Roundtable, a rapid brainstorming activity that will be introduced in chapter 5. Using a course-planning sheet (Figure 2.1) may help faculty focus their individual lesson plans. Some faculty, particularly those teaching in three-hour blocks, actually "script" the classroom activities, writing down what will happen and how long it will take. Careful planning will give faculty the self-confidence needed to introduce cooperative activities.

Course:

Structure to be introduced:

What will you do?

Why are you doing it?

Questions for Reflection/Discussion
1. How will this activity further your course objectives?
2. How will you introduce this activity to students?
3. How will you form groups?
4. How will positive interdependence be fostered (goals, resource materials, evaluation methods, roles, etc.)?
5. How will you maintain individual accountability?
6. How will you monitor students' interactions and learning?
7. What problems/challenges do you expect?

Source: South-Western College Publishing. (Reprinted with permission.)

COOPERATIVE LEARNING COURSE PLANNING

FIGURE 2.1

Confidence can also be strengthened by initially introducing low-risk cooperative-learning strategies. Eison and Bonwell (1988) have conceptualized the degree of risk involved in various classroom techniques by contrasting their various characteristics (Figure 2.2). It is advisable to begin initially with a relatively short, highly structured activity, such as the Think-Pair-Share structure described in chapter 5. Faculty should plan the activity carefully and choose concrete, relatively noncontroversial subject matter, such as asking paired students to discuss why science matters to society or to describe the symptoms of schizophrenia after students have had some exposure to the topic. Because a Think-Pair-Share activity is carefully structured and timed, it can be introduced easily. Bonwell and Eison (1991) caution that student-student interactions involve more risk than student-faculty dialogues, but that problems such as off-task behavior or shy noncontributors will lessen with planning and practice (p. 68). They consider structured small-group discussion, which engenders a high degree of active learning, to be a relatively low-risk activity.

Dimension	Low-Risk Strategies	High-Risk Strategies
Class time required	Relatively short	Relatively long
Degree of structure	More structured	Less structured
Degree of planning	Meticulously planned	Spontaneous
Subject matter	Relatively concrete	Relatively abstract
Potential for controversy	Less controversial	Very controversial
Students' prior knowledge matter	Better informed	Less informed
Students' prior knowledge of the teaching technique	Familiar	Unfamiliar
Instructors prior experience with the teaching technique	Considerable	Limited
Pattern of interaction	Between faculty and students	Among students

Bonwell, C.C. and Eison, J.A. (1991). *Active Learning: Creating Excitement in the Classroom.* ASHE-ERIC Higher Education Report No. 1. Washington, DC: The George Washington University, School of Education and Human Development.
Please call the ERIC Clearinghouse on Higher Education at 1-800-773-3742 for a complimentary publication catalog of other titles available in the ASHE-ERIC Higher Education Report Series. Also, more information on this and other higher education topics are available on the ASHE-ERIC website at http://www/gwu/edu/~eriche.

A COMPARISON OF LOW- AND HIGH-RISK ACTIVE LEARNING STRATEGIES

FIGURE 2.2

Using small-group activities can pay enormous dividends. Student-student interactions, as opposed to one-on-one student-faculty exchanges, result in what Kagan (1992) calls the principle of "simultaneity." In a traditional classroom, the teacher calls on students sequentially, a time-consuming, passive activity for all but the targeted student. Even if the faculty member encourages student-to-student exchanges during a whole-class discussion, typically only one person is speaking at a time. By initiating paired discussion, on the other hand, the teacher guarantees that virtually half the students in a classroom are actively talking; the other half are far more likely to be actively engaged in the learning processing/listening process than students involved in a whole-class discussion.

Nelson (1996) speaks convincingly of the need to alter our philosophies and our practices. He advocates a switch to alternative, non-lecture-based pedagogies, such as structured-group work and, more important, a switch to alternative paradigms of teaching and learning. Specifically, he identifies two fundamental changes: (1) measuring effective pedagogy not by what is taught, but by what is learned; and (2) viewing our roles not as weeders of the unfit and the unworthy, but as coaches and facilitators who seek the success of all students. He concludes:

> It is clear that we already know what to do first. And it is clear that much of it is doable without further delay—each of our classes can change in important and effective ways as soon as tomorrow morning. There are no risks and minimal costs in getting started. And much more than individual lives (as if that were not enough) hangs in the balance. On what grounds can we possibly justify further delay (pp. 172–173)?

SUMMARY

Despite the misgivings of some faculty, there are many compelling reasons to introduce cooperative-learning approaches into higher education class-rooms. Changing student populations and a changing workplace mean that traditional approaches to teaching no longer provide students with the necessary academic and interpersonal skills. In fact, some scholars have suggested that a paradigm shift is occurring in the teaching world, a shift to a more interactive, student-centered classroom. In keeping with this new awareness, many educators advocate more active learning, including group work. Any misgivings can be overcome when faculty begin slowly with low-risk cooperative-learning activities.

REFERENCES

Adams, M. (1992). "Cultural Inclusion in the American College Classroom." In N.V.N. Chism and L.L. B. Border (Eds.), *Teaching for Diversity: New Directions for Teaching and Learning*, No. 49. San Francisco: Jossey-Bass.

Barr, R.B. & Tagg, J. (1995, Nov./Dec.). *Change: The Magazine of Higher Learning*, 13–25.

Belenky, M.F., Clinchy, B.M., Goldberger, N.R., and Taruk, J.M. (1986). *Women's Ways of Knowing: The Development of Self, Voice, and Mind*. New York: Basic Books.

Boehm, L. (1992). "In Wake of Crisis: Reclaiming the Heart of Teaching and Learning." In T.J. Frecka (Ed.), *Critical Thinking, Interactive Learning and Technology: Reaching for Excellence in Business Education* (pp. 24–40). Arthur Andersen Foundation.

Bonwell, C.C. and Eison, J.A. (1991). *Active Learning: Creating Excitement in the Classroom.* ASHE-ERIC Higher Education Report No. 1. Washington, DC: The George Washington University, School of Education and Human Development.

Boyer, E.L. (1987). *College: The Undergraduate Experience in America.* New York: Harper & Row.

Boyer, E.L. (1990). *Scholarship Reconsidered: Priorities of the Professoriate.* Princeton, NJ: Carnegie Foundation for the Advancement of Teaching.

The Chronicle of Higher Education Almanac. (1996, Sept.). "College Enrollment by Age of Students, Fall 1993." 43(1), 17.

Combs, A.W. (1979). *Myths in Education: Beliefs that Hinder Progress and their Alternatives.* Boston: Allyn & Bacon.

Cooper, J. (1990, May). "Cooperative Learning and College Teaching: Tips from the Trenches." *The Teaching Professor,* 4(5), 1–2.

Cooper, J., Prescott, S., Cook, L., Smith, L., Mueck, R., and Cuseo, J. (1990). *Cooperative Learning and College Instruction: Effective Use of Student Learning Teams.* Long Beach, CA: The California State University Foundation.

Cottell, P.G. & Millis, B.J. (1992). "Cooperative Learning in Accounting." *The Journal of Accounting Education,* 10, 95–111.

Cottell, P.G. & Millis, B.J. (1993). "Cooperative Learning Structures in the Instruction of Accounting." *Issues in Accounting Education,* 8(1), 40–59.

Covey, S.R. (1989). *The Seven Habits of Highly Successful People: Restoring the Character Ethic.* New York: Simon & Schuster.

Cross, K.P. (1986, Mar.). *Taking Teaching Seriously.* Paper presented at the national conference of the American Association for Higher Education, Washington, DC.

Cross, K.P. (1991, Oct.). "Effective College Teaching." *ASEE Prism,* 27–29.

Culross, R. (1996, Nov./Dec.). "Remediation: Real Students, Real Standards." *Change: The Magazine of Higher Learning,* 28(6), 50–52.

Davidson, N. (1990). "The Small-group Discovery Method in Secondary- and College-level Mathematics." In N. Davidson (Ed.), *Cooperative Learning in Mathematics: A Handbook for Teachers* (pp. 335–61). Menlo Park, CA: Addison-Wesley.

Dentler, D. (1994). "Cooperative Learning and American History." *Cooperative Learning and College Teaching,* 4(3), 9–12.

Eison, J. and Bonwell, C. (1988, Mar.). *Making Real the Promise of Active Learning.* Paper presented at the national conference of the American Association for Higher Education, Washington, DC.

Ekroth, L. (1990). "Why Professors Don't Change." In L. Ekroth (Ed.), *Teaching Excellence: Toward the Best in the Academy* (Winter-Spring). Stillwater, OK: The Professional and Organizational Development Network in Higher Education.

Gaff, Jerry G. (1992). "Beyond Politics: The Educational Issues Inherent in Multicultural Education." *Change: The Magazine of Higher Learning,* 24(1), 31–35.

Giezkowski, W. (1992). "The Influx of Older Students can Revitalize College Teaching." *The Chronicle of Higher Education,* 38(29), 133–34.

Johnson, D.W., Johnson, R.T., and Smith, K.A. (1991). *Cooperative Learning: Increasing College Faculty Instructional Productivity.* ASHE-ERIC Higher Education Report No. 4. Washington, DC: The George Washington University, School of Educational and Human Development.

Kagan, S. (1992). *Cooperative Learning.* San Juan Capistrano, CA: Resources for Teachers, Inc.

Kinlaw, D. (1990). *Developing Superior Work Teams.* New York: Free Press.

Kuhn, T. (1962). *The Structure of Scientific Revolutions*. Chicago: University of Chicago Press.

Michaelson, L.K. (1992). "Team Learning: A Comprehensive Approach for Harnessing the Power of Small Groups in Higher Education." In D.H. Wulff and J.D. Nyquist (Eds.), *To Improve the Academy: Resources for Faculty, Instructional, and Organizational Development*, Vol. 11 (pp. 107–22). The Professional and Organizational Development Network in Higher Education, Stillwater, OK: New Forums Press, Inc.

Nelson, C.E. (1996). "Student Diversity Requires Different Approaches to College Teaching, Even in Math and Science." *American Behavioral Scientist*, 40(2), 165–75.

Nurrenbern, S.C. (Ed.), (1995). *Experiences in Cooperative Learning: A Collection for Chemistry Teachers*. University of Wisconsin—Madison: Institute of Chemical Education.

Perry, W. (1970). *Forms of Intellectual and Ethical Development in the College Years: A Scheme*. New York: Holt, Rinehart, & Winston.

Ryan, A. (1993, Feb.). "Invasion of the Mind Snatchers." *New York Review of Books*, 15(4), 13–15.

Wellins, R.S, Byham, W.C., and Wilson, J.M. (1991). *Empowered Teams: Creating Self-directed Work Groups that Improve Quality, Productivity, and Participation*. San Francisco: Jossey-Bass.

Widick, C., Knelfelkamp, L., and Parker, C. (1975). "The Counselor as Developmental Instructor." *Counselor Education and Supervision*, 14, 286-96.

PART TWO

· · · · · · · · ·

Classroom Management

CHAPTER 3

Planning a Cooperative Course

"Good order is the foundation of all things."

Edmund Burke

T he power of cooperative learning lies in its ability to promote what is known as deep learning. Deep learning does not occur simply because students are placed in groups. It emerges from the careful, sequenced assignments and activities "orchestrated" by a teacher committed to student learning.

The research on deep learning has been ongoing, systematic, and convergent. A project, "Improving Student Learning," sponsored by the Council for National Academic Awards in Britain, was initiated not to generate new research about student learning, but rather to encourage faculty to use the existing research and tools to strengthen their courses. The project is predicated on research indicating that:

> The students' approach to learning—whether they take a surface or a deep approach—[is] the crucial factor determining the quality of learning outcomes. Those who take a deep approach understand more, produce better written work containing logical structures and conclusions rather than lists, remember longer, and obtain better marks and degrees than those students who take a surface approach (cited in "Deep Learning, Surface Learning," 1993, p. 14).

Rhem (1995a) cites three international scholars (Ference Marton [Sweden]; Noel Entwistle [Scotland], and Paul Ramsden [Australia] who, with other colleagues, have identified the same emergent patterns in deep learning. This research suggests that, although specific implementations will vary, four key components characterize a deep approach to learning. Rhem (1995b) summarizes them as follows:

> **Motivational context**: We learn best what we feel a need to know. Intrinsic motivation remains inextricably bound to some level of choice and control. Courses that remove these take away the sense of ownership and kill one of the strongest elements in lasting learning.
> **Learner activity**: Deep learning and "doing" travel together. Doing in itself isn't enough. Faculty must connect activity to the abstract conceptions that make sense of it, but passive mental postures lead to superficial learning.
> **Interaction with others**: As Noel Entwistle put it in a recent e-mail message, "The teacher is not the only source of instruction or inspiration." Peers working as groups enjoin dimensions of learning that lectures and readings by themselves cannot touch.
> **A well-structured knowledge base**: This doesn't just mean presenting new material in an organized way. It also means engaging and reshaping the concepts students bring with them when they register. Deep approaches, learning for understanding, are integrative processes. The more fully new concepts can be connected with students' prior experience and existing knowledge, the more [likely] it is [that] they will be impatient with inert facts and eager to achieve their own synthesis (p. 4).

This research has enormous implications for college and university teaching. Researchers generally agree, for example, that group work and problem solving within the context outlined above can result in deep learning.

The cooperative activities described in this book must be viewed within the larger teaching and learning framework. Specifically, they form the heart of a carefully crafted learning sequence. The sequence can be contained within a single class period or extended to encompass out-of-class activities, including electronic exchanges. In a given class period, cooperative learning offers students and faculty a structured, on-task means to foster learner activity and learner interactions. Interestingly enough, E. D. Hirsch Jr. (1996), who is not a fan of cooperative learning, describes what he calls "dramatized instruction," which mirrors this sandwich approach. A given class period will be carefully, but not rigidly, structured, with clear objectives and a beginning, middle, and end:

> The beginning sets up the question to be answered, the knowledge to be mastered, or the skill to be gained; the middle consists of a lot of back-and-forth between student and student, student and teacher; and the end consists of a feeling of closure and accomplishment (p. 174).

This approach is validated by research presented by Sousa (1995) on how students learn. The primacy-recency effect postulates that humans, because of the limitations of working memory, tend to remember and retain information offered first in a learning sequence. We remember second-best the information presented at the end of a lesson. We remember least from the middle of a learning episode, sometimes characterized as "downtime." The length of these prime learning times and the downtime will vary based on the total length of the learning episode. Sousa recommends, among other practices, that the downtime period be used for active "processing" of the new material, particularly relating it to past learnings (pp. 37–42; 58). In other words, this is an optimum period for the learner activities and interactions with others suggested by the research on deep learning.

Student motivation, the first premise of deep learning, is enormously complex. Probably the single best article on motivation of students in higher education is Forsyth and McMillan's (1991a) "Practical Proposals for Motivating Students." Based on research, it offers practical advice in a logical, well-organized format. The authors conclude:

> Motivation is, to a large extent, a basic dispositional quality of each learner, but savvy instructors can do much to raise motivation by structuring their classrooms carefully . . . . If we can keep students intrinsically motivated, provide meaningful feedback, and encourage the development of realistic, valuable, and achievable goals that students expect to achieve, their engagement in learning should be enhanced (p. 63).

Reading these goals rests in large part on the established classroom climate. Svinicki (1991) finds that three theories of learning—cognitive, motivational, and social—coalesce around the concept of cooperation:

> In each case, the most effective learning and motivation are produced by a cooperative effort between teacher and student. In the case of cognitive theory, the teacher is helping the student to create meaning and to monitor learning. In motivational theory, the instructor works with the student to recognize his or her own potential, to select personal and realistic goals, and to feel secure in the classroom (p. 118).

The social aspects of learning have to do with the emotional context in which the learning occurs.

Creation of a secure classroom is a hallmark of cooperative-learning. Such a classroom is not necessarily placid nor built on forced consensus. Instead, it is a place of civility where opinions can be expressed and explored with honesty. Palmer (1983) describes teaching as creating a "space" that allows students and teachers to recognize truths. He states: "Our feelings may be more vital to truth than our minds, since our minds strive to analyze and divide things while our feelings reach for relatedness" (p. 85). Cognitive psychologists agree that emotions play a significant role in the learning process. Emotions can block learning, but if we like what we are learning or discover positive associations, we are more likely to remain engaged and move to higher-order thinking. Fassinger (1995) reports on the strong relationship between emotional states and social performance in the classroom. She finds that "Faculty's greatest impact on class participation stems from course designs; for example, when professors create activities that foster positive emotional climates, they are likely to cultivate interactions. . . . A positive emotional climate can enhance the likelihood of class participation (pp. 93–94).

Creating a positive, safe learning environment where students are free to interact, question, and grow involves a great deal of "upfront" planning, predicated on a commitment to cooperative interactions. As Michaelsen, Fink, and Black (1996) point out: "Many factors affect group cohesiveness, either facilitating or interfering with the team development process. Most factors are profoundly affected by faculty decisions on course design and classroom management issues" (p. 35).

This chapter will therefore focus on two issues: (1) the philosophy behind these decisions about course design and classroom management, and, (2) their expression in a course syllabus. Chapter 4 will explore other aspects of day-to-day classroom management.

Course design involves decisions about specific assignments and activities. In cooperative learning, the activities are often based on structures. Structures are essentially content-free procedures, such as the brainstorming technique, commonly called Roundtable (chapter 5), that can be used in a number of settings for a variety of purposes. When content is added to a structure—for example, when an instructor asks students to use a Roundtable structure to identify the causes of the Civil War or to suggest the challenges facing the current Congress—then it becomes a specific classroom activity. A series of activities becomes a lesson or unit plan. The Roundtable structure might be used later in another activity, perhaps with an entirely different content. The structures themselves, which will be introduced in chapter 5 and subsequent chapters, provide frameworks for content-centered activities. Structures are the classroom tools that give life to the philosophy, enabling faculty to move from insight to action.

COOPERATIVE LEARNING PHILOSOPHY

As chapter 2 suggests, faculty adopting cooperative learning must understand and embrace the paradigm shift away from competition in the learning environment. Although some might argue that our nation was founded on competition, in reality, that assumption presents a distorted view of both history and human nature. Community barn raisings and close-knit pioneer church congregations were far more common than solitary gunslingers. De Tocqueville, in fact, identified the tendency toward voluntary associations as a distinguishing American trait. Those who might argue for the value of a competitive classroom approach should recognize that competition already permeates our society. Within the last 50 years, American students have been socialized to believe in competition and independent efforts: they have had plenty of opportunities to practice these approaches in classes, on playing fields, and in neighborhood backyards or inner-city alleys. In contrast, many other societies teach students to value cooperation. In Asia, for example, children typically gather at a classmate's home where, under supervision, they work together on homework assignments. In America, most parents refuse to let little Johnny visit friends until he has finished his homework!

Cooperative learning provides a long-overdue balance to the independent and competitive models. Johnson, Johnson, and Smith (1991) applaud the fact that "we are currently leaving an era of competitive and individualistic learning. The 'me' classrooms and 'do your own thing' academic work are fading, and we are entering an era of interdependence and mutuality" (p. 1).

The term "community" has gained wide credence within American schools and within American society as a whole. In fact, Angelo (1996) sees a transformation of colleges and universities from "teaching factories" to "learning communities" where students and teachers work together toward mutual, significant academic goals in settings that de-emphasize competition (p. 1). Graves (1994) defines community as "an inherently cooperative, cohesive, and self-reflective group entity where everyone feels that he or she belongs, and whose members work on a regular, face-to-face basis toward common goals while respecting a variety of perspectives, values, and lifestyles" (p. 286). Communities in the classroom rarely emerge spontaneously. They must be carefully nurtured and cultivated. The "prime movers," at least initially, are the teachers. They must first redefine their roles (a paradigm shift) and then carefully structure the course design to allow a community to emerge.

THE TEACHER'S ROLE IN A COOPERATIVE-LEARNING ENVIRONMENT

In a cooperative-learning environment, a subtle power shift occurs away from the authority figure of the instructor to the students themselves, although the professor remains very much aware of what goes on. As Michaelsen (1992) notes, "The instructor's primary role shifts from dispenser of information to manager of a learning process" (p. 109). A number of desirable outcomes accompany this transfer. As the gap between teachers and students begins to narrow, students and instructors alike find the locus of knowledge in a learning community rather than in one individual. To put it colloquially, "None of us is as smart as all of us." Instructors can feel relaxed in this new role if they think of themselves as expanding their areas of influence rather than as abdicating responsibilities. Instead of narrowly defining themselves only as content or skill experts within a restricted discipline area, they can broaden their perspectives and their effectiveness by adding other roles to their repertoire, such as "facilitator" or "manager."

Through cooperative approaches they can dissolve what Finkle and Monk (1983) have dubbed "The Atlas Complex," a mindset of teacher-student expectations that keeps instructors firmly in the center of the classroom, bearing on their shoulders the responsibility for all aspects of the course. Nikos Kazantzakis creates an insightful metaphor of ideal teachers who "use themselves as bridges over which they invite students to cross, then, having facilitated their crossing, joyfully collapse, encouraging them to create bridges of their own." (cited in Buscaglia, 1982, p. vii). This new student-centered classroom ensures the creation rather than the transfer of knowledge. Instead of pouring knowledge into the heads of passive students, faculty members challenge them to discover, construct, and eventually transform their own knowledge.

As the focus of the classroom changes, student interdependence develops, i.e., students become actively involved not only in their own learning, but also in the learning of their peers. They receive both cognitive and motivational support from their teammates. As groups work together on common problems and projects, students benefit from their own verbalization, but they also witness a variety of thinking patterns and strategies, such as defining the problem, generalizing, drawing on past experience, or evaluating progress. Additionally, group environments provide an audience's response to students' beliefs, ideas, and attitudes, an audience that can be coached to skillfully request clarification, elaboration, and justification.

Such settings engender critical thinking because they help students to experience important activities such as identifying and challenging assumptions, and exploring and imagining alternatives (Brookfield, 1987). In fact, research conducted at the National Center for Research to Improve Postsecondary Teaching and Learning (1990) indicates that at least three elements of teaching appear to affect student gains in thinking skills: "(1) verbalizing methods and strategies to encourage development of learning strategies; (2) student discussion and interaction; and (3) explicit emphasis on problem-solving procedures and methods, using varied examples" (p. 2). All of these activities, which promote deeper learning, routinely occur in a well-designed cooperative-learning course.

THE COOPERATIVE SYLLABUS

Well-designed activities will enable faculty to avoid the dysfunctional aspects of other group learning strategies. Faculty members should, for example, include clear explanations about the nature and purpose of cooperative learning in their course syllabi. Brookfield (1991) cautions: "Being clear about why you teach is crucial, but it is not enough in and of itself; you must also be able to communicate to your students the values, beliefs, and purposes comprising your rationale. You cannot assume that students will understand your rationale or be immediately convinced that your most deeply held convictions have value for them as well" (p. 22). Brookfield's reminder reinforces the research on deep learning cited at the opening of this chapter. The quality of student learning, Ramsden contends, is dependent on the reasons you use specific teaching and assessment methods and the way your students perceive them. He emphasizes that "The key thing to understand about approaches is that they arise from the student's **perception** of the teacher's requirements." (cited in Rhem, 1995b, p. 4). Faculty must consciously foster these perceptions.

Instructors thus should prepare a syllabus which defines cooperative learning, clearly explains the rationale for its use, and explicitly delineates the standard class procedures, including classroom management techniques, such as the use of team folders. Such a syllabus cannot be sketchy. An enriched syllabus (Gabennesch, 1992) does not, like a lecture, funnel information in one direction. It opens the door, instead, for a mutual conversation. This conversation, according to Duffy and Jones (1995), "introduces a learning community into the classroom environment. It unites the professor and the students in a documented conversation, and in this way it holds both professor and students accountable for that classroom community" (p. 69).

Direct quotations from discipline-specific sources, such as the Accounting Education Change Commission, or from national scholars, such as K. Patricia Cross, will reinforce the importance of active learning, problem solving, and enhanced communication and interpersonal skills. Instructors should not overlook, either, the power of the syllabus to motivate students. Harris (1993) describes ten features of a motivating syllabus based upon the principles outlined in paired articles by Forsyth and McMillan (1991a, 1991b). She contends that a motivating syllabus: (1) conveys enthusiasm for the subject; (2) conveys the intellectual challenge of the course; (3) provides for personalization of content; (4) conveys respect for the ability of students; (5) contains attainable and positively stated course goals; (6) details grading policies that convey the possibility of success; (7) adequately specifies assignments; (8) varies assignments in terms of required expertise; (9) indicates ways in which student learning will be assessed frequently; and (10) conveys the teacher's desire to help students individually.

The syllabus should be thoroughly discussed during the first class meeting so that students have an opportunity both to digest and to question classroom approaches that may be new to them. Even more important, discussing the syllabus in a way that models cooperative, student-centered approaches sets the tone for the remainder of the course term. The following two approaches are effective.

Goal Ranking and Matching

To set up this activity, which is explained fully by Angelo and Cross (1993), instructors should consider using a form, such as the one shown in Figure 3-1. Students work individually to formulate their individual goals for the course. Then, to reinforce the cooperative-learning process and to further student connections, students discuss their goals with another person, usually someone sitting nearby. After this discussion, students will be better able to thoughtfully rank the importance of these goals prior to the second phase of the exercise.

In the second phase, the instructor shares with students her own course-related goals. It is best to offer these visually by distributing them as handouts, writing them on a chalkboard or flip chart, showing them on an overhead transparency, or using presentation software. At this point, the students, who have already shared their own goals with a partner, can determine the degree of match between their goals and the instructor's by circling the appropriate response on the right-hand portion of the form.

As the final phase of this exercise, the instructor can initiate a whole-class discussion focused on the shared goals and those student goals which do not match the instructor's. Collecting these anonymous forms will help instructors to assess the needs and desires of their students.

Angelo and Cross (1993) believe that Goal Ranking and Matching serve to assess the "degree of fit" between students' personal learning goals and the teacher's course-specific instructional goals, thereby allowing students to make informed judgments about the course and their investment in it. This activity generally motivates those who now have an enhanced awareness of their own investment in the course. Active involvement and commitment flow from these dialogues about the course's direction and aims. This activity also helps students identify and clarify their own learning goals.

Group Discussion of the Syllabus

Many instructors complain that their investments in syllabus construction are not repaid because students fail to read it. To avoid this occurrence, some instructors, in fact, tell students that they will be quizzed over the syllabus content at the next class meeting. Other faculty who want students to read and reflect on their syllabus use it as the focus of an interactive exercise during the first class session. Students jot down individually everything they want to know about the course. Invariably, concerns will involve the nature and extent of the course requirements and the grading/evaluation system. Then, the instructors ask students to form impromptu groups, introduce themselves,

What do you hope to get out of this course? Will it address your needs and expectations? This is a Classroom Assessment Technique designed to help you identify your expectations and share them with the instructor— and each other. You will also find out what the teacher's goals are for this course, and see how well those goals match yours.

1. On the lines in the left-hand column below, please list three or four goals you hope to achieve—things you hope to learn or questions you hope to raise— through participation in this course.

Your Goals for this Course	Your Ranking of their Importance	Do they Match the Teachers'?	
_____	_____	YES	NO
_____	_____	YES	NO
_____	_____	YES	NO
_____	_____	YES	NO
_____	_____	YES	NO

2. Now, using the middle column above, rank your goals in terms of their relative importance to you. Make the most important goal #1, the next most important goal #2, and so on.
3. As you hear the instructor's goals, circle "Yes" in the right-hand column next to each of your goals which matches one of those listed. If you end up with goals that the teacher has not mentioned, circle "No" next to them.
4. Prepare to talk about any important goals you have which are not included in the teacher's list of goals and/or to ask questions about those goals.

Reference: Angelo, T.A. & Cross, K.P. *Classroom Assessment Techniques: A Handbook for College Teachers*, 2nd edition. San Francisco: Jossey-Bass, 1993, pp. 290–294. (Reprinted with permission.)

GOAL RANKING & MATCHING EXERCISE

FIGURE 3.1

and share their lists and concerns. After this, the instructors pass out their syllabus, ask the students to read it carefully, and note which of the questions posed earlier by their groups have been answered. A fruitful class discussion then unfolds over syllabus components, teaching philosophies, and course approaches.

Obviously, the syllabus will contain the usual major components: course information, including how to contact the instructor; required texts and recommended readings; class schedule; course requirements, often linked to the critically important evaluation standards; and class policies, including sections on absenteeism, late assignments, and academic honesty. These components should reflect a well-thought-out course design.

Because the syllabus is such an important document, it is wise to pursue the practice of "more is better." A well-constructed, well-thought-out syllabus can protect faculty members from student complaints or grievances. Equally important, it can foster a positive learning environment when students get an immediate impression of a well-prepared, student-centered instructor. Such impressions will help establish credibility if small-group work techniques are either new to students or, worse, they have been "burned" (a common occurrence) by ill-conceived group implementations in previous classes.

The syllabus for a cooperative-learning class should be free of any classroom practices or course policies, such as "grading on the curve," that foster a sense of competition. "Grading on the curve" does not mean adjusting grades to reflect the realities of student performance; rather, it refers to the practice of establishing strict quotas (5% A's, 5% F's, etc.) unrelated to the actual abilities and performances of students within a given class. The evaluation system, as emphasized earlier, should result in individual accountability: students remain responsible for the outcomes of their learning experiences. Most instructors use a criterion-referenced grading scheme based on conventional assignments such as in-class or take-home tests, quizzes, and homework. If faculty assign group projects, they typically include ways to assess the value of individual student contributions. Instructors most comfortable with innovation have moved to completely noncompetitive grading practices such as learning contracts or mastery learning. Grading issues are discussed further in chapter 11.

In course planning, faculty should also be mindful of the fact that cooperative learning is typically an in-class pedagogy. Michaelsen, Fink, & Black (1996) offer compelling evidence why out-of-class assignments, particularly those where students work individually on pieces of a written project, can undermine group cohesiveness. Sheer "logistics" create many problems, since conflicting schedules may make it unreasonable to demand that learning teams meet for extended periods of time outside of class. Those students who are willing to "burn the midnight oil" on independent homework assignments may have difficulty scheduling out-of-class meetings that all teammates can attend, and this might lead to interpersonal, within-team conflicts. The students unable to attend meetings may feel frustration at what they perceive as unfair demands on their time and the other teammates may resent the lack of contributions from the missing students. Typically, students will meet only once to divide up the project and will then worry that unfamiliar teammates will not follow through with their fair share. Out-of-class group work also prevents faculty members from monitoring group progress directly. Such problems can be avoided by careful classroom management techniques, including formation of organized learning teams who will complete well-defined in-class tasks throughout a term.

SUMMARY

College faculty wishing to improve the effectiveness of teaching and learning processes have taken positive steps by choosing to initiate cooperative learning in their classes. If they are to succeed, teachers must have made a philosophical commitment to cooperative learning's key principles, particularly to positive interdependence and individual accountability. This commitment and enthusiasm must be clearly communicated to students through well-thought-out course designs reflected in an "enriched" syllabus intended to both inform and motivate.

REFERENCES

Angelo, T.A. (1996). "Seven Shifts and Seven Levers: Developing More Productive Learning Communities." *The National Teaching and Learning Forum*. 6(1), 1–4.

Angelo, T.A. and Cross, K.P. (1993). *Classroom Assessment Techniques: A Handbook for College Teachers*, 2nd Ed. San Francisco: Jossey-Bass.

Brookfield, S.D. (1987). *Developing Critical Thinkers: Challenging Adults to Explore Alternative Ways of Thinking and Acting*. San Francisco: Jossey-Bass.

Brookfield, S.D. (1991). *The Skillful Teacher: On Technique, Trust, and Responsiveness in the Classroom*. San Francisco: Jossey-Bass.

Buscaglia, L. (1982). *Living, Loving and Learning*. Troy, MI: Holt, Rinehart, & Winston.

"Deep Learning, Surface Learning." (1993). *AAHE Bulletin*, 45(8), 14–17.

Duffy, D.K. and Jones, J.W. (1995). *Teaching within the Rhythms of the Semester*. San Francisco: Jossey-Bass.

Fassinger, P.A. (1995). "Understanding Classroom Interaction: Students' and Professors' Contributions to Students' Silence." *Journal of Higher Education*, 66, 82–96.

Finkle, D.L. and Monk, G.S. (1983). "Teachers and Learning Groups: Dissolution of the Atlas Complex." In C. Bouton and R.Y. Garth (Eds.), *Learning in Groups. New Directions for Teaching and Learning*, No. 14 (pp. 83–97). San Francisco: Jossey-Bass.

Forsyth, D.R. and McMillan, J.H. (1991a). "Practical Proposals for Motivating Students." In R. J. Menges & M. D. Svinicki (Eds.), *College Teaching: From Theory to Practice: New Directions for Teaching and Learning*, No. 45 (pp. 53–65). San Francisco: Jossey-Bass.

Forsyth, D.R. and McMillan, J.H. (1991b). "What Theories of Motivation Say about Why Students Learn." In R.J. Menges and M.D. Svinicki (Eds.), *College Teaching: From Theory to Practice. New Directions for Teaching and Learning*, No. 45 (pp. 39–51). San Francisco: Jossey-Bass.

Gabennesch, H. (1992). "The Enriched Syllabus: To Convey a Larger Vision." *The National Teaching and Learning Forum*, 1(4), 4.

Graves, L.N. (1994). "Creating a Community Context for Cooperative Learning. In S. Sharan (Ed.), *Handbook of Cooperative Learning Methods*. (pp. 283–99) Westport, CT: Greenwood Press.

Harris, M.M. (1993). "Motivating with the Course Syllabus." *The National Teaching and Learning Forum.* 3(1), 1–3.

Hirsch Jr., E.D. (1996). *The Schools We Need: And Why We Don't Have Them.* New York: Doubleday.

Johnson, D.W., Johnson, R.T., and Smith, K.A. (1991). *Cooperative Learning: Increasing College Faculty Instructional Productivity.* ASHE-ERIC Higher Education Report No. 4. Washington, DC: The George Washington University, School of Education and Human Development.

Michaelsen, L.K. (1992). "Team Learning: A Comprehensive Approach for Harnessing the Power of Small Groups in Higher Education." In D.H. Wulff and J.D. Nyquist (Eds.), *To Improve the Academy: Resources for Faculty, Instructional, and Organizational Development,* Vol. 11 (pp. 107–22). The Professional and Organizational Development Network in Higher Education. Stillwater, OK: New Forums Press, Inc.

Michaelsen, L.K., Fink, D.L., and Black, R.H. (1996). "What Every Faculty Developer Needs to Know about Learning Groups. In L. Richlin (Ed.), *To Improve the Academy: Resources for Faculty, Instructional, and Organizational Development,* Vol. 15 (pp. 31–57). The Professional and Organizational Development Network in Higher Education. Stillwater, OK: New Forums Press, Inc.

National Center for Research to Improve Postsecondary Teaching and Learning. (1990). "Teaching Thinking in College." *Accent on Improving College Teaching and Learning,* No. 7. Ann Arbor, Michigan: NCRIPTAL.

Palmer, P.J. (1983). *To Know As We Are Known: A Spirituality of Education.* San Francisco: HarperCollins.

Rhem, J. (1995a). "Deep/surface Approaches to Learning: An Introduction." *The National Teaching and Learning Forum,* 5(1), 1–3.

Rhem, J. (1995b). "Close-Up: Going Deep." *The National Teaching and Learning Forum,* 5(1), 4.

Sousa, D.A. (1995). *How the Brain Learns: A Classroom Teacher's Guide.* Reston, VA: The National Association of Secondary School Principals.

Svinicki, M.D. (1991). "Theories and Metaphors We Teach By." In R.J. Menges and M.D. Svinicki (Eds.), *College Teaching: From Theory to Practice. New Directions for Teaching and Learning,* No. 45 (pp. 111–19). San Francisco: Jossey-Bass.

CHAPTER 4

Managing the Cooperative Classroom

"Does thou love life? Then do not squander time, for that is the stuff life is made of."

Benjamin Franklin

C lassroom management techniques are the grease that keeps the wheels rolling in unison in a cooperative classroom. They guarantee that students and faculty understand and accept their new roles, and they simplify the logistics of classroom maintenance. For instance, many professors—especially those with large classes—use team folders to return homework assignments and distribute class materials; later, students put homework and class activities in the folder, often after recording attendance and quiz grades. Before initiating such techniques, however, faculty must first organize their classroom activities around structured-learning teams.

ORGANIZING STRUCTURED-LEARNING TEAMS

The heart of a cooperative classroom lies in structured-learning teams. The critically important cooperative-learning structures promote interactions within and between these teams. The discipline-related concepts are, in turn, supported by the structures (Figure 4.1).

Although some well-known advocates of cooperative learning, such as David and Roger Johnson, recommend teams of three, most university and college level practitioners prefer heterogeneous groups of four, or "quads." Quads offer several benefits: (1) They are small enough that group members

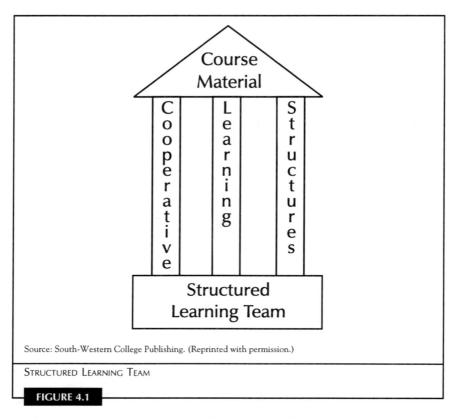

Source: South-Western College Publishing. (Reprinted with permission.)

FIGURE 4.1

tend to stay attentive and on task. Students can't "hide" or tune out as might happen, for instance, in a group of eight or, more significantly, in a typical college classroom predicated on whole-class discussion. (2) Quads are large enough to function smoothly when team members are occasionally absent. (3) Quads lend themselves well to pair work, a powerful way to stimulate student achievement and critical-thinking skills. If a class divides unevenly, faculty can add a fifth member to a team. If the teams are teacher-selected, not randomly selected, these students may not be as strong as other team members, usually because of absenteeism but sometimes because of weak academic preparation. In such teams, of course, the students should never realize who the "add-on" might be.

TEAM FORMATION

Teams may be formed in a number of ways. Some instructors prefer random assignment to teams, such as having students number off. Twenty students, for example, would form five four-person teams by calling out "1-2-3-4-5; 1-2-3-

4-5; 1-2-3-4-5; and 1-2-3-4-5." The ones would become a team, the twos a team, and so forth. Such randomness often, but not always, results in hetero-geneous teams. Students usually perceive this formation technique as fair, although some may be disappointed at being unable to work with friends. Another team formation technique, student self-selected teams, suggests that teachers are open to student wishes, but the resultant teams are rarely heterogeneous: birds of a feather tend to flock together. Furthermore, solid research suggests that such teams are likely to be unsuccessful (Fiechtner and Davis, 1985).

Sometimes, instructors can offer students a combination of student-se-lected and faculty-selected teams by asking them to identify three classmates with whom they would enjoy working, with the promise that they will be grouped with one of them. This practice is best done after students have had an opportunity to become acquainted with one another. Problems in honoring these commitments may arise, however, if large numbers of students consis-tently request the same talented classmates. As another alternative, faculty who expect students to work together outside of class—a practice not recom-mended—can group students based on propinquity or common free periods. Instructors who are concerned about learning styles can even group students based on the students' outcomes on instruments such as the Meyers-Briggs Type Indicator or the Firo-B.

Most cooperative-learning theorists and practitioners advocate instructor-selected teams, with a few caveats. Felder and Brent (1994) caution against groups where women and minorities are outnumbered. They do not recom-mend teams composed of only one woman or one minority member. Faculty should use discretion on this issue, perhaps consulting individual students to determine their preferences or potential comfort levels.

In the team formation process, regardless of when it is done, instructors should distribute students from team to team based on their academic prepa-ration and ability, their gender, their ethnic background, and any other characteristics that might prove useful. The idea is to create teams that will build on students' varied strengths. As Redding (1990) notes, students with different learning styles, can, in cooperative-learning groups, "teach each other from their special and particular perspectives" (p. 47). This type of heterogeneous grouping also provides opportunities for positive interaction. Slavin (1989–1990) concludes, "When students of different racial or ethnic backgrounds work together toward a common goal, they gain in liking and respect for one another" (p. 52).

Probably the easiest way an instructor new to cooperative learning can form heterogeneous teams is by using student data sheets. The sheets should be passed out with the syllabus at the first class meeting. The students use them to indicate academic course-related information, such as the number of courses taken in the major, relevant outside work experience, and current course and workload. In addition, students willing to share their telephone numbers for distribution in a telephone tree will facilitate out-of-class student contacts. An added benefit of the data sheets is students' appreciation for the instructor's interest in their academic and personal lives. This obvious interest helps to build the student-faculty rapport and trust needed for a cooperative classroom. To build trust even further, faculty can complete the same data sheet and distribute it to students the first class session, following the practice of self-disclosure advocated by Bonwell (1996) and others.

To help with the formation of heterogeneous teams, faculty members might want to be certain that they can identify students from diverse backgrounds. If whole-class introductions are made, instructors can jot down tactful descriptions of each student. Some instructors prefer to form teams later in a term after they have gotten a feel for students' abilities and personalities.

Other team formation processes are possible, including some that are suitable for short-term assignments. These will be discussed in later chapters. The formation of permanent structured-learning teams (ones kept intact for a full term or at least over an extended period of time) should be accomplished purposefully. Michaelsen (1996) suggests a carefully crafted lineup to ensure heterogeneity in large classes. He prioritizes his selection criteria and asks all students who meet his first criterion to line up at one corner of the room. He then extends the line by asking students to line up in turn as they match additional criteria. For example, rather than single out international students, he invites all students born outside of Oklahoma (where he teaches) to take their places in the line. Usually, he finds that individuals from specific countries tend to stand together. After all students are in place, he directs them to count off sequentially up to the specified number of teams. In a class of 240, for example, where he wants six-person teams, students initially count 1 through 40 and then begin the sequence of 1 through 40 five more times. Afterwards, all students with the same number unite to form a six-person team with highly divergent members. No one standing together in the initial line-up would work together on a permanent learning team. If lining up is too difficult, instructors can have students stand when their criterion is called and number off immediately. Those already assigned to a team would not stand again, even though they may possess another designated criterion.

Instructors in specific disciplines have developed some ingenious methods of group formation tied to their course content. Hughes (1996), for example, describes an extended process for "hiring" group members in a business management course. All students prepare a resume and submit with it a cover letter applying to be either group leaders or group members. The instructor reviews all the materials and selects group leaders for each of the projected permanent learning teams. Each team leader is then given the same amount of "money" to serve as a hiring budget, and the resumes of the remaining classmates. The leaders subsequently submit bids for the members they desire. They could, for example, spend their entire budget to acquire one desired team member. More typically, the leaders offer bids for several students. After tabulating the bids, the instructor assigns the teams. This process has several advantages: (1) The teams are likely to be heterogeneous because no one leader can afford all the optimum group members; (2) Team cohesion is promoted because no one except the instructor and the team leaders, who keep this information confidential, knows who bid what for whom. Therefore, all students assume that they are desired and valued team members; (3) Perhaps most important, the application and bidding process models "real-world" business scenarios, giving students opportunities to practice relevant skills. A process such as this divides students into two broad categories, team leaders and team members; later, students will be assigned specific roles within their teams.

ASSIGNING GROUP ROLES

Having formed the teams, faculty will want to be able to identify each team member quickly and easily, so that roles can be assigned to accomplish specified tasks. The easiest way to establish quick student identifications within given teams is to have students number off (one, two, three, four). Many faculty prefer to identify teams and team members through the use of playing cards, which can be distributed as the teams are assembled. The playing cards allow the instructor to communicate readily to the students their group assignments (by the rank of the card) and the roles they are to play within that group (by the suit of the card). Instructors can enliven discussions by having students draw cards from another deck: the person whose card is drawn then is called upon. The playing cards enable faculty to easily keep track of students they have called upon directly—a serious equity concern— by checking off from an ongoing list, for example, the Jack of Hearts or the Two of Clubs. When instructors add extra team members, bringing some team totals to five, they can use jokers—carefully designated as "wild cards" because of the connotations— for the fifth member or can cannibalize a second desk of cards. In the latter case, a team composed of five deuces might contain two "hearts," which can be distinguished by the color of the back of the playing card, usually blue or red.

The roles assigned within the groups are rotated frequently to form positive interdependence. This practice discourages domination by one person, a problem common in less-structured group work, and gives all students an opportunity to practice various social, communication, and leadership skills. This emphasis on rotating roles prepares all students for success, not only in the cooperative-learning classroom, but also in the "real world" of society, where teamwork is essential. Miller (1996) gives an additional rationale for role rotation. Research she has conducted using Gordon's cognitive-style typology suggests that students respond differently to course materials and to cooperative-learning tasks based on their cognitive styles. Permitting groups to assign members' roles often allows students to opt for tasks that come easily and to circumvent tasks that challenge them. Assigning rotating roles in a group, a practice perceived as equitable, allows all students to be stretched by a variety of tasks (p. 13).

It is often useful to give the rationale for these rotating roles, which will differ from institution to institution and from discipline to discipline. At the U.S. Air Force Academy, for example, the following paragraph provides a rationale for the practice of rotating roles:

> In the Air Force you will hold a number of different positions and play many different roles. Learning to assume responsibly for the duties associated with these roles is a key part of your cadet experience in your squadrons, on the athletic fields, and in your classrooms. To ensure that everyone has an opportunity to experience different responsibilities, the roles in this class will rotate each week to a different team member.

The following defined roles work well in college and university classrooms:

Group Facilitator

These students are responsible for moderating all team discussions, keeping the group on task for each assignment, and ensuring that everybody assumes their share of the work involved. They must also be certain that everyone benefits from an optimal learning situation: everyone should have the opportunity to learn, to participate, and to earn the respect of their teammates.

Group Recorder/Folder Monitor

These students are responsible for picking up the team folder and checking it carefully. They distribute all material other than the student data sheets or any other items that are to remain permanently in the folder. They also distribute all class materials and return all papers, assignments, or notes to their teammates. At the end of the class session, they make sure that all relevant class materials are in the team folder before returning it to the instructor. The Recorders keep all necessary records, including attendance and homework check-offs, and record any assigned team activities. They also prepare the group's activities, completing work sheets or written assignments or summarizing discussions for their group's oral reports or for submission to the instructor.

Group Reporter

If no other specific spokesperson is designated by the instructor, these students will assume that role and orally summarize the group's activities or conclusions. They also routinely assist the Group Recorder with the preparation of group reports and worksheets.

Timekeeper

The Timekeeper is responsible for keeping the group aware of time constraints for any activities. With the facilitator, they help the group remain on task, consulting with other teams when needed. They are also responsible for leaving the team's work area in good condition and assuming the role of any missing group members, if no fifth member is available to fill in.

Wild Card

These students assume the role of any missing member or fill in however they are needed.

The student roles are more realistic when they match disciplines. Accounting students, for example, enjoy roles with titles that correspond to executive positions in business organizations. Thus, the facilitator becomes the Chief Executive Officer (CEO); the Chief Financial Officer (CFO) acts as the timekeeper; the Controller serves as the recorder; and an Executive Vice President (EVP) serves as the reporter. Other roles can be added, based on the discipline needs. For example, the fifth student in a group, the Wild Card, could serve as a lawyer, who acts as the group's skeptic by questioning assumptions and conclusions. These assigned roles give all students a sense of importance, raising individual self-esteem while simultaneously building group cohesion

In addition to the ongoing responsibilities associated with specified roles, the real work of the teams will be to complete, cooperatively, a variety of assignments and activities designed to help members learn the course content. Instructors can use the teams, for example, as a basis for short-term activities such as the Think-Pair-Share structure which will be discussed more fully in chapter 5. For example, an instructor might pose a significant question, such as "How does the digestive system work?" or "Define 'due process'" or "Explain why the human brain operates like either a sponge or a sieve," allowing 30 seconds of wait time before initiating a three-minute discussion. To identify pairs for the discussion, the instructor might ask the heart to pair with the student holding the diamond and the club to pair with the person holding the spade. For the final portion of this activity, the instructor might call on a volunteer or two to share the paired conclusions with the entire class, or the sharing might be done within the quad.

As indicated in chapter 1, these heterogeneous structured-learning teams typically remain in place for at least half a semester. Most practitioners agree that groups must remain together long enough to establish rapport and undergo the "forming, storming, norming, performing" interactions described in the group dynamics literature. Most theorists agree that groups undergo various stages of development. Charrier (1965), for example, identifies five stages of group maturation characterized by (1) politeness (getting acquainted, sharing values, trust, etc.); (2) goal setting (Why are we here? goals, objectives); (3) bid for power (influence, competence); (4) cooperation (constructive, open-mindedness, accepting differences); and (5) esprit de corps (unity, cohesion, high spirits). These stages, whatever they are called, require students to work together for an extended period of time. The research of Watson, Michaelsen, and Sharp (1989) suggests that groups tend to rely heavily on their most competent member until they adapt more cooperative behaviors after 20–25 hours together. Furthermore, culturally heterogeneous groups rarely cohere as rapidly as more homogeneous groups: effective functioning may not begin until 35–40 hours of extended teamwork (Watson, Kumar, and Michaelsen, 1993).

Forming new groups at the midterm point, however, does offer students the opportunity to work with different individuals, a useful skill in the workforce. It can also eliminate the predictability of groups that have fallen into set patterns. Furthermore, it gives teachers an opportunity, after having become better acquainted with students' talents, learning styles, and personalities, to put together more functional groups. If new groups are to be formed, a convenient time is after an hour test or after the midterm, when the achievement levels will be more obvious. At this point, the faculty member should assign to each group one student who performed well on the exam, one who performed poorly, and two or three who performed close to the mean. Once again, additional heterogeneity can be built into the groups by dividing the students as evenly as possible with respect to gender and ethnicity. Personality factors can be taken into account as well.

Often, when teams are formed, students will find their own working space in the classroom. Students should sit as close together as possible to allow for face-to-face interaction. If possible, the groups should be arranged so that the instructor can circulate among them to monitor team progress and behaviors. This direct student-faculty contact also sends a clear signal that the instructor values student learning. Because the architects who design classrooms often have unenlightened views of learning options, many classrooms are not conducive to group work, particularly those with seats bolted to the floor in rigid rows. Other than opting for another room, instructors can do little to change these configurations. However, through careful planning, instructors can still facilitate planned group activities, even in an auditorium. A seating chart, such as the one depicted in Figure 4.2, allows students to work within learning teams, including pairs, with a minimum of physical movement.

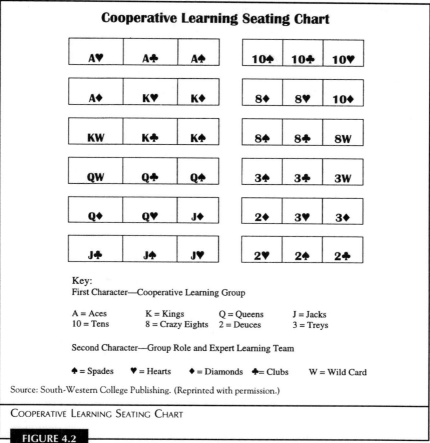

Cooperative Learning Seating Chart

A♥	A♣	A♠

A♦	K♥	K♦

KW	K♣	K♠

QW	Q♣	Q♠

Q♦	Q♥	J♦

J♣	J♠	J♥

10♠	10♣	10♥

8♦	8♥	10♦

8♠	8♣	8W

3♠	3♣	3W

2♦	3♥	3♦

2♥	2♠	2♣

Key:
First Character—Cooperative Learning Group

A = Aces	K = Kings	Q = Queens	J = Jacks
10 = Tens	8 = Crazy Eights	2 = Deuces	3 = Treys

Second Character—Group Role and Expert Learning Team

♠ = Spades   ♥ = Hearts   ♦ = Diamonds   ♣= Clubs   W = Wild Card

Source: South-Western College Publishing. (Reprinted with permission.)

COOPERATIVE LEARNING SEATING CHART

FIGURE 4.2

ESTABLISHING CLASSROOM NORMS

A culture for cooperative learning must be fostered at the onset. Most students come from academic backgrounds that reward competitiveness rather than cooperation. In a cooperative-learning class, students should understand and follow these fundamental rules: You have the right to ask questions or ask for help in your group; you have the responsibility to provide assistance in your group. These rules can be extended class-wide, so that students feel free to consult other groups.

Because most students view instructors as the source of truth and wisdom, they tend to turn to them immediately when questions arise. To discourage this, faculty members should advocate another class norm: Look first to teammates and classmates for answers; consult the instructor only when everyone in the group has the same question. Many instructors carry this edict even further and require groups to send a group member, such as the Recorder, to another team to ask them if they know the answer. As a classroom rule, students can be required to consult three other sources before turning to the instructor. Kagan (1992) calls this guideline "three before me." When such parameters are enforced, students quickly learn that much of the knowledge they seek may be found within the collective wisdom of the group itself. Therefore, a subtle shift occurs, moving the instructor off center stage and into the role of coach or helper.

Establishing group and class norms at the beginning of the semester is a positive way to build team cohesiveness and also to head off potential team dysfunctions down the road. Thus, before the newly assembled teams get down to the serious discipline-related tasks that will be their primary focus for the next eight weeks or so, many instructors set aside class time to determine group norms. Students then identify and establish guidelines to help their teams function more smoothly.

Solomon has developed a worksheet (Figure 4.3) to help students focus on the task of clarifying their own expectations, the expectations they have of their learning team, and finally, the collective expectations they have for their

---

Individual Expectations

_____

_____

_____

Paired Expectations

_____

_____

_____

Team Expectations

_____

_____

_____

---

* Solomon, R., Davidson, N. & Solomon, E. (1993) *The Handbook for the 4th R: Relationship Activities for Cooperative & Collegial Learning*, Vol. III. Columbia, MD. National Institute for Relationship Training. (Reprinted with permission).

WHAT BEHAVIORS DO YOU EXPECT FROM YOUR TEAMMATES?

FIGURE 4.3

classroom experiences. Similarly, Towns (1996, personal correspondence) has students first answer questions independently and then work toward team expectations. As part of the process, the students also discuss the advantages and disadvantages of working in groups, a good way to get issues out in the open (Figure 4.4).

Team-building exercises such as this help students establish "ownership" of the group process. Initially, every group member must contribute to the group consensus. But perhaps more important, because team norms are recorded (those using team folders usually staple them to the inside cover), they remain a viable reference point for team cohesiveness. A team, for example, might decide that all members should have a voice in decisions. If, later in the term, a team member suggests that a peer's input was ignored, the group can feel comfortable about turning to that student to be certain they have included her alternative viewpoint. Many groups will establish norms such as "We will

---

Chemistry 344

Name _____ Date _____

Working in Groups—Your Viewpoint

[Date] will be our first problem solving session. During these PSS you will work with four or five other students to solve a problem. In order to prepare you for working in a group, answer the questions below. **Take some time to really think about what you believe your responsibilities are to your group mates and what the group's responsibility is to each member.**

1. List what you believe your responsibilities are to the group.
2. List your group's responsibilities to each member.
3. Describe the advantages of working in a group or as a team.
4. Describe the disadvantages of working in a group or as a team

Working in a Group

We believe an individual member of our group has the following responsibilities to the group.

We believe our group has the following responsibilities to each individual member.

Names _____   _____

                _____   _____

                _____   _____

Towns, M. T., Assistant Professor of Chemistry, Ball State University. (Reprinted with permission.)

TEAM-BUILDING ACTIVITY BASED ON SHARED COMMITMENTS

FIGURE 4.4

respect one another's opinions"; "We will all contribute our fair share"; "We will contact one another if we must be absent"; "We will help one another succeed"; and "We will all listen attentively." Regardless of their previous education or life experience, all students should feel that they are contributing group members. Group norms and expectations not only establish a climate in which students can feel their contributions are heard; but they also motivate students to offer more to the team.

TEAM BUILDING

Because group cohesion is such an important part of successful team learning, many instructors will spend some time on activities calculated to promote positive relationships and foster interdependence. This investment is a judgment call individual faculty members must make: their decision will probably depend on how confident they feel about asking students to do unexpected exercises. Many instructors feel that time invested upfront in teambuilding— a concept echoed in the corporate world—is time well spent. A decision to deliberately foster team cohesiveness will likely be made only by instructors who are themselves convinced that such activities are not "Mickey Mouse," "grade schoolish," or "hold-me-touch-me-feel-me." But, faculty willing to accept the value of team building and experiment with some specific activities generally find that they encounter fewer student-student problems.

Abrami, Chambers, Poulsen, Howden, d'Apollonia, De Simone, Kastelorizios, Wagner, and Glashan (1993) divide team-building activities into three broad categories: (1) icebreakers, used initially to help team members get acquainted; (2) appreciation activities that help teammates discover each others' talents; and (3) goal setting or visioning activities that aim for deeper cohesion based on shared goals and agreed-upon procedures.

Bonwell (1996) advocates icebreakers for the first class session because they help students grow accustomed to public speaking and aid students' comfort levels by enabling them to get acquainted with one another. An icebreaker that leads to shared appreciation might be a team-naming activity. Cooperative-learning professors may decide to provide ten minutes of class time to allow students to determine team names. Although some may regard this exercise as too frivolous or too risky, students tend to bond more quickly when the team name gives them a sense of cohesion. Often the students come up with team names by identifying elements they have in common, a good way to strengthen ties within a heterogeneous group. Teams, might, for instance, dub themselves the "No Accounts" if all of them have misgivings about the course challenges in a foundation accounting course; or, they might focus on common personal characteristics or hobbies, evidenced by names such as "The Hip Hops" or "Travelers."

Kagan (1992) recommends a team-building activity called "Uncommon Commonalities" (Figure 4.5) where students list things that team members have in common (close family members who are ichthyologists; fears of flying; passions for pistachio ice cream). If three students share a passion for surfing, then the word "surfing" goes in column three. If only one person is a Buffalo Bills fan, then the words "Buffalo Bills" are entered in the first column. Students strive to find as many commonalities as they can, so that the fourth column (or fifth, if there are five members) will have the most entries. After identifying points in common, each team can try to reach consensus on a team name, usually one based on those points. Kagan (1992) suggests that the team-naming project should follow these guidelines: (1) Each team member has a voice in the decision; (2) Consensus must be reached; (3) Consensus does not imply coercion. (4) Any team members having serious objections to the group decision should not consent to it (pp. 8:3–8:5).

Uncommon Commonalities			
1	2	3	4

Team Name

Solomon, R., Davidson, N. & Solomon, E. (1993) *The Handbook for the 4th R: Relationship Activities for Cooperative & Collegial Learning*, Vol. III. Columbia, MD. National Institute for Relationship Training. (Reprinted with permission).

TEAM-BUILDING ACTIVITY BASED ON SHARED INTERESTS

FIGURE 4.5

If team folders are used, the teams may spontaneously decorate the covers based on the team name, an action that aids classroom management because teachers and teams can readily identify the folders. Students may also bring in personal photos, stickers, or other decorations for the front cover.

THE QUIET SIGNAL

Because structured-group work rarely occupies all of the allotted class time, instructors find that a class usually alternates between the lecture mode, when the class's attention is focused upon the instructor, and the group mode, when students are actively learning within their teams.

With well-designed instructions, transfer from the lecture mode to the group mode presents no difficulty. A prearranged quiet signal provides a convenient and uncomplicated way to regain the class's attention when they are actively engaged in group activities. Instructors simply explain the need for the signal and then invite students to choose among several options or to identify their own signal. Most often, students will opt for a raised hand. Instructors wishing to capture the class's attention raise their hand. When students notice the signal, they complete any unfinished sentence, raise their own hands, and signal those around them to also raise their hands. Within seconds, this raised-hands technique can transform the noisiest classroom into one of attentive silence. An auditory signal, such as a tinkling brass bell, can serve as an alternative or a supplement to a raised hand. To provide comic interlude and to prevent students from tuning out a familiar sound, one accounting instructor uses a collection of unusual bells which he alternates throughout the term. The variety of signals keeps student attention from waning. Even flickering lights can prove effective, provided instructors are not in a computer lab!

A timer with a shrill auditory signal serves as a particularly efficient quiet signal because it can, at the same time, allow the instructor to monitor timed tasks. The timer also helps students understand that they must complete tasks within the allotted time. Instructors must be careful, however, that they do not unintentionally annoy or offend students by overuse of any of these signals.

COOPERATIVE HOMEWORK CHECK: AN EXAMPLE TO MODEL A WELL-MANAGED COOPERATIVE CLASSROOM

The point of a cooperative classroom is to enhance student learning. College and university faculty new to cooperative learning should be certain that all exercises related to the structured-learning teams involve students in meaningful activities. A good starting point is to use cooperative-learning activities as a stimulating alternative to the ponderous, teacher-dominated task of reviewing assigned homework problems. During a Cooperative Homework Check, students review homework assignments in their structured-learning teams. Here is how this activity might unfold in a typical precalculus class:

Ten minutes before class begins, Dr. Allison is placing the session's agenda on the chalkboard. Stacked on the front desk are colorful file folders, including some neon ones, with sheets stapled to the front covers indicating the various team numbers. "Hi, Sally!" "Good morning, Zeke." Smiling cheerfully, Dr. Allison turns to greet each entering student. Students laugh and joke with one another as they enter the classroom and take their seats within their structured-learning teams. While they stow backpacks and remove notebooks, the team Recorder/Folder Monitors pick up the team folders and carefully pass out to the team members the homework turned in the previous class period. The checkmarks indicate that Dr. Allison has glanced over each student's work. The Folder Monitors also distribute worksheets that their teams will use later in the class period to do sample problems after Dr. Allison has offered a mini-lecture on power functions. Team Three has a bright orange folder with a decorated front cover sporting the words "Number Crunchers" and a shark-toothed PacMan. Bill, Team Three's facilitator, glances at the clock and says, "Are we ready?" The three other students nod eagerly and, like other teams in the room, they begin a systematic review of the homework they will turn in this class period. "Okay, what did we come up with for number one?" asks Bill. The team members chorus "509 years," identical answers. "Great!" says Bill. "Number two?" Again, there is agreement. "Number three?" This time, Shawn has a different value for the growth constant than his teammates do. "Okay, let's have a look," smiles Bill. "You may have discovered the ultimate, awesome answer." The four heads pore over Shawn's paper. "I see it!" exclaims Melissa. "Look at this step." She then explains to Shawn where the calculation went astray. "Oh, I see it now," responds Shawn. "Thanks!" "Okay," says Bill. "Number four?" As the students work, Dr. Allison is moving silently from team to team, listening and observing.

About midway through the review period, Dr. Allison raises her hand as a quiet signal and the class comes to attention. "From my monitoring, it is obvious that most of you had trouble with Number 17. Let me review the principles behind it and then have the Reporter from Team Six—that's Vanessa, isn't it?—explain the steps involved. Team Six really got into this problem in depth."

As the Homework Check continues, the Timekeepers for each group remind their teammates of the need to pace their coverage of the assigned problems. At one point, the members of Team Eight discover that they cannot agree on the correct solution for Number 15. The Timekeeper consults with Team Five and is able to clarify the discrepancies in their team's answers up to a point. Since none of them can resolve the entire computational impasse, all team members raise their hands, signaling to Dr. Allison that they need help. She cheerfully provides the necessary information.

At the conclusion of the specified time, each Group Recorder marks on a sheet at the back of the folder the number of problems each student got correct. Dr. Allison and the class had previously established ground rules emphasizing academic honesty for this procedure. The Recorder/Folder Monitor sees that the corrected homework problems for each team member are placed in the folder. Dr. Allison will skim them, place checkmarks on the papers, and return them via the folder at the next class session. The class then proceeds to the next phase indicated on the agenda, the mini-lecture on power functions.

This Cooperative Homework Check replaces the typical homework review where the instructor asks the entire class if anyone had trouble working any of the problems. Often the problem specified and then put on the blackboard is one that many students answered correctly, so their time is wasted. Often, too, the slower students do not want to call attention to their deficiencies and will never identify perplexing problems.

A Cooperative Homework Check, like other group-oriented activities, results in several positive effects. Because of peer pressure, more students come to class prepared. Students are more likely to work on assigned problems if they know they will let their team down if they are unprepared. Also, many more students become more actively involved in the learning process than under a traditional model where the teachers asks students to identify difficult problems and then works them on the board while students watch passively.

Another advantage of reviewing problems within the team is the positive impact of immediate feedback and peer tutoring. Students focus only on those problems that gave them trouble and provide on-the-spot coaching for any students needing special attention. Such coaching benefits both the coaches— who conceptualize and verbalize the steps—and the students who receive the coaching. Because of the individualized, focused coaching, students appear to learn and retain course concepts far better. Perhaps best of all, activities such as the Cooperative Homework Check allow students to assume responsibility for their own learning and that of their classmates.

SUMMARY

Practical classroom-management logistics, such as group formation and duration, the role of students, and the role of the teacher, make for a smooth-running class. Team-building activities that lead to team norms, or guidelines, provide perimeters for expected behavior as well as establish faster group cohesiveness. Once the climate is set for a cooperative classroom, instructors can use the structures described in the following chapters as tools to implement cooperative learning.

REFERENCES

Abrami, P., Chambers, P.C., Poulsen, C., Howden, J., d'Apollonia, S., De Simone, C., Kastelorizios, K., Wagner, D., and Glashan, A. (1993). *Using Cooperative Learning.* Montreal: Concordia University: Centre for the Study of Classroom Processes.

Bonwell, C. (1996). "Building a Supportive Climate for Active Learning." *The National Teaching and Learning Forum.* 6(1), 4–7.

Charrier, G.C. (1965). *Cog's Ladder: A Model of Group Growth.* Unpublished paper at Proctor and Gamble Co.

Felder, R.M. and Brent, R. (1994). *Cooperative Learning in Technical Courses: Procedures, Pitfalls, and Payoffs.* Eric Document Reproduction Service Report ED 377038. Online at <http://www2.ncsu.edu/unity/lockers/users/f/felder/public/Papers/Coopreport.html>. Downloaded 27 June 1996.

Fiechtner, S.B. and Davis, E.A. (1985). "Why Groups Fail: A Survey of Student Experiences with Learning Groups." *The Organizational Behavior Teaching Review,* 9(4), 58–73.

Hughes, C. (1996). "The Dynamics of Group Formation: An Applied Method for Selecting Team Membership." *USAFA Educator,* 4(3), 8;10. Reprinted in *Cooperative Learning and College Teaching.*

Kagan, S. (1992). *Cooperative Learning.* San Juan Capistrano, CA: Resources for Teachers, Inc.

Michaelsen, L. (1996). *Problems with Learning Groups: An Ounce of Prevention.* Preconference Workshop. Annual Conference of the Professional and Organizational Development Network in Higher Education. Snowbird Resort and Conference Center, Salt Lake City, UT.

Miller, J.E. (1996). "Cognitive Styles and their Relevance in Improving Cooperative Learning Courses." *Cooperative Learning and College Teaching,* 7(1), 11–14.

Redding, N. (1990). "The Empowering Learners Project." *Educational Leadership,* 47(5), 46–48.

Slavin, R.E. (1989–1990). "Research on Cooperative Learning: Consensus and Controversy." *Educational Leadership,* 47(4), 52–55.

Solomon, R., Davidson, N., and Solomon, E. (1993). *The Handbook for the Fourth R: Relationship Activities for Cooperative and Collegial Learning,* Vol. III. Columbia, MD: National Institute for Relationship Training.

Watson, W.E., Kumar, K., and Michaelsen, L.K. (1993). "Cultural Diversity's Impact on Group Process and Performance: Comparing Culturally Homogeneous and Culturally Diverse Task Groups." *The Academy of Management Journal,* 36(3), 590–602.

Watson, W.E., Michaelsen, L.K., and Sharp, W. (1991). "Member Competence, Group Interaction, and Group Decision-making: A Longitudinal Study." *Journal of Applied Psychology,* 76, 801–09.

PART THREE

· · · · · · · · ·

Structuring the Cooperative Classroom

CHAPTER 5

Beginning Structures

"If you don't know where you are going, you will probably end up somewhere else."

Laurence J. Peter and Raymond Hull

Cooperative-learning structures are the "meat" in an educational sandwich. They offer faculty opportunities to design lessons that enrich students' learning through a range of educational activities. Pioneered by Spencer Kagan, the structural approach to cooperative learning is most effective when the structures allow students to process and elaborate on information to which they have been exposed earlier but need to commit to deep memory. As emphasized earlier, structures are the content-free building blocks, or tools, of cooperative learning. Instructors add their own content-specific information to create a classroom activity tied to course objectives. Many structures actively used by teachers at all levels of education are effective in college and university courses. Because much of the early work on cooperative learning was done at the K–12 level, the nomenclature, unfortunately, does not always suggest the rigor associated with postsecondary courses. Faculty members committed to the principles of cooperative learning and the positive effects it will have on student achievement and affective behaviors must simply remain open-minded and ignore the sometimes "cutesy" terminology. The point is: cooperative learning works, call it what one will.

The cooperative-learning structures discussed in this and subsequent chapters are powerful tools to achieve specific classroom objectives. Obviously they can remain nameless or can be renamed, but best of all, structures can be modified, or new ones invented, to serve specific course-related needs. This chapter concentrates on some basic introductory cooperative-learning structures that may be implemented easily into college courses.

The five structures discussed in this chapter—Think-Pair-Share, Roundtable, Value Line, Corners, and Three-Step Interview—are relatively simple to implement. All of these structures, however, require careful planning.

STRUCTURE! STRUCTURE! STRUCTURE!

Structure is essential to the cooperative-learning environment. The more organization built into classes, through focused structures and through classroom management techniques, the more meaningful active learning becomes. When structure is lacking or haphazard, which may have occurred too often in students' previous group work experiences, students wander off task: uncommitted learners revel in the opportunity to "blow it off" as more serious students chafe at the wasted time and question the validity of small-group work. Using a variety of cooperative-learning structures prevents boredom and provides varied learning opportunities. To eliminate the problem of off-task students, instructors should build into every structure an extra topic, assignment, problem, or step, called an extension activity, for groups that work more rapidly than others.

Therefore, besides initially "selling" students on the value of group work in theory, particularly by emphasizing that it develops the teamwork skills needed for success in life, instructors should gradually acquaint students with some of the structures outlined in this and subsequent chapters. The instructions for each activity, as indicated earlier, must be clearly articulated, preferably in writing. Worksheets or graphic organizers, particularly if used one-per-team, focus group work and emphasize the importance of positive interdependence.

Graphic Organizers

Graphic organizers are handouts or worksheets that help students organize information and ideas by providing a practical framework for given tasks. They furnish a visual, holistic representation of facts and their relationships. Instructors wishing to view many practical examples of graphic organizers should consult Bellanca (1990; 1992) and McTighe (1992). Several accounting-specific graphic organizers are included in Appendix A.

Graphic organizers enhance student learning in cooperative-learning settings by providing a focal point for discussion in the structured-learning teams. They offer a common frame of reference for thinking. After using the graphic organizer, members of the structured-learning teams have a tangible product of the team's discussion which can provide a basis for further reflection and thinking. This aspect aids the group-processing component of cooperative learning.

Graphic organizers are also useful for whole-class sharing. Each team can be given, for instance, a transparency acetate for a report-out using an overhead projector. Graphic organizers foster positive interdependence because only one worksheet is provided per team. Time on task is also enhanced because the pre-prepared worksheet clarifies the nature of the task and focuses the discussion. Graphic organizers, like concept mapping (chapter 12) where students jointly prepare a visual depiction of an abstract concept, help them become more aware of the creative, logical links between ideas, because this normally invisible part of the thinking process becomes perceivable. Besides offering examples of various types of graphic organizers (charts, spider maps, continuums, and chains), Prescott (1993) also underscores their value for students whose learning styles "need a visual stimulus to release their powers of critical thinking" (p. 9).

SEQUENCED LEARNING

As indicated in chapter 3, it is crucial to design learning activities that foster a deep approach to learning. Johnston (1995) provides a useful summary of the factors affecting deep learning. They are:

> The degree of interest, relevance, and challenge provided by the subject content, a workload which is not perceived as excessive by students, clarity and organisation [sic] of classes, provision of a framework through the use of concept maps which demonstrate interrelationships, assessment instruments which reward deeper learning, and student involvement in their own learning through the use of strategies such as group work or negotiation of topics for subject assessment tasks. Teachers need to surrender some control if the learner is to become independent and in this respect a "developed" approach to teaching is required (p. 6).

Developed theories of learning have been formulated by Baird (1992), Svensson and Hogfors (1988), and others. Essentially, those espousing developed theories see learning as a mutual journey undertaken by students and teachers. Students assume much of the responsibility for factors such as "pace, directions, objectives, and process" (Johnston, 1995, p. 1) with the teacher serving as a knowledgeable, experienced mentor or guide. Such flexible learning considers students' former experiences and knowledge as the journey unfolds. Johnston notes that "the teacher's role has changed from being an infallible expert responsible for a final product to being a guide who is more responsive to the context in which the learning is occurring" (p. 2).

In this book, we use the term "sequenced learning" to represent a deliberate structuring of course assignments and activities. The sequence refers to the stages in student learning that result in a deeper approach. In a typical college or university setting, students target their learning toward meaningful content which is usually identified or specified by the more knowledgeable teacher. In many cases, however, the content becomes more meaningful when students have some choice. They can then grapple with this content, often studying and learning independently. In an ideal sequence, the instructor designs activities that allow students to "process" this material at a deeper level, thereby increasing the likelihood that the new learning will be transferred to the brain's long-term memory, with sufficient retrieval cues. The cooperative-learning activities we advocate serve this purpose, particularly when they include another all-important aspect of sequenced learning: feedback on what is learned. The final phase of student learning requires meaningful assessment, bringing the process full circle because we cannot assess unspecified goals. Several later chapters deal with assessment. A key document in the assessment movement, "Principles of Good Practice for Assessing Student Learning," (Astin, Banta, Cross, El-Khawas, Ewell, Hutchings, Marchese, McClenny, Mentkowski, Miller, Moran, and Wright, 1992), specifies: "Clear, shared, implementable goals are the cornerstone for assessment that is focused and useful" (p. 1).

Because the tenets outlined above are so germane to student learning, other scholars have advocated them under different names. For example, Massey (1996) considers "Systems Thinking" crucial to student learning. He refers to faculty as "process designers" and "process managers." In fact, he carries the learning sequence (goals, content, teaching and learning activities, feedback, and assessment) a step further by considering inputs other than faculty, such as campus support staff, capital equipment, and purchased services and software.

Michaelsen, Fink, and Black (1996), using a form of structured-group work called "team learning" (chapter 9), have developed an instructional activity sequence that involves individual study, individual and group tests offering immediate feedback, and application-oriented activities. Creed (1996), a cognitive psychologist, advocates purposeful out-of-class assignments followed by cooperative-learning activities during class. Such activities offer varied opportunities to use specific information, thereby increasing the likelihood that such practice will lead to greater problem-solving abilities in the future.

THINK-PAIR-SHARE

Think-Pair-Share is probably the best-known and most widely used cooperative learning structure. Many people use it without connecting it to cooperative learning or realizing that one person, Frank Lyman (1981), was responsible for its creation and dissemination. Because of its simplicity and versatility, Think-Pair-Share offers an entry point for college instructors new to cooperative-learning. It is a relatively low-risk activity.

In Think-Pair-Share, a cooperative learning structure encouraging in-creased student participation and higher-order thinking skills, students learn a new response cycle to questions raised in class, one based on student interac-tion and hence, active learning. This easy-to-use technique has wide applica-tions, even in large lecture classes.

To initiate a Think-Pair-Share activity, the instructor poses a question which cannot be answered facilely with a response based on rote memoriza-tion; often the question is a probing one without a single definitive answer. Typically, students are given time, usually 30 seconds to a minute, to **think** of a response. The importance of this "think time" cannot be overemphasized. Instructors new to cooperative learning may find that moments of silence in a class seem overly long. However, they must resist the temptation to hurry the process, since these moments allow students to retrieve memories from long-term storage. Retrieval time varies, based on a number of factors, including where and how these memories are stored. Storage is related to how students have linked information to their past learning. Thus, calling on the students whose hands shoot up first, a common pedagogical practice, is detrimental, according to Sousa (1995), for two reasons:

> First, the slower retrieving students feel that they are not getting teacher recognition, thereby lowering their self-concept. Second, by not retrieving the information into working memory, they miss an opportunity to relearn it (p. 48).

Compelling research by Rowe (1974, 1978) offers further incentives to respect this "wait time." She discovered that extending the wait period to at least five seconds increased the length and quality of student responses and resulted in more participation by slower learners, more higher-order responses, and more evidence to support inferences. The teachers who increased wait time also exhibited to their students positive qualities of using more higher-order ques-tioning, showing more flexibility in evaluating student responses, and improv-ing their expectations for the performance of slow learners.

An instructor may prefer that this "think" period be used to allow students to write their responses, a practice ensuring that most students are on task. This practice also helps instructors fulfill calls for writing across-the-curricu-lum. Additional benefits occur when these individual responses are collected at the conclusion of the class, reviewed, and returned. The instructor gains valuable insights into the level of student processing and retrieval and, when the instructor's comments are quickly jotted down on these written responses, students gain valuable feedback.

In the second stage of the Think-Pair-Share sequence, students **pair** with another classmate, often a member of their structured-learning team, to discuss their responses to the question. This phase of Think-Pair-Share rein-forces the principle of simultaneity in the college classroom. In the lecture and recitation technique, only two people, the instructor and a designated student, interact. Other students may or may not be attentively listening or mulling over their own responses. In Think-Pair-Share, all persons are simultaneously involved in paired discussion: 50% of a class are vocal.

This paired discussion also has cognitive benefits. Presselsen (1992) emphasizes that the collaborative nature of cooperative learning involves both a group processing of the content information and a shared response to the cognitive processing of each individual member. These benefits occur because students, in explaining how they have derived an answer or reached a conclusion, must scrutinize their own thought processes: "Students engaged in cooperative learning need to reflect on what they think about the particular tasks of instruction, but they must also consider how they arrived at such thoughts and what the significance of a particular act happens to be" (p. 2). Thus, students are engaging in metacognitive processes, learning about learning, a step essential to the construction of knowledge and essential for deep learning.

In the third phase of Think-Pair-Share, the instructor invites students to **share** their responses. If the sharing is done with the class as a whole, instructors will find that students, whose ideas have been reinforced, refined, or challenged through discussion with a peer, will be eager to volunteer. Instructors will no longer face a paucity of student participants but will have the "problem" of which of many respondents to recognize. Furthermore, the level of responses is far more intellectually rich than responses typically coming from a situation where an instructor merely tosses off a question and waits for the hands of the most assertive students to shoot skyward. As a general rule, it is wise to limit a whole-class followup to four to six responses in order to avoid repetition, particularly if the question encouraged complex answers.

Responses during the share period do not necessarily need to involve the whole class, however, particularly if instructors have organized students into ongoing structured-learning teams. Because much of the benefit from this activity comes from the reflection and subsequent verbalization, instructors can simply ask that students share their paired discussions within the small, but safe, framework of their teams.

A Think-Pair-Share activity with random pairs can be initiated quickly and easily during a lecture when an instructor recognizes a need for students to "process" or reflect on the material. However, instructors who are committed to the formation of structured-learning teams sometimes deliberately pair stronger and weaker students by assigning the former to major suits (hearts and spades) and the latter to minor suits (diamonds and clubs). Suit colors may then be used as the basis for pairs, or dyads, called "suit partners." For example, within the structured-learning team, the club would have been assigned to the student who had performed poorly and the spade to the student who had performed well. These students would form one dyad while the students who had performed about the mean, holding diamonds and hearts, would form the other dyad. In groups of five, the student holding the wild card would replace any missing group member or join with the black suits to form a triad. Students, of course, should not be aware of these instructor-designed internal structures. These stronger-weaker designations also prove useful with other structures such as Jigsaw, to be discussed in chapter 8.

Other sharing alternatives for Think-Pair-Share enhance its flexibility. One obvious option is to eliminate the final share phase, having accomplished the most important elements of the activity by having students reflect upon and then verbalize their responses. Too often, instructors assume that students expect every contribution to be acknowledged and validated publicly. These whole-class sharings are often unnecessary and time-consuming. Thus, the Think-Pair-Share activity can be initiated without structured-learning teams in virtually any setting where people are seated together. In fact, many public speakers have used its power to generate active audience engagement.

Even in its simplest form, Think-Pair-Share offers benefits to students and instructors alike. At a minimum, students have valuable wait time to think questions through before any discussion begins. Moreover, students have an opportunity to rehearse responses mentally and orally with a peer before being asked to share publicly. This process enhances oral communication skills and confidence. All students have an opportunity to share their thinking with at least one other person, thereby increasing their sense of involvement. The Think-Pair-Share structure is particularly powerful when used for reciprocal teaching, an approach receiving increasing attention in higher education.

Instructors also benefit, since students spend more time actively learning course-related material. Students who might have "tuned out" during a traditional lecture and recitation presentation actively listen to each other during Think-Pair-Share activities. Thus, simultaneous learning transpires in a busy, animated classroom. After rehearsing in pairs, students are more capable of volunteering well-thought-out responses. Instructors also have more in-class time to think themselves. They can concentrate on asking higher-order questions, observing reactions, and listening to responses. Think-Pair-Share is easy to learn, easy to use, and creates a more relaxed atmosphere than calling on individual students.

The Think-Pair-Share structure can also be used for complex, extended student exchanges. It can be used, for example, to reach consensus by asking students to agree upon a single solution for a problem. Johnson, Johnson, and Smith (1991) find that "Pairs create a new answer that is superior to each member's initial formulation through the process of association, building on each other's thoughts, and synthesizing" (p. 5:13). For issues, students can conversely be asked to play devil's advocate with their partner and draw out deeper informed responses by carefully phrased probing questions from an opposing viewpoint.

Think-Pair-Share also can build learning skills through paired problem solving. A problem-solving period can be extended by asking students to solve exercises using a variation of this structure. Exercises developed in Think-Pair-Share sessions replace the more traditional, but less effective practice of placing a numerical example on the blackboard or on an overhead for students to mechanically duplicate in their notes. Because students actively derive solutions and their underlying concepts, rather than copying them, they feel ownership and are more likely to retain the knowledge.

Lyman (cited in Millis, Lyman, and Davidson, 1995) offers three college-level scenarios that provide a closer look at the implementation and effectiveness of Think-Pair-Share.

In a college physics class, the instructor provides a visual model with two possible exit trajectories for an object moving rapidly through a concentrically curved tube. She asks the students to take three minutes to predict the path of the object by drawing it on paper and to derive and write down the governing principle of force (think). After this independent work, the students attempt to come to a consensus with a pre-selected partner (pair). After two minutes of pair discussion, during which the instructor circulates to observe, a spokesperson for each pair indicates by a hand signal the path the pair predicted (share). Since most pairs predicted incorrectly, the teacher offers the correct answer but now repeats the learning process by asking the students to derive the principle for the correct answer, independently (think) and then discuss it with their partners (pair). She concludes the session with a whole-class discussion elaborating on the governing principles (share).

The above scenario contains the essential elements of Think-Pair-Share: independent thinking, structured-pair cooperative talk, and large-group discussion. The Think-Pair-Share structure allows all students to participate in high-level concrete-to-abstract thinking. Furthermore, it fosters the principle of simultaneous interaction, with 50% of the students talking at any given time and the other 50% listening. It also provides both students and teachers with critical feedback to guide the subsequent learning.

As another example, a history class is studying nationalism by focusing upon causes and effects of the European public mood preceding World Wars I and II. When the history students enter the class, they spend three minutes writing what they remember about the public mood prior to World War I from a previous lecture on this topic and from their reading. Upon a cue, they read a partner's comments, and from paired discussion, they add to their notes anything new from the partner's recollection. After four minutes of pair work, the instructor begins a lecture on the causes of nationalistic fervor in World War I. Ten minutes later, she stops the lecture and asks the students to prepare to teach their partners the causes of nationalistic fervor by using examples from their prior knowledge; that is, by connecting the cause(s) she just amplified with the effects they wrote about and discussed earlier. During a whole-class discussion, the teacher asks students to share their examples, so that they are adding to what she has just taught. The instructor then makes further cause-effect connections in another short lecture, and after six minutes asks the students to add, orally, any examples she didn't mention. She concludes by using a similar strategy for World War II and having the students independently create a Venn diagram to compare the public moods before the two wars.

During the next class period, the students will attempt to reach consensus on the Venns with a partner, justifying their conclusions, before they hear the instructor's views.

This history scenario illustrates complex uses of Think-Pair-Share structures. The bridging activities at the beginning and end of the class create continuity with what has been studied and with what will subsequently be discussed. Pair-add-on, pair-alternate, and pair-teach allow students to compare, to exemplify, and to connect cause and effect. Thus, the instructor uses a form of "metacognitive anchoring" to give students direction on exactly how their minds are to function as they think, thus preventing the "cognitive drift" that occurs with vague prompts such as "find supporting details." Typically, students feel empowered and more curious when their thinking precedes the lecture. They are also likely to be more attentive when they know they may have to, at any moment, think, write, and talk with a partner about the content.

A final scenario from a literature class illustrates the fit of Think-Pair-Share to the self-assessment and constructivist, or theory-making, aspects of learning. It also models the effective practice of having students spend the "think" portion of the activity by writing.

The English literature instructor's objective is to teach students to create quality descriptive writing and to recognize the quality. The instructor reads aloud five descriptive passages from "great" literature as the students read the scenes independently. He then displays five scenic pictures and asks the students to pick one and make it come to life in writing. After they have written for ten minutes (think), the instructor directs students to bracket their three best descriptive phrases or sentences. Partners then read each other's papers and bracket the three phrases or sentences they consider to be the most effective. The pairs then compare and justify their choices to each other (pair). The students then write a description of one of the other scenic pictures and repeat the evaluative process. This process is repeated again until each student has written and analyzed three descriptions and has read and analyzed those of her partner. The task now changes. Using a Think-Pair-Share sequence, the students derive individually, in pairs, and finally with another pair (in a quad) a set of criteria for quality descriptive writing. During a whole-class lecture/discussion, students may now compare their team-generated rubric to that of the instructor's. As a class, they create a concentric circle diagram which connects each criterion for quality descriptive writing to examples from the "great literature" and from their own writings. The instructor and students will subsequently use this theoretical design to assess descriptive writing.

This Think-Pair Share process replaces a common scenario where students are simply handed the criteria for quality descriptions and exhorted to "go and do likewise." It also replaces a second scenario where the literature teacher provides a few limited examples and then encourages a "rush to rubric," in which self-selected students derive the criteria during a whole-class discussion. With the extended Think-Pair-Share activities, the instructor emphasizes the efficacy of modeling and of student-constructed theory, thereby revealing to the students their own power to learn both the practice and theory of any process. Such activities also encourage student "buy-in" to the theory.

Think-Pair-Share, a multifaceted cooperative structure, becomes a vehicle for learning to learn as well as for learning. Students receive a positive message about their own cognitive and social competence when they bring a thought-out response to a cooperative discourse in which everyone has had a chance to respond. The ingredients of structured, independent think time and pair interaction create an opportunity for a truly responsive college classroom, one in which all students take responsibility for learning. Having mastered a basic, and yet cognitively sophisticated structure such as Think-Pair-Share, faculty are ready to move on to other structures suitable for higher education classrooms, such as Roundtable.

ROUNDTABLE

Roundtable, a cooperative-learning structure useful for brainstorming, reviewing, or practicing a skill, requires the use of a single sheet of paper and pen for each group. Students respond in turn to a question or problem by stating their ideas aloud as they write them on paper. Students should vocalize ideas because (1) silence in a setting like this is boring, rather than golden; (2) other team members need to be reflecting on the proffered thoughts; (3) variety results when teammates learn immediately that someone has come up with an idea they had planned to offer; and (4) hearing the responses spoken means that students do not have to waste valuable brainstorming time by reading the previous ideas on the page.

Team members ideally should not skip turns, but if their thoughts are at a standstill, it is better to pass rather than turn the brainstorm into a brain drizzle. To encourage participation, the pass option can be limited to one round. As the paper circulates clockwise, team members record ideas as rapidly as possible, resulting in the quick generation of ideas. As with other brainstorming activities, students should not slow the flow of creative ideas by stopping to explain, question, or evaluate. Before report-outs occur, however, instructors should allow teams to review their ideas, making certain that all members understand all contributions.

As a variation of Roundtable, instructors substitute a piece of acetate and a transparency pen in the exercise. Students rapidly record responses on the acetate using the Roundtable procedure. For the summary, the instructor asks one or two designated reporters to share their groups' results with the entire class using an overhead projector. In another variation, the students stand over a desk and brainstorm in Roundtable fashion, recording their ideas in turn, using markers on a large piece of flip chart paper. The sheets can either be left in place or posted.

Many creative uses can be made of the ideas generated, depending on their nature. Roundtable is particularly useful when faculty wish to develop sequenced activities that lead to higher-order thinking. For example, students identify, using a Roundtable, the most important ethical issues facing people in professions such as law, medicine, accounting, or academic counseling. The faculty member then assembles a composite of all the ideas and uses them later in a problem-solving structure, to be discussed in chapter 6, called Send-a-Problem. Students can generate ideas for research paper topics which later can be listed and circulated to all students.

In Roundtable, the multiple answers encourage creativity and deeper thinking. Thus, students familiar with the concepts will still find the group exploration challenging. A structure such as this, by its organizational format—one piece of paper and one pen per group—reinforces the concept of positive interdependence and also serves as a team-building exercise, because group members feel a sense of accomplishment when reviewing their team-generated list.

Examples of Roundtable topics are widespread. Some suggested topics might be outlining the various international roles played by the United Nations; identifying the defining characteristics of Gothic architecture, impressionistic painting, or early photography; listing the various symptoms of schizophrenia, AIDS, or co-dependency; summarizing the most important events of 1918 or any other significant year; or providing examples of well-known engineering trusses. Roundtable topics can also be multiple; for example, students circulate a graphic organizer with three subheadings: "Doric, Ionic, Corinthian." The directions read: "Circulate this sheet rapidly, with each team member adding distinguishing elements of these types of Greek architecture."

Keenan and Maier (1995) offer a multiple Roundtable in their economics courses. Students receive one worksheet per team with the following directions: "Pass this sheet of paper around your team." Each team member writes down one idea, then passes it on. The paper heading is "Medical Care in the U. S." and the sheet contains two subheadings with space for answers underneath: "Examples of market allocation of medical care in the U.S. today" and "Examples of non-market allocation of medical care in the U.S. today." After the Roundtable is complete, the team discusses the question: "Do you think medical care should be treated as a product or as a 'right' for everyone?" (p. 2).

USING COOPERATIVE-LEARNING STRUCTURES FOR GROUP FORMATION

The structures just discussed, Think-Pair-Share and Roundtable, do not require the use of structured-learning teams. Instructors may wish, however, to form groups through meaningful class activities. Three cooperative-learning structures—Value Line, Corners, and the Three-Step Interview—can help instructors rapidly create heterogeneous teams. These teams may or may not become the semi-permanent structured-learning teams that form the heart of the cooperative classroom. To give students the opportunity to work with other classmates, instructors may create temporary teams for brief in-class assignments and interactions. These three structures lend themselves well to rapid, varied team formation. They also permit students to engage substantively with the course content.

Value Line

A Value Line ascertains students' opinions in a quick and visual way by asking them to line up according to how strongly they agree or disagree with a statement or proposition. In an undergraduate course, for example, instructors may ask students to respond to the following statements:

- The United States was justified in dropping the second atomic bomb on Nagasaki.
- Business majors should be required to take more liberal arts courses.
- Funds should be diverted from other medical research into AIDS programs.
- Every woman is entitled to abortion on demand.
- The United States should adopt a flat income tax rate.

Clear instructions reinforced by visual aids are particularly important for implementation because many students are unaccustomed to active learning that involves active movement.

To initiate the structure, which is diagrammed in Figure 5.1, instructors briefly give students arguments for or against the proposition and show them a five-point Likert scale on an overhead. After a moment of "think time," instructors ask students to choose the number that best describes their position on the issue. To avoid indecisiveness, it is a good idea to have the students jot down their number before the next step. Instructors next ask students who have chosen "one" to stand at a designated point along the wall of the room. The students who have chosen "two" follow them, and so forth until all students are lined up, but not bunched together.

Group Formation with a Value Line

Step 1. Form a rank ordered line and number participants as follows:

Strong Agreement   **Strong Disagreement**

1 2 3 4 5 6 7 8 9 10 11 12 13 14 15 16 17 18 19 20

Step 2. Locate the midpoint of the line:

1 2 3 4 5 6 7 8 9 10 11 12 13 14 15 16 17 18 19 20

↑
midpoint

Step 3. Form heterogeneous groups of four members by assigning the above numbered value line participants as follows:

| 1 | 10 |
| 11 | 20 |

Group 1

| 2 | 9 |
| 12 | 19 |

Group 2

| 3 | 8 |
| 13 | 18 |

Group 3

| 4 | 7 |
| 14 | 17 |

Group 4

| 5 | 6 |
| 15 | 16 |

Group 5

Source: South-Western College Publishing. (Reprinted with permission.)

VALUE LINE

FIGURE 5.1

After the students have formed a continuous line based on their opinions, instructors must identify the midpoint. The easiest way to do this is to ask students to ignore the original number they selected as the basis for their location in the line so that they can count off sequentially, calling out numbers from one end of the line-up to the other. Following this "count-off," each student now has a unique identifying number. The instructor finds the median number by dividing the last number by two.

The next steps are critically important. The instructor forms the first group of four students by taking one from each extreme of the line and two from its midpoint. To ensure the rapid and accurate identification of these four students, it is helpful to use an overhead that allows the instructor to draw lines through the numbers who have been assigned to teams. A simple numerical grid (Figure 5.2) works well. In a class of 70, for example, the instructor calls the numbers 1, 70, 35, and 36, and crosses them off the grid. For the next team, she calls 2, 69, 34, and 37, again crossing the numbers off the grid. If the group is large, instructors can ask a student from the first group formed to record the numbers on the blackboard or a flip chart as they are called out: Team One: 1, 70, 35, 36; Team Two: 2, 69, 34, 37.

1	2	3	4	5	6	7	8	9	10
11	12	13	14	15	16	17	18	19	20
21	22	23	24	25	26	27	28	29	30
31	32	33	34	35	36	37	38	39	40
41	42	43	44	45	46	47	48	49	50
51	52	53	54	55	56	57	58	59	60
61	62	63	64	65	66	67	68	69	70

Source: South-Western College Publishing. (Reprinted with permission.)

Numeric Grid

FIGURE 5.2

Playing cards are not essential to the Value Line structure, but many faculty members find that using them can simplify some of the "logistics" of organizing the newly formed teams. If cards are used, students approach the instructor when she calls their numbers, and each of the four team members receives a playing card of the same rank but a different suit (e.g., team one would be composed of four aces: heart, diamond, spade, and club; the second team would be composed of four deuces: heart, diamond, spade, and club, etc.). Role assignments can also be designated at this time. If the group is unusually large, instructors may ask a designated assistant to seat the teams and the playing cards can be distributed later.

Once teams are formed, they should sit closely together. If the instructor uses playing cards and wishes to assign seats, she can place cards identical to those handed out directing the formation. The cooperative-learning seating chart discussed in chapter 4 can guide the seating locations. Students quickly find their seats by locating the card that matches the one they hold. Alternatively, the instructor can designate the location of each team by placing tent cards marked Aces, Twos, Threes, etc., around the room.

Instructors continue to form teams with this procedure until all students have been assigned to a team and have found their designated seats. Any students left over join a team as a fifth member.

A Value Line lends itself well to paired discussion, also. To form pairs where students can exchange viewpoints on various topics, instructors have the students line up as before, based on their stance on a controversial issue. This time, instead of pulling four students from the ends and midpoints to form a quad, the instructor breaks the line at the midpoint and literally doubles it back around so that the two students at each end are paired, and so on (e.g., 1 and 70 pair; 2 and 69 pair; 3 and 68 pair, etc.). Although not all students pair with partners having extremely divergent views, many will. Pairing students of opposing viewpoints allows them to stretch their perspectives and to learn to examine at least two sides of an issue. These monitored exchanges promote critical-thinking skills by helping students to recognize the validity of alternate viewpoints and to identify and question their own assumptions before exploring alternative patterns of thought.

When planning to use a Value Line, instructors must remember that this is a highly public structure. Students can neither run nor hide. Thus, teachers will want to select appropriate topics that will not cause students discomfort. It would be awkward to have students take sides on controversial issues in which they are personally involved. It would be unwise, for example, to have students line up on the issue of impeaching Mayor Jones when Suzie Jones, his daughter, is in the class. A structure such as Corners presents far less controversy.

Corners

Although heterogeneous groups are advocated for long-term structured-learning teams or for discussions where multiple viewpoints can be aired, in some cases homogeneous grouping, particularly for short-term activities, may be productive. The structure Corners can facilitate homogeneous placement. It can also lead to later heterogeneous grouping.

To initiate Corners, instructors ask students to join a group based on a mutual interest, preference, or question solution. Often the choices, usually four, are designated by a specific corner of the room. These groups are thus homogeneous based on the selection criteria. In a principles accounting class, for example, students may select a group based on their academic majors. As an alternative, students may select a group based on their agreement with one of four responses to statements such as: "The greatest value of college life comes from: (a) academic subjects studied; (b) social skills acquired; (c) networks formed with peers and professors; (d) the opportunity to interact with people of differing backgrounds, cultures and views." In a history class, they might select a corner based on the following prompt: "America's greatest president is (a) George Washington; (b) Abraham Lincoln; (c) Franklin D. Roosevelt; (d) Harry S. Truman." Instructors should choose options carefully, so that the groups are roughly equal. The size of the group in each corner will not matter for paired or whole-group discussions, but the group sizes should be fairly uniform if Corners will be used for group formations.

Instructors announce the four options and make certain that students clearly understand them. In addition, a visual aid, such as a sign posted in each corner or area of the room, helps students know exactly where they should move. As in the Value Line formation, the instructor first provides "think time" before asking students to choose a corner at a given signal. While in their corners, students might briefly discuss the topic which generated the group formation. After each group reaches consensus or finishes sharing relevant ideas within an allotted time span, the instructor can ask a representative from each corner to share its best ideas with the rest of the class.

The team formation occurs when the instructor pulls one person from each corner to form structured-learning teams. There, students with divergent opinions or differing content expertise can study designated course material. These newly formed teams perform problem-solving activities that will capitalize on each student's opinion or area of expertise. For example, the history students reviewing the four presidents could explain why they each selected a different person. In defending their choices, the students might discuss the differing leadership strengths, personal values, and issues faced. The students might then summarize this discussion by creating a profile of the ideal president. Students in a biology, physiology, or psychology class might initially self-select corners based on their confidence in their knowledge about a certain brain part. Then, when the teacher formed six-person structured-learning teams, they would bring their expertise on the characteristics and functions of their part of the brain: corpus callosum, cerebrum, amygdala, hippocampus, brain stem (RAS), and cerebellum. Working together, the students all come to an understanding of the brain as a whole.

Three-Step Interview

A structure called the Three-Step Interview guides students into student-selected heterogeneous groups. Three-Step Interview builds from pairs (dyads) into groups of four. It is an excellent "icebreaker" for an initial class meeting, provided that the students perceive interview questions as interesting and course-related. Faculty ask students to find partners whom they don't know well. After finding a partner, they sit down, so that the instructor can help any stray class members to find partners. If the class has an uneven number of students, then the instructor can suggest that three students work as a triad.

The students decide who will be the initial interviewer or the instructor may designate that person. Students interview their partners for a specified amount of time, depending on the complexity of the interview questions. Besides requesting some introductory background information, such as name, hometown, and intended major, the interviewer asks for opinions on class-related topics: Should premed students study holistic medicine? What do you consider the most important role of the House Ethics Committee? Why do astronomers need to study calculus? How do you use writing in your daily life?

At the prearranged quiet signal, the two switch roles and the other person conducts the interview, asking the same questions for the same number of minutes. The instructor then asks each pair to join another pair to form a quad. For the specified time, the members of these newly formed groups introduce their partners to the other group members, succinctly sharing their partner's ideas. Students cannot recap the entire interview in the allotted time, so they need to highlight the points of most interest to the other team members.

During this final step, any triads join a pair to form a group of five. A trickier problem occurs when the class paired evenly for the reciprocal interviewing steps, but one pair is left over after the quads are formed. In this case, it may be necessary to split a pair, with apologies, so that each of these two students can be added to another group as a fifth member. Instructors should try to anticipate this problem as soon as the pairs are formed so that they can identify the two students to be split up and alert them early in the process that they will be reassigned due to the uneven breakdown of numbers of students.

The interview topics for the Three-Step Interview should allow each student to contribute to the discussion: that is, the initially interviewed student cannot give away "the answer." As with Roundtable, the possibilities for topics are endless: Should Nora in *The Doll's House* have left her husband? What are the most important qualities of an effective leader? Do you feel students achieve more under an intrinsic or extrinsic reward system? Was the United States' invasion of Grenada justified?

In this activity, as in others, instructors should provide what is often called a "sponge," or an "extension." This is an extra question, problem, or activity to be completed by groups working more rapidly than others. The knowledge that there is an expectation of on-task behavior and added responsibilities keeps students from rushing through tasks in order to "goof off."

If the Three-Step Interview is used during the course term rather than as an icebreaker at the beginning, more complex interview questions can help students learn the course material in greater depth. This use promotes sequenced learning by having students "process," through the interview questions, the material that they read outside of class. The students discover immediately how well they understand the material when they must respond to their partner's questions. Because the questions are open-ended, students benefit from the perspectives provided by their partners on the same question. Teachers, perhaps, benefit most of all: by listening to the paired responses and team discussions, they get a clear idea of their students' levels of preparation, misconceptions, and depth of knowledge.

The Three-Step Interview also provides an excellent opportunity to practice and reinforce effective listening skills. If students have to summarize information provided by their partners, they are more likely to pay attention and also to be certain that they understand the viewpoint. Instructors, too, should be listening so that they can compliment, and therefore reinforce, use of effective teamwork skills, such as asking probing questions or providing positive reinforcement. When instructors discover the depth of their students' knowledge, they can begin their lectures at an appropriate level. The structure promotes team bonding as students share ideas and experiences. It is reinforcing to hear one's ideas enthusiastically expressed by a partner. And finally, the Three-Step Interview focuses attention on important course-related topics by allowing students to "connect" with the material in a personal way.

SUMMARY

College faculty committed to the philosophical basis of cooperative learning and willing to invest in the planning needed to manage a student-centered classroom can now gradually introduce some of the structures that help students to master complex subject matter. They can do so knowing that such structures, because they are part of a sequenced assignment, can foster in-depth mastery.

Perhaps the most basic, lowest-risk cooperative-learning structure is Think-Pair-Share. Yet, this structure is cognitively complex. In Roundtable, an extremely versatile structure, students brainstorm ideas which may be shared or applied in a number of ways. Neither of these techniques requires permanent structured-learning teams.

Three other structures—Value Line, Corners, and the Three-Step Interview—can be used to form learning teams. Value Line, probably the most logistically difficult to manage with large classes, results in a human Likert scale after students take a stand on a particular topic or issue. Instructors can then form teams composed of students with divergent opinions. Similarly, teachers can form divergent teams in Corners by pulling students from each of the corners to form heterogeneous quads. The Three-Step Interview is useful for team formation, but it offers other benefits as well, such as giving students and teachers immediate feedback on students' understanding of assigned readings.

Regardless of the structure chosen, the secret to a successful cooperative-learning classroom is careful planning and organization. All of the activities must be carefully explained to students and clearly tied to course objectives. The classroom management techniques discussed in chapters 3 and 4 will assure smooth implementation of the structures discussed in this chapter.

APPENDIX A

Graphic Organizers in Accounting

Types of Organizations	
Users	**Accounting Information Needs**
External Users	
Top Management	
Functional and Division Managers	
Middle managers	
ACCOUNTING INFORMATION USERS	

EXAMPLE 1

Type of Information	Cost Leadership Requirements	Product Differentiation Requirements
Costs for Performance Assessment		
Perceived Importance of Meeting Budgets		
Product or Service Cost as an Input to Pricing Decisions		
Marketing Cost Analysis		
Analysis of Competitors' Costs		

ACCOUNTING INFORMATION AND CORPORATE STRATEGY

EXAMPLE 2

Tool	Role in Strategic Cost Management

NEW DECISION MAKING TOOLS FOR THE NEW BUSINESS ENVIRONMENT

EXAMPLE 3

Category	Examples
Unit Level	
Batch Level	
Product Level	
Facility Level	

OVERHEAD COST HIERARCHY

EXAMPLE 4

Type	Brief Description	Performance Measures
Cost Center		
Revenue Center		
Profit Center		
Investment Center		

RESPONSIBILITY CENTERS

EXAMPLE 5

REFERENCES

Astin, A.W., Banta, T.W., Cross, K.P., El-Khawas, E., Ewell, P.T., Hutchings, P., Marchese, T.J., McClenny, K.M., Mentkowski, M., Miller, M.A., Moran, E.T., and Wright, B. D. (1992). *Principles of Good Practice for Assessing Student Learning.* Washington, DC: American Association of Higher Education.

Baird, J. (Ed.), (1992). *Shared Adventure: A View of Quality Teaching and Learning. Second Report of the Teaching and Learning Science in Schools Project.* School of Graduate Studies, Monash University.

Bellanca, J. (1990). *The Cooperative Think Tank: Graphic Organizers to Teach Thinking in the Cooperative Classroom.* Palatine, IL: Skylight Publishing.

Bellanca, J. (1992). *The Cooperative Think Tank II: Graphic Organizers to Teach Thinking in the Cooperative Classroom.* Palatine, IL: II/Skylight.

Creed, T. (1996). *Empowering Learners: Transforming Faculty and Student Roles* (with Millis). Presentations at 1996 Faculty Regional Workshops, Council of Independent Colleges, Raleigh, SC (May 29–31) & Cleveland, OH (June 6–8).

Johnson, D.W., Johnson, R.T., and Smith, K.A. (1991). *Active Learning: Cooperation in the College Classroom.* Edina, MN: Interaction Book Company.

Johnston, C. (1995). *Fostering Deeper Learning.* Economics Department, University of Melbourne. Online at <http://www.econ.unimelb.edu.au/ecowww/fost.html>. Last modified 19 Sept. 1995. Downloaded 30 July 1996. No longer available.

Keenan, D. and Maier, M.H. (1995). *Economics Live! Learning Economics the Collaborative Way.* 2nd Ed. New York: McGraw-Hill.

Lyman, F. (1981). "The Responsive Classroom Discussion." In A.S. Anderson (Ed.), *Mainstreaming Digest.* College Park, MD: University of Maryland College of Education.

Massey, W. (1996). *From Handicraft to Systems Thinking.* Presentation at the AAHE Summer Quality Academy, Breckenridge, CO, July 27–31.

McTighe, J. (1992). "Graphic Organizers: Collaborative Links to Better Thinking." In N. Davidson and T. Worsham, (Eds.), *Enhancing Thinking through Cooperative Learning.* (pp. 182–97). New York: Teachers College Press.

Michaelsen, L.K., Fink, D.L., and Black, R.H. (1996). "What Every Faculty Developer Needs to Know about Learning Groups." In L. Richlin (Ed.), *To Improve the Academy: Resources for Faculty, Instructional, and Organizational Development,* Vol. 15 (pp. 31–57). The Professional and Organizational Development Network in Higher Education. Stillwater, OK: New Forums Press, Inc.

Millis, B.J., Lyman, F.T., and Davidson, N. (1995). "Cooperative Structures for Higher Education Classrooms." In Harvey C. Foyle (Ed.), *Interactive Learning in the Higher Education Classroom: Cooperative, Collaborative, and Active Learning Strategies.* (pp. 204–25). Washington, DC: National Education Association.

Prescott, S. (1993, Fall). "Troubleshooting Cooperative Learning." *Cooperative Learning and College Teaching,* 4(1), 6–9.

Presselsen, B.Z. (1992). "A Perspective on the Evolution of Cooperative Thinking." In N. Davidson and T. Worsham (Eds.), *Enhancing Thinking through Cooperative Learning,* (pp. 1–6). New York: Teachers College Press.

Rowe, M.B. (1974). "Wait-time and Rewards as Instructional Variables: Their Influence on Language, Logic, and Fate Control." *Journal of Research on Science Teaching,* 2, 81–94.

Rowe, M. B. (1978). "Wait, Wait, Wait . . .." *School Science and Mathematics,* 78, 207–16.

Sousa, D.A. (1995). *How the Brain Learns: A Classroom Teacher's Guide.* Reston, VA: The National Association of Secondary School Principals.

Svensson, L. and Hogfors, C. (1988). "Conceptions as the Content of Teaching: Improving Education in Mechanics." In P. Ramsden (Ed.), *Improving Learning: New Perspectives* (pp. 255–72). London: Kogan.

CHAPTER

Structures for Problem Solving in Teams

"The most significant question which can be asked about any situation or experience proposed to induce learning is what quality of problem it involves."

John Dewey

The structures in this chapter entail "taking a bigger bite," moving toward semi-permanent or permanent structured-learning teams. We want to recommend, however, that teachers take small steps in implementing additional cooperative learning. Too often, swept away by enlightened enthusiasm, instructors will launch into a new pedagogy without sufficient preparation. When the results are less than optimal, some instructors react by retreating, "Oh, I've made a good-faith effort to try small-group learning, and it just doesn't work." Such well-intentioned efforts are counterproductive for both students and faculty. It is far better to become familiar with the theory and practice of cooperative learning by reading materials such as this book and by talking with colleagues and observing their courses. Then, some of the more basic structures can be introduced gradually.

Having uttered these cautions, however, we hope that most readers are ready to establish structured-learning teams, a crucial step for building cooperative classrooms. With such teams in place, faculty can consider more advanced cooperative-learning structures. They can assign student roles that will make all students accountable for their own learning and for the learning of teammates. Smith and Waller (1997) suggest four specific ways that these structured-learning teams achieve positive interdependence:

Positive interdependence is typically structured by asking the group to prepare a single product (goal interdependence), asking the students to make sure each person in the group can explain the groups' answer (learning goal interdependence), giving the group one copy of the assignment (resource interdependence), and assigning a special role to each member (role interdependence) (p. 202).

This chapter focuses on three advanced cooperative-learning structures that are carried out within the context of ongoing structured-learning teams: Structured Problem Solving, Discovery Learning, and Send-a-Problem. All three of these versatile structures are particularly useful in promoting problem-solving skills.

STRUCTURES USEFUL IN BUILDING PROBLEM-SOLVING SKILLS

Cooperative learning is ideally suited for building problem-solving skills. Such skills, as all of us recognize, are essential in an increasingly complex world where simple solutions are rarely evident. The United States Air Force Academy, for example, has identified as one of its seven educational outcomes, "Framing and resolving ill-defined problems." As the term "framing" implies, an important facet of problem solving lies not just in the solutions, but in what Smith (1993) calls "problem identification, problem formulation, and building models to predict, explain, understand, etc." He cites Albert Einstein:

> The mere formulation of a problem is often far more essential than its solution, which may be a matter of mathematical or experimental skill. To raise new questions, new possibilities, to regard old problems from a new angle requires creative imagination and marks real advance in science (p. 11).

Larkin and Chabay (1989) conclude also that mature problem solvers do not launch into immediate action based on obvious superficial elements:

> Scientists' problem-solving starts with redescribing the problem in terms of the powerful concepts of their discipline. Because the concepts are richly connected with each other, the redescribed problem allows cross checking among inferences to avoid errors (p. 158).

Helping novice problem solvers learn to adopt the approaches of more experienced problem solvers (the experts) in a given discipline poses a challenge for all teachers.

There are many problem-solving approaches, but most of them have important elements in common. Depth of processing, something that occurs in well-structured group work, can make the difference between poor and good problem-solving approaches (Whimbey, 1984). Such depth involves both knowing problem-solving strategies and knowing when to apply them. In many cases metacognitive strategies—self-consciously monitoring and evaluating thought processes—can strengthen students' awareness of their own approach to problems. Small groups offer an opportunity for students to explain, justify, and elaborate on their rationale for reaching conclusions. Several studies suggest that talking aloud about the steps in solving a problem can be beneficial, particularly when an unstructured problem is not so simplistic that the process is automatic (Gagne and Smith, 1962; Berry, 1983, Bender, 1986.) Research also suggests that approaching problems from different perspectives can cause creative breakthroughs, a finding that reinforces the value of problem solving within heterogeneous groups.

Although researchers caution that no single problem-solving heuristic is applicable to all disciplines (Groner, Groner, and Bischof, 1983), some broad-based steps seem useful in most educational settings. Woods (1994), for example, outlines these eight tasks to be completed in self-directed, interdependent small groups:

1. Explore the problem, create hypotheses, identify issues. Elaborate.
2. Identify what you know already that is pertinent.
3. Identify what you do **not** know.
4. As a group, prioritize the learning needs, set learning goals and objectives, and allocate resources; members identify which tasks each will do.
5. Individualize self-study and preparation.
6. Return to the group, share the new knowledge effectively so that all the group learn the information.
7. Apply the knowledge to solve the problem.
8. Assess the new knowledge, the problem solution and the effectiveness of the process used. Reflect on the process (pp. 6–1).

Although this model is used for complex, long-term problem solving, involving out-of-class study, the broad stages are useful for in-class group problem solving: (1) think through the task, identifying what is known and what is not known; (2) identify the resources of the group and set priorities and objectives; (3) share knowledge; (4) use the knowledge to solve the problem and/or complete the task; (5) assess the value of the end-product and the processes involved in deriving/producing it. Students in structured-learning teams will find these steps useful as they work through problems, tasks, and issues.

Principles Behind an Effective Problem-Solving Environment

Although they are speaking specifically of Problem-Based Learning, to be discussed in chapter 9, Savery and Duffy (1995) recommend eight instructional principles, based on constructivist theory to guide teaching and the design of the learning environment. These principles are relevant for any cooperative problem-solving activity:

1. Anchor all learning activities to a larger task or problem;
2. Support the learner in developing ownership for the overall problem or task;
3. Design an authentic task;
4. Design the task and the learning environment to reflect the complexity of the environment they should be able to function in at the end of the learning.
5. Give the learner ownership of the process used to develop a solution;
6. Design the learning environment to support and challenge the learner's thinking;
7. Encourage testing ideas against alternative views and alternate context;
8. Provide opportunity for and support reflection on both the content learned and the learning process (pp. 145–46).

These principles can be applied in many well-thought-out cooperative activities. An activity developed by Meyers (1988), for example, for an English class would become an authentic career-oriented problem in an adult education advertising class. He asks teams of three students to write and deliver a one-minute commercial intended to "sell" an audience on buying a specific gift (an invented product with a name such as "Sparkum," "Onadi," "ZYX," etc.) for a targeted person (mother, teacher, boss, girlfriend, etc.) on a specific occasion (Valentine's Day, Hanukkah, Moving, "Just Because," etc.) Each team draws three cards, one identifying the hypothetical product name; another pinpointing the recipient, and the third indicating the occasion. The give-and-take creativity within each team, as they refine their commercial, underscores the value of multiple perspectives within a group that is exploring alternatives. To aid reflection, after the commercial is acted out, with all team members participating, the other students offer a sentence or two of feedback, noting especially if the commercial was convincing for the target audience (pp. 133–37). Reflection on the team interactions that created the final product would add an assessment/group processing component to this sequence.

Identifying problems and providing a supportive, yet challenging context for solving them become important goals in cooperative learning. The structures that follow allow instructors to organize learning tasks within a structured cooperative framework.

Structured Problem Solving

Within the structured-learning teams that form the basis of a cooperative classroom, many activities promote problem-solving ability. Effective use of these teams depends in part on the assignment of numbers, playing card suits, or some other designator to identify group members quickly and relatively anonymously. Kagan (1992) has named the structure we will describe "Numbered Heads Together," terminology that may be a turnoff for college-level students. The Johnson, Johnson, and Smith (1991) term for the structure, "Problem Solving Lesson," again smacks too much of the primary or secondary level. We prefer to call it Structured Problem Solving.

Although Structured Problem Solving requires structured-learning teams, it is a fairly easy structure to initiate. Students within quads are assigned identities. These can be achieved by numbering off or by some other method, such as playing card suits or colored tablet sheets. The instructor poses a question or problem or clearly assigns a specified task. She also announces a time limit.

The question is often posed as a directive because the power of Structured Problem Solving lies in the peer coaching that occurs within the team. In an accounting class, for instance, instead of asking, "What is a journal? What is a ledger?" the instructor might say: "Be certain that everyone on the team knows the definition of a journal and a ledger, and two ways they might interact." It is useful to build in, as with Think-Pair-Share, a few seconds of reflective time, allowing some students to collect their thoughts and others to think more deeply. The students then work together for the specified amount of time, which can vary depending on the complexity of the questions or problems to be mastered.

Students must understand that they have two tasks: (1) to complete the specified assignment cooperatively, and (2) to be certain that all team members can serve as spokespersons for the team results. At the end of the time period, the teacher calls a number, a playing card suit, or a color and those designated students respond on the group's behalf.

The responses can vary. For example, the instructor asks that the students holding the clubs raise their hands if the team can provide an answer. If a limited number of hands go up, instructors provide a few additional minutes of teamwork with the admonition, "Be certain that the club on your team can represent the team's viewpoint." Then the instructor calls on two to six people—depending on the complexity of the question or problem—to respond before the class as a whole. In other cases, those designated might go to the blackboard or whiteboard to work through the problem.

Structured Problem Solving has many benefits. For instance, it encourages full and even participation because the instructor can easily keep track of the students called upon by noting the number, suit, or color selected and the specified team responding during a whole-class share. More important, however, it shifts the focus in a classroom to a cooperative rather than a competitive mode. In a typical whole-class discussion, the teacher poses a question and waits, sometimes for an uncomfortably long period of time, for hands to shoot upward. Usually, only a few students will compete for the teacher's attention. The rest may simply tune out. When one student is selected, the others in competition for the instructor's attention are often secretly thinking, "I hope he botches it, so that I can share my ideas." This kind of negative scenario does not occur with Structured Problem Solving. Instead, students prepare their team response together, resulting in a more sophisticated caliber of responses. Rather than individuals competing for the instructor's attention, there is an expectation that everyone is potentially able to respond to the question. Because the response is team-generated, students randomly selected as the team spokespersons find their role far less threatening than when they are called upon for individual responses. It is also less threatening to hear a teacher call for responses from the diamonds, for instance, than to be singled out by name. Students who normally do not participate feel far more comfortable speaking up under this structure. Because team members are responsible for the learning of others, positive interdependence is fostered. Furthermore, students are likely to remain attentive if they know they may be the team spokesperson. Because students may be individually tested on the material covered, individual accountability is fostered as well.

Some additional benefits have been identified by Ziegler (1996), who typically sequences learning by offering short lectures in his computer science classes, followed by one or two examples. He then has students solve problems in their structured-learning teams without knowing who will serve as the spokesperson. His approach augments lectures in much the same way as Think-Pair-Share. Ziegler gives these reasons for using Structured Problem Solving:

> I think the immediacy of problem solving is a great help. They get to try out my method right away and this seems to reinforce concepts MUCH better than looking at notes 20 hours later. In addition, the students feel much less inhibited about asking questions in only a group of two or three other students and I hear their "dumb question" rather than the whole class. Each student knows she or he may have to do a presentation so there is a fair bit of pressure to learn that may not have been there before. In addition, "pride of group" becomes a factor. Since no one wants their group to fail, each student actively tries to ensure that all members of the group understand. I quickly find out when I have not explained something well. If several students ask the same question based on an imperfect understanding of what I said, I can immediately stop the group activity and do another example or expand on my explanation (p. 1).

Structured Problem Solving at first glance seems to be sabotaged by the use of predesignated and rotated team roles. Upon entering class, students know in which capacity they must act for the day, thus potentially eliminating the element of positive interdependence in Structured Problem Solving because the reporters, who furnish oral responses, are already identified. The solution here is simply to tell students that, for this activity, their usual roles are no longer operative. Group reporters or spokespersons will be chosen at random, perhaps by drawing a card from another deck. The role of leader is particularly important in Structured Problem Solving because that individual is responsible for checking to see that all group members understand and can summarize the discussion points and/or problem solutions. The instructor may wish to assign that role in advance with the understanding that any team member, including the leader, may be the reporter.

An Option for Structured Problem Solving

Before turning to some discipline-specific examples of Structured Problem Solving, we would like to mention a classroom management technique, Talking Chips, that can potentially enhance Structured Problem-Solving activities.

Talking Chips

Talking Chips encourages full and even participation from members of cooperative-learning groups, particularly when the issue is controversial. Each group member has a token, the "talking chip," although instructors may feel more comfortable with different nomenclature. A pen or paper clip or even the playing card identifying group membership works well as a talking chip. The chip serves as a ticket giving its holder permission to share information, contribute to the discussion, or make debating points. After having contributed, the student must surrender the talking chip by laying it down in full view of the other team members until all students in the group have participated. After all students have spoken in random order and all chips have been laid down, the students retrieve their talking chips and the next round of discussion ensues. Once students are accustomed to this somewhat artificial approach, the conversation flows freely, but evenly, as students quickly relinquish their chips, wait until others have contributed, and then make their next point.

Talking Chips builds listening, communication, and interpersonal proficiency. Group members, especially those who tend to "spout off," consider more carefully what they have to say before speaking, since they surrender the right to talk afterwards. Reticent students, because they understand the ground rules, participate in a safe environment where they are encouraged to contribute. If discussion is delayed because they are not comfortable responding, they may pass, but team members, particularly the group leader, should ask direct, but gentle questions to draw the person into the discussion. Groups might initiate a "one pass only" rule. They might also allow a student who has nothing original to contribute to use his turn to paraphrase the response of another teammate.

Instructors need not confine their use of Talking Chips to controversial issues. They can use this structure any time they desire equitable discussions. Student team members, too, may request the use of Talking Chips during any group activity, including Structured Problem Solving. Faculty members should encourage the group leaders, who are responsible for keeping the teams on task and for ensuring learning opportunities for all group members, to use this option.

The use of Talking Chips helps students learn the importance and mechanics of an equitable discussion. Once students have mastered these skills, Talking Chips may no longer be necessary.

Examples of Structured Problem Solving from Various Disciplines

A number of computer science instructors have turned to cooperative-learning methods. Many use Structured Problem-Solving approaches. Not surprisingly, a number of these innovative faculty members have also posted their teaching ideas on the World Wide Web. For example, BradyLink (1996), in her computer science courses, has structured-learning teams implement a HyperCard stack consisting of a narrative and story board HyperCard. In the space of a single class period they must design the stack, produce a short development log, and prepare a demonstration.

To help computer science students learn to look for ambiguity in requirements and to understand the need to clarify a software specifications document via interactions with the customer, Smith (1996) gives each group a one-page, user-generated specifications document for a software design. Each group reviews the document and for fifteen minutes brainstorms a series of clarifying questions. Group reports last ten minutes. After this activity, each group member should understand the need for formalism; the need for accurate communication; and the role of the customer in defining requirements.

Using groups of three when the class divides evenly, Tenenberg (1995) uses these Structured Problem-solving assignments:

- Write a program to sum and output a sequence of integers read in from a file (a 30-minute activity in a computer science 1 course)
- Write, debug, and execute an exception handler for divide by zero on the M68020, and write a test code that will generate the exception. (a 100-minute exercise in a computer structures course)
- Draw a game tree for tic-tac-toe, 3-ply deep, starting from an empty board, and use *alpha-beta* pruning on it applying the following static heuristic function on states (heuristic function provided). (a 75-minute activity for an artificial intelligence course).

In a general biology I course, Miller (1995) of Worcester Polytechnic Institute uses a group problem-solving approach. Her syllabus identifies a pattern of activities to help teams find solutions under clearly specified timelines: (1) clearly state the problem and establish a goal; (2) gather all the relevant information; (3) generate possible solutions to the problem; (4) list constraints on what can be accomplished; (5) choose a possible solution; (6) analyze the important factors that must be considered in the development of the detailed solution; (7) create (synthesize) a detailed solution; (8) evaluate the final solution.

To involve students directly in scientific thinking, Miller assigns the following problem for the unit on Molecular Biology of Aging:

- Devise an experiment or series of experiments that would help to distinguish between the genetic program and the error theories of aging.
- Start by summarizing the essential features of the genetic program theory and the error theory of aging. Explain the uncertainties (i.e., inconsistencies, or things we don't know) in each of the two theories you have selected. Identify an important point of difference or disagreement between the two theories you have described. Suggest two or three experimental strategies you could use to distinguish between the two theories.
- Choose one of the strategies you have devised to test the two theories, and describe it in more detail. Your experimental design should include:
  1. a clearly stated and concise objective;
  2. a description of the experimental system (i.e., what cells or organism(s) you will use;
  3. a general description of the methods to be used in conducting the experiment (i.e., what will be done to each of the control and experimental groups);
  4. a description of the results you might expect to obtain and how you would interpret them.

Rhoades and McCabe (1991) offer a number of activities from various disciplines that could be completed in Structured Problem-Solving teams. They suggest, for example, that student teams could create or augment captions for textbook pictures, stressing important concepts just covered in class. To ensure individual accountability and positive interdependence, each student could be responsible for a sentence:

A sociology class might describe the different norms for behavior they would expect to find in the photographs of people shown in various settings. A biology class studying ecosystems could have each person on a team hypothetically remove a different element from the habitat illustration and then teammates predict a specific impact on that community. An

economics class studying current trade policy could interpret the graph
showing past and current U. S. import-export figures by incorporating at
least four key words (concepts) assigned by the instructor (p. 6).

In his political science course at Glendale Community College in Los
Angeles, Weaver (1997) delivers a brief lecture on the U. S. Supreme Court's
obscenity guidelines. The students then listen attentively to a broadcast of the
Howard Stern radio show and, in groups of four, apply the guidelines to the
broadcast to determine if it can be banned.

Discovery Method

Davidson (1990), a mathematician, describes what he calls the Discovery
Method. He found that calculus students placed in structured-learning teams,
can, with initial guidance and an adequate foundation, derive complex theorems and proofs on their own without having seen the instructor demonstrate
them. He also discovered that students participating in this kind of learning
situation retain far more than students taught through traditional mathemati-
cal methods.

Many diverse students, like calculus students, can benefit from the Discovery Method. Just as calculus students can discover complex theorems and
proofs on their own, students studying other disciplines, given a few fundamental principles, can discover a method, model, or system on their own.

Because the Discovery Method involves experiential learning that promotes transfer into long-term memory it results in retention of material
covered. Self-esteem rises also because students assume ownership of the
concepts or methods that they have discovered. Furthermore, because they
can attribute their success to mutual effort, their sense of competency and
control increases. This process of working with unstructured problems and
cases fulfills key educational objectives. Perhaps most important, the Discovery Method is both challenging and fun for students.

Examples from Three Disciplines

Instructors may use the Discovery Method to enhance student learning early
in a principles of accounting course. One objective could be for students to be
able to identify the purpose of accounting. Prior to assigned reading on the
subject, the instructor, without providing a numerical example, delivers a
mini-lecture briefly describing concepts about business transactions, recording
transactions, calculating account balances, and reporting information found
in accounts.

The instructor then gives students a simple list of transactions which
typically occur in a business—sale, cost of products sold, cost of renting
equipment, maintenance, and utilities. The instructor asks each structured-

learning team to prepare a brief report which would tell the reader whether this company had created any value and, if so, how.

After the prearranged time has elapsed, the instructor gets the students' attention with the quiet signal and randomly calls for two or more group reports. The instructor then leads a whole-class discussion, pointing out the similarities and differences of methods the students have "discovered." Finally, the instructor introduces the income statement to the students, emphasizing the similarities between the information "discovered" by the students and the information contained in the income statement.

The Discovery Method can also be used fruitfully in a first-year composition course, where students are typically uncertain about the demands of the course and the qualities of effective writing. Instead of lecturing, the instructor asks students in structured-learning teams to review and evaluate successive models of effective writing from various disciplines. From each brief piece (Willie Morris' "Two Hearts," paragraphs from Stephen Jay Gould, etc.), the students identify the characteristics of clear, creative prose. They must be certain that everyone understands the reasons for the principles they discover. After each team has analyzed four pieces, they work together on a composite list of the most germane characteristics of effective writing. The teacher calls on a spokesperson from each team (by number) to write these characteristics on the board and to explain the rationale for each entry. By comparing and contrasting the various entries and reaching consensus on the most important elements, the class as a whole "discovers" the principles of effective composition.

Lawlor (1997) uses the Discovery Method to teach the anatomical and cultural evolution of the genus *Homo*. Four species, *Homo habilis* (early *Homo*), *Homo erectus, Homo sapiens sapiens,* (modern *Homo sapiens*), and archaic *Homo sapiens* (including Neanderthals), are the objects of study. Prior to the discovery activity, students have already studied some human evolutionary trends and cranial anatomy related to the australopithecines. Each group receives a cranial cast of one *Homo* species; a set of casts of tools representing the variety of artifacts associated with that species; some brief supplemental readings, with relevant parts flagged; one or more relevant transparencies (e.g., maps); and a card with the following questions:

1. Please give the scientific name and any popular names associated with this species.
2. When and where did this species live? (Name regions and important sites.)
3. What is the average cranial capacity? Range of cranial capacities? What cranial features distinguish this species from other species in the genus?

4. How would you describe the artifacts associated with this species? How or why might they have been made? What do they say about the lifestyle of this species?

The groups have 20 minutes to prepare a presentation. During that time, the instructor draws a timeline and a chart on the board which the students embellish during their reports. She also circulates to monitor progress and answer any questions. After each group makes a 5-to-10-minute presentation, the class as a whole examines the chart and the timeline to discover overall trends. Lawlor concludes: "This approach makes students apply the concepts in a way no lecture can. Most of my students seem to retain more this way, with more informed, clearer discussions and better test grades as a result. It is a pleasure to see formerly uninvolved students argue with authority over brow ridges and blade technology!"

Send-a-Problem

The Send-a-Problem structure gives students the opportunity to identify or focus on their own issues or problems and to participate in the problem-solving process in the context of community. The exact source of this structure is unclear, but a version of it was generated by the Howard County, Maryland Staff Development Center in 1989, inspired by Kagan's (1989) high consensus-oriented Send-a-Problem structure which used rotating flashcards for content review.

To initiate Send-a-Problem, instructors must have at hand a list of problems or issues for which the structured-learning teams can generate solutions. The instructor can identify the issues, but students have far more "investment" in the Send-a-Problem activity if they have direct input. Using the Roundtable or Structured Problem-Solving structures, teams can compile a lengthy list of possible topics to be solved during that class session or in a subsequent one.

To begin the problem-solving segment of Send-a-Problem, the instructor brings to class file folders or envelopes with one problem posted on each one. She announces the activity and its time limits. She distributes the folders, one per team. In large classes, several teams can work simultaneously on the same problems with the caveat that they cannot be seated close together.

In smaller classes, each team can select its own problem, if time permits. The instructor posts the problem options on flip chart paper, a blackboard, or an overhead. Each structured-learning team then rank-orders their preferred choices. Topics are crossed off as teams select them. If time is limited, instructors might arbitrarily call on one team member (identified by a number, playing card, or color) to make the selection for their team. When flip chart paper is used, these specified team members rush to the posted sheets and cross off the issue their team will address.

Once each team has a specific problem to focus upon, the activity proceeds in a highly structured manner: (1) Each team discusses its particular problem and generates within the given time frame as many solutions as possible; the solutions, recorded on a sheet of paper, are placed in the folder or envelope on which is written the problem addressed. The team name can go at the top of the sheet. (2) The folders are then passed clockwise to another team which does not open the folder. That team, seeing only the problem identification but not the solutions generated by the previous team, follows an identical procedure and brainstorms solutions, placing their recorded conclusions in the folder or envelope. (3) The folders are passed again, but this time, the team opens the folder and reviews the ideas/solutions generated by the other two teams. They can add additional ideas of their own or consolidate those already suggested by the two other teams. Their primary task, however, is to identify the two most viable solutions to the given problem or issue. If desired, they can place a star or a check next to the best solutions.

Each step is carefully timed. Instructors need to make judgment calls about the total time allotment. Send-a-Problem can be used successfully as a brainstorming activity with each team "blitzing" through as many solutions as possible within a narrow time limit. Most often, however, the structure is used as a vehicle for meaningful discussion, thoughtful synthesis and evaluation, and creative problem solving. Those familiar with Bloom's Taxonomy (1956) will recognize that this activity brings students to the top level of critical thinking because the final step requires sophisticated evaluation.

Group reports can provide useful closure. The reporters announce the issue their quad discussed, the two solutions they have chosen, and, if desired, the team or teams that suggested them. The creativity and multiplicity of solutions reinforces the value of structured teamwork.

Send-a-Problem can serve multiple purposes. As Kagan (1994) emphasizes, cooperative-learning structures can further both academic and social objectives. Instructors will find Send-a-Problem useful for reviews prior to examinations. The instructor brings to class old quiz or examination questions stapled to folders or envelopes, or the students themselves can generate possible questions. The activity proceeds as described above, but in the final step, students synthesize a composite answer or merely select the best one in the folder. To offer more practice, the folders can be passed more than twice. With five passes, each team solves five different problems.

Examples from Various Disciplines

Instructors will find that Send-a-Problem activities are limited only by their imaginations. Virtually all disciplines lend themselves to problem-solving activities where "many heads are better than one." As a variation of the traditional model outlined above, for example, the teams could be asked to discuss and record problem identification and problem formulation ideas: What things would a clinician need to know before considering a diagnosis of Attention-Deficit Disorder/AIDS/Alzheimer's? What features would an art historian look for to authenticate an original Rembrandt/Renoir/Klee? Biology students might be asked to design various experiments, including a list of equipment, such as: compare the rates of growth of two different kinds of bread molds; compare the rates of growth of fruit fly populations receiving different vitamin supplements; compare the rates of growth of two hybrid varieties of bean plants.

Quantitative disciplines, such as math and accounting, can rotate challenging problems with multiple approaches to the "bottom line." Issues-oriented courses can circulate a number of thorny problems that have no one correct solution. For example, a class in religion might identify dilemmas facing the Roman Catholic Church today (challenges to Papal authority; the declining priesthood, etc.), and the students may discuss the ramifications of these issues and propose possible solutions. A class in history might outline the various claims to territory of the ranchers, the farmers, and the Native Americans. A class in literature might break down various aspects of a novel or short story with teams locating and explaining examples of things such as color imagery, symbols, and figures of speech. Literature students could also define key terms such as *Protagonist, Round Characters, Flat Characters, Static Characters,* and *Dynamic Characters.* Or, the teams could tackle complex interpretations of characters in a story, such as "Theft" by Joyce Carol Oates: (1) What do we learn about Marya in the opening pages? What can we deduce about her character/personality? (2) How does Marya feel about herself? How do we know? (3) How are Marya and Imogene Skillman different? (4) In what ways are Marya and Imogene Skillman similar? (5) Explain what kinds of thefts are occurring in the story.

The Send-a-Problem concept need not be limited to issues only. In place of the folders, geologists can pass around rocks needing identification; paralegal instructors can have teams fill out worksheets on various legal books; and ESL teachers can have teams caption various cartoons, using the target language.

BRINGING CLOSURE: SOME REPORT-OUT METHODS

As indicated earlier, closure is critically important to learning. Students must feel that their discussion and group activities have added to their knowledge, skills, and abilities. Often the instructor's summarizing mini-lecture will do the trick, particularly if he weaves into it the comments, products, and ideas generated by the students in their small groups. With the three problem-solving structures in this chapter, student reports are appropriate. Unfortunately, such reports are always time-consuming, usually uneven, often tedious and repetitious, and sometimes provoke intense anxiety for the speaker. They should be used with care. Often faculty members can take up materials generated through in-class group activities and either compile a summary for the next class period or comment—very quickly!—on individual or team products.

The report-out methods that follow offer rapid alternatives to the traditional whole-class report approach where a spokesperson from each group summarizes their work.

Stand Up and Share

This report-out method should be rapid and energetic. It works best when students have completed an activity, such as Roundtable, that lends itself to a single-statement summary. It relies on students having an easily designated identity within each team so that teachers can call on the "Number Twos" or the "Hearts" to serve as spokespersons. These designated students then rise and respond on behalf of the group. Each team answers in turn, giving only one response, in rapid round robin fashion. Depending on the number of answers and the number of teams involved, teams may go through another rotation, with other group members sharing one group idea (the "Number Fours" or the "Clubs" this time).

All students must pay attention to the sharing because they may serve as the next spokesperson. No ideas should be repeated. If student spokespersons find that all the topics on the team's list have been covered, they merely sit down and the rotation continues. Besides allowing for rapid exchanges (sometimes this activity becomes a "Stand Up and Shout"), the value of positive interdependence (teamwork) is emphasized.

Three-Stay One-Stray

Like "Stand Up and Share," this structure by Kagan (1992) requires the easy identification of a team member who will become the group's spokesperson. It too builds on another structure, such as Structured Problem Solving, but in this case the topics can be far more complex. After the problem-solving discussions are complete and all team members indicate that they can give the team's report, the teacher designates the student from each team who will "stray." That is, one student from each group (such as the "Number One" or the "Diamond") leaves it and rotates to an adjoining team to give the report. In large classes, it is essential that the order of rotation is clear. Playing cards work particularly well because the "Aces" know to rotate to the "Deuces," the "Jacks" to the Queens," and so forth.

The designated student, who is welcomed as a visitor, shares with this new team the results of his original group's discussion, giving proposed solutions to problems or summarizing findings. A second rotation may be desirable if the topic prompted divergent thinking and solutions.

Three-Stay One-Stray offers a low-threat forum where students can exchange ideas and build social skills, such as asking probing questions. It also offers students the opportunity to learn by teaching. Placing the report-out responsibility on the students reinforces the valuable concept that knowledge resides within the learning community, not just with the "authority-figure" instructor. Perhaps its greatest value lies in its efficiency. Instead of, for example, 10 sequential 5-minute reports to the entire class (50 minutes, plus transition time), individual students are simultaneously giving 5-minute reports throughout the room.

Team Rotation

Based on a structure by Kagan (1992), called "Inside/Outside Circle," Team Rotation offers a rich but timesaving report-out method. The team presentations must have been prepared ahead of time, perhaps at a previous class session. Students should pay serious attention to using creative visual aids, prompts, etc., to stimulate student learning. The length of time devoted to each portion of the report-out will depend in part on the complexity of the material to be communicated. The report-out steps can also be extended over two or more class periods. The steps are as follows:

1. Teams are randomly matched and the first team offers its presentation.
2. The listening team asks related or amplifying questions, requests clarifications, and provides constructive feedback intended to strengthen the presentation.
3. The second team offers its presentation and receives commentary from the first team.
4. Each team now reworks its presentation based on the feedback received.
5. A second cycle of reports occurs, with teams randomly rematched.
6. Teams make their revised presentations and then receive feedback from the listening teams.
7. The listening team now presents and, in turn, receives its feedback.

The time sequence for moderately complex material might look like this for a course scheduled in 50-minute class sessions: Day One: Team A makes its presentation (10 minutes); Team B offers constructive feedback, questions, clarifications (5 minutes); Team B makes its presentation (10 minutes); Team A offers constructive feedback, questions, clarifications (5 minutes); Teams work on revisions of their presentations based on feedback (15 minutes). Day

Two: Team A makes its presentation (10 minutes); Team C offers constructive feedback, questions, clarifications (5 minutes); Team C makes its presentation (10 minutes); Team A offers constructive feedback, questions, clarifications (5 minutes). Thirty minutes remain free in this second class period for instructor and peer feedback, plus other topics.

Team Rotation, like many other cooperative structures, capitalizes on the Principle of Simultaneity. If ten teams had offered ten-minute presentations with five minutes of feedback, twice, then the report-outs would have stretched over six class periods. Multiple presentations also would have meant that a majority of the class members were passive for extended periods of time and were therefore likely to be inattentive.

Many students find presenting to a small group of people, rather than an entire class, less threatening. The small group setting also increases the likelihood of more focused feedback. The listening team members tend to ask valid questions that they may not have felt comfortable posing before a whole group for fear of embarrassing either themselves or the presenting team. Perhaps the greatest advantage of Team Rotation is the time built in for revision. Students learn to rely on peers for helpful feedback. Their presentation skills are honed by rehearsal, revision, and repetition. All students benefit from having an opportunity for peer coaching and learning. Peer feedback forms, to be discussed in chapter 11, prove useful for team and teacher assessment.

Gallery Walk

A Gallery Walk requires a report-out that can be visually depicted, preferably on butcher paper. It can be an outline, a concept map, or any other written product. In this case, a designated student stays by the desk or table (or next to the butcher paper if it is taped to the wall) and serves as the group spokesperson. The other students move around the room, examining the products of other teams' thinking and asking questions of the designated spokesperson. The spokesperson role should be rotated so that no one is left without the stimulation of exploring the different student creations.

This structure is efficient, and it engenders a sense of team cohesion as each group displays the product of their "group think." The variety of the end products emphasizes the value of critical/creative thinking.

Teachers can use a variation of "Gallery Walk" with required individual or team longterm products. Rather than having time-consuming report-outs, all students provide a summary of their project, which will be circulated to the class beforehand. Each product, such as a term paper or student portfolio, is assigned to a specific work area, as in a conference poster session. Then the students spend a class period examining one another's work. To provide feedback, each student or student team leaves a comment sheet next to the product, and browsers write a brief, usually complimentary, response.

SUMMARY

Instructors who have read this chapter may be ready to use one of these three problem-solving structures. Structured Problem Solving, for example, is ideal for mutual problem solving. At the same time, it fosters peer teaching, greater student involvement, and positive interdependence leading to greater team rapport. The Discovery Method leads to greater student mastery and retention. Send-a-Problem fosters application, synthesizing, and evaluation skills under a format that appeals to students. The four report-out methods offer creative options that can save time and add interest.

Faculty who are considering cooperative-learning structures to supplement their traditional presentations need to realize that these structures, although proven to be effective, take careful planning and are enhanced by the use of ongoing structured-learning teams rather than random reformation of teams whenever an activity seems desirable. Once faculty are both committed and comfortable with cooperative-learning techniques, they rarely return to a method of teaching that relies exclusively on lecture punctuated by random, whole-class discussion.

REFERENCES

Bender, T.A. (1986). "Monitoring and the Transfer of Individual Problem Solving." *Contemporary Educational Psychology*, 11, 161–69.

Berry, D.C. (1983). "Metacognitive Experience and Transfer of Logical Reasoning." *The Quarterly Journal of Experimental Psychology*, 35A, 39–49.

Bloom, B.S. (1956). *Taxonomy of Educational Objectives (Cognitive Domain)*. New York: Longman.

BradyLink, A. (1996). *Cooperative Learning in Computer Science: Assignment for General Education or CSO Course.* Online at <http://bingen.cs.csbsju....egler/CSO.hypercard.html>. Downloaded 25 June 1996. No longer available.

Davidson, N. (Ed.),(1990). *Cooperative Learning in Mathematics: A Handbook for Teachers*. Reading, MA: Addison-Wesley.

Gagne, R.M. and Smith, E.C. (1962). "A Study of the Effects of Verbalization on Problem Solving." *Journal of Experimental Psychology*, 63(1), 12–18.

Groner, R., Groner, M., and Bischof, W.F., (Eds.), (1983). *Methods of Heuristics*. Hillsdale, NJ: Lawrence Eribaum Associates.

Johnson, D.W., Johnson, R.T., and Smith, K. (1991). *Active Learning: Cooperation in the College Classroom*. Edina, MN: Interaction Book Company.

Kagan, S. (1989). *Cooperative Learning Resources for Teachers*. San Juan Capistrano, CA: Resources for Teachers, Inc.

Kagan, S. (1992). *Cooperative Learning*. San Juan Capistrano, CA: Resources for Teachers, Inc.

Kagan, S. (1994). "The Structural Approach." In S. Sharan (Ed.), *Handbook of Cooperative Learning Methods* (pp. 114–33). Westport, CT: Greenwood Press.

Larkin, J.H. and Chabay, R.W. (1989). "Research on Teaching Scientific Thinking: Implications for Computer-based Instruction." In L.B. Resnick and L.E. Klopfer (Eds.), *Toward the Thinking Curriculum: Current Cognitive Research* (pp. 150–72). Alexandria, VA: Association for Supervision and Curriculum Development.

Lawlor, E.J. (1997). *Small Group 'Research' on Biocultural Evolution of the Genus* **Homo**. Presentation at the 1997 Regional Conference on College Teaching: Using Cooperative Learning in Discipline-Specific Settings. Feb. 21-22, 1997, Occidental College, Los Angeles.

Meyers, G.D. (1988). "A Lesson in Rhetoric: Writing and Performing TV Commercials." In J. Golob (Ed.), *Focus on Collaborative Learning: Classroom Practices in Teaching English* (pp. 133–37). Urbana, IL: National Council of Teachers of English.

Miller, J.E. (1995, Oct. 10). Syllabus sent with private correspondence.

Rhoades, J. and McCabe, M. (1991). "Practice Activities and Your Textbooks." *Cooperative Learning and College Teaching*, 2(1), 6–8.

Savery, J.R. and Duffy, T.M. (1995, Sept./Oct.). "Problem-based Learning: An Instructional Model and its Constructivist Framework." *Educational Technology* (pp. 31–38.). Reprinted in *Educational Psychology 97/98 Annual Editions* (pp. 143–51). Guilford, CT: Duskin/McGraw-Hill.

Smith, K.A. (1993, Winter). "Cooperative Learning and Problem Solving. *Cooperative Learning and College Teaching*, 3(2), 10–12.

Smith, K.A. and Waller, A.A. (1997). "Cooperative Learning for New College Teachers." In W.E. Campbell and K.A. Smith (Eds.), *New Paradigms for College Teaching* (pp. 183–209). Edina, MN: Interaction Book Company.

Smith, P. (1996). *An Exercise in Designing Software from Specifications.*Online at <http://bingen.cs.csbsju....SoftwareEngineering.html>. Downloaded 25 June 1996. No longer available.

Tenenberg, J.D. (1995). *Using Cooperative Learning in the Undergraduate Computer Science Classroom.* Paper to appear in the Proceedings of the Midwest Small College Computing Conference, 1995.Online at <http://phoenix.iusb.edu/...coop/papers/mwscc95.html>. Downloaded 25 June 1996. No longer available.

Weaver, M. (1997). *The First Amendment and the Howard Stern Show.* Presentation at the 1997 Regional Conference on College Teaching: Using Cooperative Learning in Discipline-Specific Settings. Feb. 21–22, 1997, Occidental College, Los Angeles.

Whimbey, A. (1984). "The Key to Higher Order Thinking is Precise Processing." *Educational Leadership*, 42(1), 66–70.

Woods, D.R. (1994). *Problem-Based Learning: How to Gain the Most from PBL.* Waterdown, ON: Donald R. Woods.

Ziegler, L. (1996). *Cooperative Learning: A Normal Class Day.* Online at <http://bingen.cs.csbsju.edu/~lziegler/normal.html>. Downloaded 25 June 1996.

CHAPTER 7

Basic Paired Teaching

Education should be viewed "as a social enterprise in which all individuals have an opportunity to contribute and to which all feel a responsibility."

John Dewey

Reciprocal teaching has been receiving a lot of attention in higher education. As indicated earlier, the dynamics of Think-Pair-Share can have a profound impact on student learning. McKeachie, Pintrich, Lin and Smith (1986), for instance, conclude: "The best answer to the question, 'What is the most effective method of teaching?' is that it depends on the goal, the student, the content, and the teacher. But the next best answer is, 'Students teaching other students'" (p. 63).

On a basic level, reciprocal teaching can be used efficiently when a vast body of information, such as technical concepts and terminology, needs to be committed to long-term memory. Students study the body of material independently, but to ensure mastery, some in-class time is permitted for paired coaching. Many of the structures discussed in this chapter are intended for mastery learning. The body of knowledge to be mastered will vary in complexity, but these reciprocal teaching methods promote deep learning because they focus on integrating knowledge, active learning, student-student interactions, and immediate feedback. The peer support also bolsters motivation to learn. This motivation can even be fostered by flashcard-type learning.

FLASHCARD TUTORING

Students prepare flashcards, often for pretest coaching, with a word, concept, or short-answer question on the front of the card and the answer on the back. The activity is meaningful only if students deliberately pick topics they need to master. Otherwise, the task of creating flashcards will be perceived as busy work. Giving a practice test to pinpoint areas where students need to concentrate their efforts reinforces the value of flashcard tutoring.

Working in pairs, one student assumes the role of tutor, holding up, in rapid succession, the cards prepared by her partner with the question prompts. If the "tutee" gives an accurate response, he or she receives the card. If the answer is incorrect or partially correct, the tutor shows the flip side of the card and allows time for study and reflection. The two might discuss ways to master the elusive definition or answer, such as through a mnemonic device. The card is then placed at the back of the deck for a subsequent response. During the next round, only the incorrectly answered cards are displayed and the tutor gives appropriate hints or clues. After the final round, when the tutee has earned all of the cards through correct responses (without the hints), the roles are reversed until both partners have mastered the material. For elementary students, Kagan (1992) offers a more structured version of this method, called the flashcard game.

Flashcard Tutoring is suitable for relatively low-level thinking (the knowledge and comprehensive levels of Bloom's well-known Taxonomy). Thus, it is particularly useful for memorization in courses such as astronomy or biology that require students to understand a number of terms, or in foreign language or ESL courses, where vocabulary building is critical. Faculty worried about "spoon-feeding" students by using class time for material they should presumably have mastered on their own need to remember that, without peer coaching, some students will never master some or all of the key terms/concepts. Or, class time may be squandered by quizzes to "force" students to study, a punitive rather than reinforcing practice.

SCRIPTED COOPERATIVE DYADS

Dansereau and colleagues (Dansereau, D.F.,1986; Larson and Dansereau, 1986; Larson, Dansereau, O'Donnell, Hythecker, Lambiotte, and Rocklin, 1985) have done elaborate studies with a tightly structured cooperative technique where pairs exchange repeated oral summaries of sequential text material, one or two pages at a time. A "cooperative-learning script," which is often supplied to both members of the dyad, is as follows:

1. Flip a coin to determine who will be partner A or B.
2. Both partners read Passage #1.
3. When both are finished, put the passage out of sight.
4. Partner A orally summarizes Passage #1.
5. Partner B detects and corrects any errors in Partners A's summary (the **metacognitive** step).
6. Both partners work together in developing analogies, images, etc., to help make the summarized information memorable (the **elaboration** step).
7. Both partners read Passage #2.
8. Repeat steps 4–6 with partners reversing roles.

Among undergraduate general psychology students, these techniques were found to significantly influence learning, especially with regard to the metacognitive activities which help the achievement performance of the **listener**. The **elaborative** activities also facilitate transfer of learning to other material and situations:

1. If possible, students should be paired with partners whose level of verbal ability differs from their own;
2. The cooperative-teaching script should be used if mastery of content is desired;
3. The cooperative-learning script, with its emphasis on the elaboration step, should be used if transfer to individual reading and studying is the goal;
4. Students should be encouraged to tailor the scripts to their own needs in developing individual study plans;
5. Transfer from the cooperative experience can be facilitated by switching partners and analyzing videotapes.

Johnson, Johnson, and Smith (1991) have developed a similar structure called "Read and Explain Pairs," which asks students to concentrate on one paragraph at a time. After Partner A summarizes the paragraph to Partner B, the two identify the question being asked in the paragraph and agree on a summary that answers the question. They actively relate the meaning of the paragraph to previous learning before moving to the next paragraph, where the procedure is repeated.

COOPERATIVE NOTE-TAKING PAIRS

Johnson, Johnson, and Smith (1991) describe a useful paired activity to help students master lecture material. Called "Cooperative Note-Taking Pairs," the activity begins with the research-supported premise that students' notes are likely to be incomplete, inaccurate, or both. Poor note-taking can result from students' inability to keep information in working memory while they encode notes; from information overload, due sometimes to unfamiliarity with the material or from too many complex visual diagrams; from unskilled note-taking practices; or from students' complacency about their ability to recall information later. The procedure unfolds as follows:

> After exposure to a lecture segment, one partner summarizes his or her notes to the other, who in turn adds and corrects. Students may ask one another, "What have you got in your notes so far? "What are the three key points made by the instructor?" "What was the most surprising thing the instructor said?" The **rule** is that each member must take something from the other's notes to improve his or her own (pp. 5:20–21).

At the conclusion of a lecture, students can follow a similar process called "Closure Note-Taking Pairs" (p. 5:25).

THINKING-ALOUD PAIR PROBLEM SOLVING

Focused on problem solving, thinking, and metacognition, Thinking-Aloud Pair Problem Solving (Whimbey and Whimbey, 1975; Lochhead and Whimbey, 1987) helps facilitate transfer of information by encouraging students to abstract the principle from practice. Svinicki (1991) states that "If students can articulate the steps they are taking to solve problems, or if they can extract an underlying concept from a set of examples, then they will be more likely to use that abstraction in a different context. This is known as decontextualizing . . ." (p. 34). Working in pairs, one student serves as the problem solver and the other as the monitor. The teacher often precedes the pair work with instruction. Multiple problems are then posed. Sherman (1994) offers this example from a science lesson: The teacher discusses the three different temperature scales (Kelvin, Fahrenheit, and Celsius), explains the correlation between cricket chirps and air temperature, and tells students how to determine the air temperature in degrees Celsius by counting the chirps per minute, adding 30, and dividing by seven. She then poses a series of conversion questions depending on the level of the students. The problem solver talks through his reasoning procedures as he attempts to solve the first problem. The monitor, or listener, encourages him to think aloud and articulate key steps in the problem-solving process. The two then switch roles. After most students have solved all the problems, the pairs discuss in their structured-learning teams the strategies they used and the stumbling blocks they encountered (p. 233).

THINK-PAIR-SQUARE

A modification of Think-Pair-Share, Think-Pair-Square (Lyman, 1981) provides instructors with a useful structure when they desire group interaction, but not a full-class discussion. Instructors will find Think-Pair-Square particularly useful for solving simple problems where the answer is either right or wrong. It can be used successfully, however, with more complex problems as well. Robertson, Davidson, and Dees (1994), in fact, find "partner problem solving . . . particularly appropriate for open-ended problems that provide opportunities for students to have many interpretations, strategies, and solutions" (p. 253).

In Think-Pair-Square, students are given time to consider a response and to share it with a partner. The two may also work together on paired problem solving. If playing cards are used, the suit partners that were described earlier work well here. The difference between Think-Pair-Share and Think-Pair-Square occurs in the last phase where students share each other's responses in their structured-learning teams instead of in front of the whole class, a less time-consuming, often more focused activity.

This within-team sharing is important in determining that the pairs have solved the problem(s) correctly. Even if one pair in the group has gone astray, they are likely to catch their errors and understand the nature of them when they compare their conclusions and problem-solving steps with the other pair in the team. Think-Pair-Square is a more advanced structure than Think-Pair-Share because of its reliance on structured-learning teams. Whereas a Think-Pair-Share activity can be conducted spontaneously with partners who have not previously been acquainted and then brought to closure through whole-class sharing, Think-Pair-Square relies upon student familiarity with a predesignated partner within a structured learning team. Thus, in Think-Pair-Square, students assume greater responsibility for learning.

This structure is useful for virtually any discipline where problem solving is important. For example, two pairs of engineering students within a structured-learning team might work simultaneously on this problem and then compare their answers: Point "0" is the origin of a set of reference axes x and y (2-D problem). Point A is 8 *feet* along the positive x-axis. Force P, unknown magnitude, is in the first quadrant at 30 CCW from the positive x-axis. Determine the force P. Also, using the principle of moments (only), find the perpendicular distance from point A to force P. As a sponge or extension activity, a pair working faster than the other pair could move on to this question: Determine the moment of the force F tending to twist the frame in the two brackets (i.e., find the moment of the force about the y-axis) (Lewis, 1995, p. 22).

Another math example is designed to provide cognitive dissonance (pose a problem that challenges students' prevailing assumptions and beliefs). Each pair within the structured-learning team could be challenged to solve this problem and then compare their answers:

> In class yesterday, 80 percent of you agreed with this statement: "The maximum speed of a sailboat occurs when the boat is sailing in the same direction as the wind." However, that intuitive answer is wrong. Sailboats can actually go much faster when they sail across the wind. How so? Using what you have been learning in vector algebra, explain why sailboats can sail faster when the wind blows sideways to their direction of travel rather than from directly behind them. Make your explanation clear enough for the general public to understand. You can use diagrams if that helps (Bean, 1996, p. 27).

Worksheets or memory matrices (Angelo and Cross, 1993, p. 142) are particularly useful with a Think-Pair-Square structure because they focus student learning, particularly when recall is important. They also make it easy to cross-check during the "squaring" portion of this activity. Figure 7.1 offers two illustrations.

In a literature class, pairs of students can identify examples of color imagery in *The Great Gatsby* and then compare their results with the other pair in their structured-learning team to develop a composite list. In a composition class, students could prepare complex bibliography cards in pairs and then compare their results with the other working pair. As part of this process, they may end up editing one another's cards.

PEER EDITING

Johnson, Johnson, and Smith (1991) have evolved a complex series of steps for peer editing (pp. 4:18–4:19; 8:21), which involves mutual outlining. Working in pairs, each student describes to the other their ideas for the paper they intend to write. The listening student takes notes, asks clarifying questions, and produces an outline of the other student's composition. The two then research their individual papers, keeping in mind material that might prove useful to their partner. Working together after the research stage, the two students compose the opening paragraphs for each composition or research paper. The two students then write their own papers, coming together later for serious peer editing. This peer editing includes commentary on all aspects of effective writing such as a clear thesis, well-constructed topic sentences, coherent transitions, a logical organization, full support, plus surface corrections (including grammar, spelling, and punctuation). Then, the two students make revisions. They give each other's papers a final reading before submis-

Key Literary Movements

	Characteristics	Key Authors	Typical Works
Determinism			
Realism			
Impressionism			

Manned Space Exploration

	Spacecraft Design	Launch Vehicles	Spacecraft Recovery
Soviet			
American			

Thanks to Curtis Hughes for helping to develop these ideas.

MEMORY MATRICES

FIGURE 7.1

sion, signing their names to indicate that the mutual tasks have been completed with care.

RECIPROCAL PEER TUTORING

Reciprocal Peer Tutoring (Fantuzzo, Dimeff, and Fox, 1989; Fantuzzo, Riggio,
Connelly, and Dimeff, 1989) extends the reciprocal teaching beyond a single
lesson plan. Students remain randomly paired with partners throughout a
semester, quarter or other academic unit. Before each class unit exam, each
partner prepares a ten-question multiple-choice test based on the most salient
points in the material covered through readings and lecture. As in the
flashcard procedure discussed earlier, each student prepares a 3 x 5 card with
the question on the front and the correct answer on the back, including
relevant references to the book(s) or lecture segment. During tutoring sessions, the partners administer the tests to one another, simulating normal
examination procedures. They then mark one another's exams, explaining in
detail the correct answers to any missed or partially incorrect question responses. The instructor collects all test materials prior to her own whole-class
examination.

PAIRED ANNOTATIONS

Paired Annotations, an activity based on the double-entry journal recommended by writing-across-the-curriculum and classroom assessment experts,
is best used on an ongoing basis so that students gain skill in the technique.
This "front-loading" activity motivates students to read important chapters or
articles prior to a class session. It can even be used to summarize lectures. This
structure thus enables teachers to sequence learning in meaningful ways. It
builds critical-thinking and writing skills by having students analyze and then
compare their responses to the same piece of writing. It has the additional
virtue of being relevant to virtually any discipline.

The teacher identifies a pool of articles on a specific topic under consider-
ation or the students themselves can identify important resources. Topics
could include ethical issues in accounting, the population control controversy,
or interpretations of *Hamlet*. Each student, working individually out-of-class,
prepares a reflective commentary on one of the articles or chapters. They do so
using a double-column format where they cite major points excerpted from the
original source on the left-hand side and reactions, questions, commentary,
and connections with other readings on the right (the columns might not be
the same length) (Figure 7.2). When students come to class, the teacher
randomly pairs them with other students who have read and analyzed the
same material. The two partners now read one another's reflective commen-

taries, comparing both the key points they have identified and their specific responses to them. They discuss their reasons for the choices they made. Then, working together, they prepare a composite annotation summarizing the article or chapter.

Critical Points	Response

Annotated Summary

PAIRED ANNOTATION

FIGURE 7.2

This activity should be repeated several times during the semester, pairing different students. It enables students to reflect on their own thinking skills (metacognition) and to compare their thinking with that of other students. The more paired annotations they complete, the more skilled students become at identifying important points in an article.

Paired Annotations is deliberately structured to promote both individual accountability and positive interdependence, hallmarks of cooperative learning. The student pairs submit their individually prepared double-columned analyses along with their jointly prepared annotation. Although the bulk of the writing is done outside of class, students will need class time to compare and discuss their responses if the activity is to have critical-thinking value. Instructors need not assign a letter grade to each piece of writing. Students can receive x number of points applied toward a criterion-referenced final grade, assuming that their double-columned analyses and paired annotations are of sufficient quality. Informal, handwritten comments on the pieces by the instructor will reinforce student thinking and provide feedback that will lead to more sophisticated writing. It is useful to share appropriate examples with the class as a whole. If students come to class unprepared, they must complete their analysis individually while their classmates work together, and they receive no credit, of course, for a paired annotation. Fortunately, such instances are rare.

Using writing to promote critical thinking helps students examine, evaluate, verify, analyze, weigh alternatives, and consider consequences as ideas develop. Writing and thinking cannot be separated. Pulitzer prize winner Don Murray (1978) contends: "I believe increasingly that the process of discovery, of using language to find out what you are going to say, is a key part of the writing process." It is also a key part of the thinking process. All of the activities discussed in this chapter foster critical-thinking skills and all are applicable to virtually any discipline.

TEAM ANTHOLOGIES

Millis (1994) has described an extended variation on Paired Annotations which involves structured-learning teams in a longer, ongoing semester assignment. Team Anthologies are intended to teach the research process without, however, having students actually produce a research paper. Frequently, writing research papers is a time-consuming, product-centered effort coming too late in a semester to allow for meaningful processing and feedback. The Team Anthology assignment sends students to the library, either physically or electronically, to research a given topic and to evaluate and analyze the original sources.

In this activity, quads select a discipline-specific topic, one which typically might be chosen for a term paper. They are given the task of preparing a team research anthology that contains a bibliography and annotations of the most valuable articles or chapters.

The process works systematically, using combinations of independent effort, pair work, and team approaches:

1. Each team agrees on a discipline-specific topic for research.
2. Each team member, working individually, identifies the most important sources on the topic. This bibliography is submitted independently.
3. The team compiles a team research bibliography drawn from the work of all four members: to do this, they debate the relative merits of each entry, including its relevance, currency, and value.
4. Each team member, working individually, prepares a reflective commentary on an article, using a double-entry journal format. The teacher collects these commentaries to insure individual accountability, but the students also retain a copy for future pair work.

5. Team members then pair, exchanging the articles they have just analyzed. Each reads her partner's article (but not her reflective commentary at this point) and prepares a double-entry journal response, which is submitted to the teacher. The student also retains a copy.

6. The two teammates now read each other's double-entry journals, comparing their responses to the same article. Together, they prepare a composite annotation summarizing the article.

7. Steps 4, 5, and 6 are repeated several times, pairing different students within the structured-learning team, until the team as a whole has completed the desired number of annotations.

8. Working together, the team now prepares its work for publication by adding three elements to the bibliography and annotations: (a) a cover; (b) an introduction, stating the purpose of the anthology and its value for the intended audience (fellow students); and (c) a conclusion, giving suggested uses or applications of the anthology and recommended future research on the topic, including unanswered questions. Students might also include their own plans for future research within the discipline.

9. To promote whole-class sharing, the anthologies can be duplicated for each class member, depending on class size and budget constraints; shared through a gallery walk; or placed on reserve in the library.

Team Annotations promote deep thinking and hone critical-thinking skills by their sequenced nature. This extended activity is deliberately structured to capitalize on independent work outside of class (the bibliographies and double-entry journals) followed by pair and team work within class. Teachers and teammates must monitor the steps carefully to ensure that all students perform their fair share of the work, but the individual submissions promote accountability. The team anthology cannot be completed without the contributions of all team members, thus ensuring positive interdependence.

RECIPROCAL LETTER WRITING

In this activity, advocated by Toby Fulwiler, a Writing-Across-the-Curriculum scholar, students write about issues identified through sentence stems or prompts. It involves letter exchanges between students.

The instructor prepares an activity sheet with the prompts (sentence stems) for reflection. These can be presented as individual handouts for out-of-class assignments or projected on an overhead for in-class writing. Because these exchanges can be composed fairly rapidly, they are often effective as an active learning/reflective in-class activity that lasts about thirty minutes. All assignment sheets begin with a salutation (Dear X) and end with a P. S.: "One personal thing about me you may not know is:

Typical prompts might be:

- *Military Ethics.* The 'Just War' tradition has relevance today because _____;
- *Political Science or Speech Communications.* I think President Clinton's State of the Union addresses succeeded because _____. His strongest point was _____;
- *Composition.* I plan to write my classification on the topic of _____. My major points will be _____. My reservations about this assignment are _____;
- *Accounting or Computer Science.* Unreliability in a computer accounting system can be caused by events such as _____;
- *Ecology, Biology, Ecoomics.* The spotted owl controversy involves the following issues _____. I think the most important issue is _____, because _____;
- *Psychology or Pre-Medicine.* I do/do not feel that Prozac should be frequently prescribed because _____;
- *Sociology.* The causes for homelessness are _____. I think we should attack the _____ issue by _____.

Paired students, working simultaneously in class or outside of class, write a personal letter to their partner based on the sentence stems. They exchange letters, read them, and write a response focused primarily on the issues, but they may also address in their own P. S. a response to the personal comment made by their partner. The partners again exchange letters so that they can read each others' responses. (No one likes to write a letter without getting a reply!) The letters can be kept by the students without teacher review, but more often they are taken up, read informally, and eventually become part of an ongoing class journal.

SUMMARY

Too often, well-meaning instructors teach as they were taught, which typically means lecturing and using whole-class discussion. The latter can be intimidating, however, for many students who remain silent or even inattentive. Howe (1988) reminds us that:

> Moving too quickly towards expecting pupils to talk openly in a large group is rather like throwing a whole class into the deep end of a swimming pool. As well as the few non-swimmers who might drown (never to be heard from again?!), there will be others who are unhappy out of their depth. Whilst a few strong, natural swimmers splash about happily, the nervous ones are so anxious about drowning, or so conscious and embarrassed about their lack of finesse as swimmers, that they lose all confidence and cling silently on to the side of the pool. They need to be gradually brought to the deep end (p. 34).

A famous quip, "It's hard to get left out of a pair," has particular relevance for this chapter. Peer teaching can positively affect students' learning outcomes and their attitudes toward the subject matter. The secret lies in appropriate structuring and monitoring so that students remain on task, engaged in their reciprocal learning. All of the activities described in this chapter contribute toward these ends by focusing on cooperative problem solving and metacognitive strategies. In the next chapter, we will look at more complex variations of peer teaching and coaching.

REFERENCES

Angelo, T.A. and Cross, K.P. (1993). *Classroom Assessment Techniques: A Handbook for College Teachers.* 2nd Ed. San Francisco: Jossey-Bass.

Bean, J.C. (1996). *Engaging Ideas: The Professor's Guide to Integrating Writing, Critical Thinking, and Active Learning in the Classroom.* San Francisco: Jossey-Bass.

Dansereau, D.F. (1986). *Dyadic and Cooperative Learning and Performance Strategies.* Paper presented at the annual meeting of the American Educational Research Association, San Francisco.

Fantuzzo, J.W., Dimeff, L.A., and Fox, S.L. (1989). "Reciprocal Peer Tutoring: A Multimodal Assessment of Effectiveness with College Students." *Teaching of Psychology,* 16(3), 133–35.

Fantuzzo, J.W., Riggio, R.E., Connelly, S., and Dimeff, L.A. (1989). "Effects of Reciprocal Peer Tutoring on Academic Achievement and Psychological Adjustment: A Component Analysis." *Journal of Educational Psychology,* 81(2), 173–77.

Howe, A. (1988). *Expanding Horizons: Teaching through Whole Class Discussion.* Sheffield, England: National Association for Teachers of English.

Johnson, D.W., Johnson, R.T., and Smith, K.A. (1991). *Active Learning: Cooperation in the College Classroom.* Edina, MN: Interaction Book Company.

Kagan, S. (1992). *Cooperative Learning.* San Juan Capistrano, CA: Resources for Teachers, Inc.

Larson, C.O. and Dansereau D.F. (1986). "Cooperative Learning in Dyads." *Journal of Reading,* 29, pp. 516–20.

Larson, C.O., Dansereau, D.F., O'Donnell, A.M., Hythecker, V.I., Lambiotte, J.G., and Rocklin, T.R. (1985). *Effects of Metacognitive and Elaborative Activity on Cooperative Learning and Transfer,* 10, 342–48.

Lewis, R.B. (1995). *Practical Applications of Critical Thinking in the Engineering Classroom.* Booklet to accompany workshop given at the United States Air Force Academy.

Lochhead, J. and Whimbey, A. (1987). "Teaching Analytical Reasoning through Think-Aloud Pair Problem Solving." In J.E. Stice (Ed.), *Developing Critical Thinking and Problem-Solving Abilities.* (pp. 72–93) *New Directions for Teaching and Learning,* No. 30. San Francisco: Jossey-Bass.

Lyman, F. (1981). "The Responsive Class Discussion." In A. S. Anderson (Ed.), *Mainstreaming Digest.* College Park, MD: University of Maryland College of Education.

McKeachie, W.J., Pintrich, P.R., Lin, Y., and Smith, D.A. (1986). *Teaching and Learning in the College Classroom: A Review of the Research Literature.* Ann Arbor: The University of Michigan.

Millis, B. J. (1994, Spring). "Increasing Thinking through Cooperative Writing." *Cooperative Learning and College Teaching,* 4(3), 7–9.

Murray, D. (1978). "Internal Revision: A Process of Discovery." In C.R. Cooper and L. O'Dell (Eds.), *Research on Composing: Points of Departure.* (pp. 85–104) Urbana, IL: National Council of Teachers of English.

Robertson, L., Davidson, N., and Dees, R.L. (1994). "Cooperative Learning to Support Thinking, Reasoning, and Communicating in Mathematics." In S. Sharan (Ed.), *Handbook of Cooperative Learning Methods.* (pp. 245–66) Westport, CT: Greenwood Press.

Sherman, S.J. (1994). "Cooperative Learning and Science." In S. Sharan (Ed.), *Handbook of Cooperative Learning Methods.* (pp. 226-44). Westport, CT: Greenwood Press.

Svinicki, M.D. (1991). "Practical Implications of Cognitive Theories." In R. J. Menges and M.D. Svinicki (Eds.), *College Teaching: From Theory to Practice: New Directions for Teaching and Learning,* No. 45 (pp. 27–37). San Francisco: Jossey-Bass.

Whimbey, A. and Whimbey, L. (1975). *Intelligence Can be Taught.* New York: Innovative Science.

CHAPTER 8

Reciprocal Teaching

"Learning and teaching are constantly interchanging activities. One learns by teaching; one cannot teach except by constantly learning."

Kenneth Elbe

As emphasized earlier, cooperative-learning structures enable faculty members to use the content of their own disciplines to promote thinking skills developed within the context of the subject matter students are mastering. A recent review of the research literature on long-term retention of classroom-taught content (Semb and Ellis, 1994) suggests that classroom approaches, including peer tutoring, that "involve actively engaging learners in an enriched, contextualized-learning environment . . . should result in differential retention by making it easier for students to assimilate new information into existing memory structures or to create new, well-organized ones" (p. 278).

As the following Jigsaw structure will suggest, students actively enhance their own learning as they come to understand material deeply enough to teach it to fellow students. Gartner, Kohler, and Riessmann (1971) emphasize that various cognitive processes occur when someone prepares to teach effectively. First of all, teachers must review the material, resulting, one assumes, in a deeper understanding. Second, teachers must organize the material in order to present it to others unfamiliar with it. In this process, they will likely seek creative ways to get their points across. They may discover or design, for instance, relevant anecdotes, concrete examples, visual or oral illustrations, graphic organizers, charts, and classroom or homework activities. Third, teachers are also likely both to identify and subsequently to reorder or rearrange the salient facts, resulting in an in-depth understanding and, sometimes, in a reconceptualization of the subject.

As faculty can verify, the learning process continues as teachers become involved with the actual teaching. This effect is probably even more pronounced on individuals whom Whitman (1988) identifies as "co-peers," students who teach other students. The clarification and amplification, including stretching to find clearer examples, helps students enlarge their own understanding. Webb (1983, 1991) has found that giving detailed, elaborate explanations increases student achievement. Additional benefits of peer teaching/coaching have emerged. Working with peers can reduce the sense of working in an isolated vacuum for an artificial audience, usually the teacher. Gere (1987), in speaking of the power of writing groups, emphasizes that "The peer who says 'I don't understand' establishes—more powerfully than any theory, instructor's exhortation, or written comment can—the 'otherness' of the audience and pushes writers to respond to this otherness by more effective ways to convey ideas" (p. 68).

Thus, faculty who care deeply about student learning can use peer teaching techniques such as Jigsaw to promote higher-order thinking skills (playfully abbreviated as HOTS in the K–12 literature) and depth of knowledge. Newmann and Wehlage (1993) describe development of such thinking skills in these words:

> Higher-order thinking (HOT) requires students to manipulate information and ideas in ways that transform their meaning and implications, such as when students combine facts and ideas in order to synthesize, generalize, explain, hypothesize, or arrive at some conclusion or interpretation. Manipulating information and ideas through these processes allows students to solve problems and discover new (for them) meanings and understandings. When students engage in HOT, an element of uncertainty is introduced, and instructional outcomes are not always predictable (p. 9).

Such higher-order thinking can occur when faculty deliberately structure tasks to capitalize on student peer coaching and on interactions where they encounter alternative viewpoints that challenge existing beliefs and assumptions. The Jigsaw structure accomplishes these aims.

JIGSAW

Many courses require demanding problem-solving skills that force students to confront complex, challenging topics involving multiple pieces of information necessary for final, overall mastery. Even if a definitive answer is neither possible nor desirable, students need to come to an understanding of in-depth issues. Such problems are ideally suited for the cooperative-learning structure, Jigsaw.

In this structure, each member of the structured-learning team assumes responsibility for a specific part of a problem. They are responsible for more than just mastering or knowing their part. As "specialists," they must also be able to teach it to their fellow teammates. Thus, working together, the group merges the various portions to solve the "puzzle."

In a basic Jigsaw activity, students temporarily leave their structured-learning teams (called "home" teams in the K–12 literature) to form expert teams which may be organized, for example, like the suits of playing cards. The student holding the heart from each of the groups meets with all the other hearts in the classroom. Those holding spades, diamonds, and clubs form similar expert teams. Figure 8.1 illustrates how a class of twenty can be quickly transformed from five structured-learning teams into four expert teams with five members, one from each of the original groups. If classes are larger, then students can form two or more expert teams on the same piece of the puzzle. If the original structured team consists of five members rather than four, then two students pair and work as a unit in their expert team and when they return to their original team.

In the expert teams, students have two tasks: they must master the material, and they must also develop, as a team, creative ways to teach the other members of their "home" structured-learning teams the material they have mastered. They must be able to respond knowledgeably and positively to questions raised by their teammates. Figure 8.1 shows how students holding playing cards are arranged in home and expert teams.

Jigsaw, as Clarke (1994) notes, was initially developed by a team of teachers, administrators, and researchers as a way to develop equal opportunities for participation and achievement in desegregated classrooms. To reduce the emphasis on "winners" and "losers" in a typically competitive classroom, the Jigsaw inventors sought to develop methods of ensuring that students relied on one another as valuable resources. Many versions of Jigsaw have been developed since Aronson, Blaney, Stephan, Sikes, and Snapp (1978) first published their work. In the 1980s, for example, Slavin (1986) and Kagan (1989) popularized several variations, including those in Slavin's models emphasizing an extrinsic reward system. Regardless of the variation, higher education faculty will find that the value of Jigsaw lies in the teaching and peer coaching process.

Jigsaw also reinforces the most basic tenets of cooperative learning. Positive interdependence is fostered since students must work together and teach one another in order to get the "big picture"—all of the information and skills they will need to solve the problem, or in some disciplines, to function effectively on

Students Organized into
Structured Learning Teams

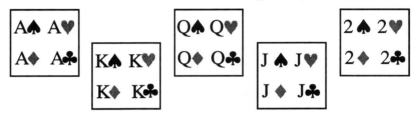

Students Form Expert
Learning Teams by Suit

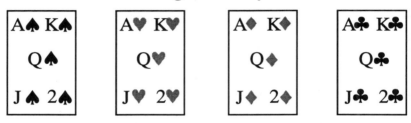

They complete their task and prepare to teach it

Students Teach their Portion in
Structured Learning Teams

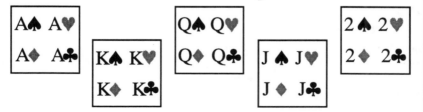

Source: South-Western College Publishing. (Reprinted with permission.)

JIGSAW

FIGURE 8.1

the job. At the same time, individual accountability is reinforced because students must learn all the information, not just their own portion, since they are tested individually. Students interact within two different groups, reinforcing the idea of heterogeneity as a way to bring multiple perspectives to a given problem. The positive interactions that result from these brief, but intense encounters in the expert groups help to develop the skills students will need in the "real world." Because expert teams have the responsibility of making certain that all members can successfully teach the materials/conclusions, the important concepts of group processing and accountability are also reinforced.

Teachers must decide with care what content to deliver with a Jigsaw structure. Because of the complexity of the structure, it should not be overused or used superficially. Cuseo (1994) suggests that if instructors seek to develop students' higher-order thinking skills, then the learning task should focus on: "(1) ill-structured problems that may not be readily resolved, (2) issues to be discussed or debated, or (3) decision-making tasks that require exploration of, and determination from, equally appealing alternatives" (p. 5). Examples from several different disciplines will illustrate suitable kinds of material and appropriate approaches.

Jigsaw Examples

In an upper-level undergraduate history course on the American Civil War, the 27 students, who are already in four-person structured-learning teams (three teams have an extra member), are asked to select a specialized topic that they wish to explore in depth. From a list of topics generated through the Roundtable structure, the class decides to focus on Civil War photography. All class members agree to explore the general topic of Civil War photography and to come to the next class session with appropriate subtopics. Each team subsequently discusses in class the subtopics suggested by their members and selects and refines their best options. A recorder from each team puts these on the blackboard. During the ensuing student-directed discussion, the class decides that the topic of Civil War photography is far too broad. After further discussion, they choose to focus on the photography documenting a single battle, the Battle of Gettysburg. Next, they debate the most appropriate way to jigsaw the assignment: should each expert team look at the photographers themselves or at other issues, such as what portions of the field were covered and when or how the various photographers interpreted their subject matter? When the objectives of the study are defined—to complete a systematic examination of the Gettysburg series as a group—the class decides to have each expert group concentrate on the photographers themselves (Gardner and his men; Mathew Brady; The Tyson brothers; and miscellaneous photographers such as Frederick Gutekunst and Peter S. and Hanson E. Weaver).

They decide to examine their work systematically so that the same topics are examined for each photographer or group of photographers.

The expert groups meet several times, sharing, analyzing, and refining the historical data they have uncovered. Next they prepare exhibits and charts that will help each team member "teach" their complex data to the home team members. The carefully monitored teaching occurs within each home team, with each member discussing the different photographers their expert teams investigated. Each student then takes an individual test. Because the work was done as a group project, the students ask if they may also retake the examination, pooling their knowledge in composite answers. The teacher agrees, knowing that they will benefit from the immediate feedback and from the exchange and debate of ideas. Both grades are recorded—the team grades in all cases are higher—and contribute toward the final course grade.

Jigsaw also works well in Modern Children's Literature, an upper-level undergraduate survey course where a key goal is to develop students' proficiency in close textual readings. After a mini-lecture on characterization, which explains and models close textual analysis, the instructor uses a required course book, such as *Charlotte's Web*, with four strong characters (Fern, Charlotte, Wilbur, and Templeton), and asks each student in a four-person structured-learning team to choose one character. If a team has five members, then two students work with the same character. To focus their reading and subsequent discussion, students receive a graphic organizer (Figure 8.2) on which, as a homework assignment, they list on the extending arms each trait that describes their character. In the corner boxes, they list (with page numbers) each episode or event that provides evidence for this trait. In the subsequent class meeting, all the students studying the same character compare their charts in expert groups of three to five students and each expert group completes a second chart, using the best ideas of all members. At a signal, each expert member returns to the home structured-learning team where they explain in-depth their character's four key traits and the evidence in the text that supports this interpretation.

This activity helps students learn to pay close attention to textual clues. They learn from one another in the expert teams by comparing and contrasting their different approaches to the same homework assignment. They also learn to offer textual evidence for their assertions. The analysis is far deeper than if each team had merely worked on four character charts or if the instructor had lectured on the character traits.

This assignment can be evaluated by giving points toward a criterion-referenced grading scheme. Both charts (the individually prepared one done at home and the expert team-generated one) are collected in the home team folders at the end of the class session.

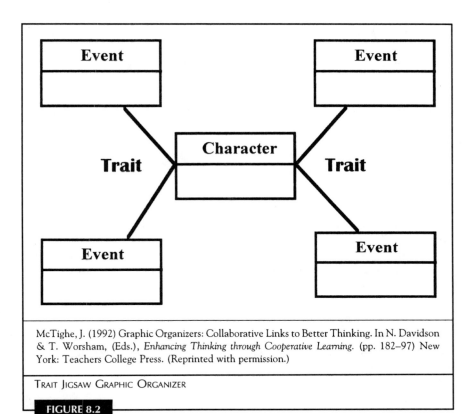

McTighe, J. (1992) Graphic Organizers: Collaborative Links to Better Thinking. In N. Davidson & T. Worsham, (Eds.), *Enhancing Thinking through Cooperative Learning.* (pp. 182–97) New York: Teachers College Press. (Reprinted with permission.)

TRAIT JIGSAW GRAPHIC ORGANIZER

FIGURE 8.2

Examples of Jigsaw are common in virtually every discipline. In a general anthropology course for non-majors, an instructor assigns students to teams of four and has each team member research one branch of anthropology: cultural, linguistic, physical, and archaeology. Students are encouraged to identify important researchers and relevant topics for study. During the following class period, the expert teams meet to pool their knowledge and prepare to teach their teammates information about their branch. In the original home teams, each student teaches the others, round robin style. This activity replaces a teacher-generated lecture on the four branches. It is far more likely to engage students with the discipline, because they are actively involved and because they can also select examples of interest to themselves and their classmates.

M. S. Rivkin (1994) uses a Jigsaw in her mathematics/science classes for students in early childhood education. Preferably conducted outdoors, this activity asks each different "expert" within the teams—(mathematicians, scientists, artists, and poets) to respond to a natural phenomenon (a stream, flowers, a tree) from their appropriate perspective (e.g., by counting measuring, drawing, or writing). After the expert teams have met and prepared their representations—inspired by tools such as calculators, measuring devices, graph paper, reference books, pH kits, markers, paints, clay, or writing paper—the structured-learning teams reassemble, and each expert shares their "creation" and the rationale behind it. Rivkin finds that this activity fosters student-student teambuilding and helps her appreciate the different attitudes and aptitudes students bring to an education course, one in which they need to learn that all perspectives children bring to a classroom must be cultivated and valued.

Jigsaw works extremely well in science courses where information and experiments are often highly complex. In a chemistry lab on absorption spectroscopy in which several different-colored solutions are studied, Sandra Laursen of Western Michigan University requires each home team member to change one variable in the experiment (i.e., the effect of concentration; the path length of a cell; a varied cpd.) Working in expert teams, each member formulates a hypothesis about the effect of their variable and designs an experiment to test the effect of this variable on a measurable (absorbency). After performing the experiment, members of the expert teams process the results and decide how to share them with their respective home teams. After each member of the home team shares the result of their experiment, the home team prepares a compilation of the results.

Pete Jones (1991) uses a Jigsaw approach to structure mock trials in his French classes. He takes classic fairy tales such as *Little Red Riding Hood* and has students meet in expert groups based on the four main characters—Little Red Riding Hood, her grandmother, the wolf, and the hunter. In these groups, the four students answer character question sheets with a goal of judging who is guilty in the wolf's death. When they return to the home team, all students take turns as the prosecuting lawyer. They use a Structured Problem-Solving approach to determine who will deliver their deliberations and verdict to the entire class. All conversations are conducted in French, of course.

Jigsaw opportunities abound in virtually all disciplines, including the sciences and social sciences, where topics can be logically broken down into three or four subtopics. Activities such as the literature example for Jigsaw model what might be called "front loading": getting students to perform meaningful, thought-provoking activities prior to a class where they can then "process" them. Too often, faculty will simply exhort students to read a chapter and be prepared for class discussion or a lecture. Without direction, students have no incentive to do the preparation, particularly if they know the material will be covered by the instructor and that they can hide in a large class where the odds of their being called upon are relatively slim if they don't volunteer.

WITHIN-TEAM JIGSAW

In Within-Team Jigsaw (Figure 8.3), pairs formed within the structured-learning team work on different aspects of a learning task. Any fifth member (sometimes identified with a wild card or joker) joins a pair to form a triad. If instructors are using playing cards to identify team roles, the suits can be used for pairing, black suits forming one pair and red suits the other. These suit partners function as smaller expert-learning teams, similar to their larger counterparts formed in Jigsaw.

Instructors who use Think-Pair-Square should understand the difference between that structure and Within-Team Jigsaw. In Think-Pair-Square, students simultaneously work on the same task and verify their answers in the structured-learning team. In the more complex Within-Team Jigsaw, suit partners work on two distinct parts of a problem-solving "puzzle." Their task in the structured-learning team is to put together the pieces to arrive at a solution, and to teach other members of the structured-learning team their portion of the problem and its solution.

Within-Team Jigsaw is easier to implement than Jigsaw. Its disadvantage lies in the fact that the "puzzle" can have only two pieces. In Jigsaw, the number of pieces is limited only by the imagination of the instructor and the number of students in the class. Within-Team Jigsaw, however, can be a creative, efficient way to ensure content mastery.

Biochemistry instructors, for example, can offer students direct instruction on organic molecules: carbohydrates, lipids, and proteins, which are polymers of carbon. Such instruction can be punctuated by various Think-Pair-Share questions, such as Define or describe a *polymer* or Give five examples of proteins in the body. For the Within-Team Jigsaw activity, each pair within a

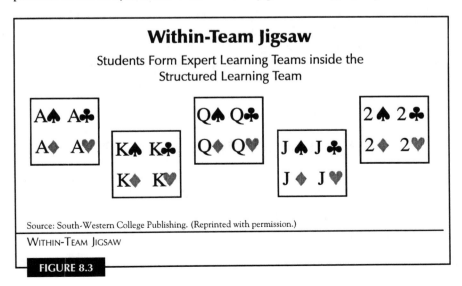

Within-Team Jigsaw

Students Form Expert Learning Teams inside the
Structured Learning Team

Source: South-Western College Publishing. (Reprinted with permission.)

WITHIN-TEAM JIGSAW

FIGURE 8.3

structured-learning team selects from a container a paper diagram of an amino acid. They must then build a model of the amino acid they picked. After the instructor has checked the models, the team works together to do a lasso chemistry dehydration synthesis and make an amide bond. The challenge is to have each team create a protein based on the work of the two sub-teams (Gibsen, 1995).

Accounting instructors, after a brief expository lecture on the differences between cash accounting and accrual accounting, can assign pairs interlocking problems. One pair within the structured-learning team calculates net flow from operations while the other pair calculates net income. Students know that they are responsible not just for calculating the correct figures, but also for being able to explain to their paired teammates how to accomplish the calculation. Therefore, the pair work is devoted to two tasks: performing the accurate calculation and devising a teaching strategy.

After the quiet signal signifies the conclusion of the specified work time, the students regroup in their structured-learning teams, where the teaching occurs. The students should be coached to extend their learning by comparing and contrasting the results and discussing their implications.

Historians might use Within-Team Jigsaw by having pairs within a team research the campaign for Northern Africa from the perspectives of Generals Rommel and Montgomery. Prior to their work as expert pairs, the team as a whole would decide on the criteria to be investigated, such as battle objectives, tactics, and outcomes. Similarly, teams in a literature class might identify the relevant criteria each team will apply for an in-depth analysis of two characters in a novel (e.g., Alexis Zorba and the narrator in Nikos Kazantzakis's *Zorba the Greek* or Tom Sawyer and Huckleberry Finn in Mark Twain's *The Adventures of Tom Sawyer*). Combining the Discovery Method with Within-Team Jigsaw can produce in-depth knowledge. For example, teams looking at the leadership qualities of Rommel and Montgomery could reconvene to determine the overall characteristics of an effective leader. Theater students could view in separate pairs two films, such as Leni Riefenstahl's *The Triumph of the Will* and Frank Capra's *Why We Fight*, and after teaching one another what they learned about each work of art, the team could determine the elements of the propaganda film.

DYADIC ESSAY CONFRONTATIONS (DEC)

In addition to building student critical-thinking skills, Dyadic Essay Confrontations (DECs) allow instructors to incorporate meaningful writing assignments in their courses. Probably their most important use is to ensure that students read and understand the assigned material, thereby freeing class time for mastery and processing activities.

Developed by Sherman (1991), a DEC assignment requires students to master complex material such as a chapter from the course text or other specialized readings. Sherman states, "As originally conceived, this highly structured cooperative-learning technique grew out of three concerns: (1) the need for students to encounter from classmates diverse opinions and unique perspectives on the required readings; (2) their need for meaningful integrative experiences to connect differing text materials; and (3) my desire—and certainly theirs!—for a more active and dynamic classroom environment" (Millis, Cottell, and Sherman, 1993, p. 12).

A DEC proceeds through a series of steps. Students are responsible outside of class for the following: (1) reading and reflecting on the assigned material; (2) formulating an integrative essay question that encourages comparisons between the current material and material previously covered; (3) preparing a model response to their own question, no longer than one page, single-spaced; (4) bringing to class a copy of their essay question and, on a separate page, their model answer.

During class time, students are responsible for: (5) exchanging essay questions with a student with whom they are randomly paired; (6) writing a spontaneous essay in response to the question they receive from their partner; (7) reading and commenting on both the model answer to the question they received and on the spontaneous answer provided by a classmate to the essay question they formulated, looking in each case for divergent and convergent ideas; and (8) participating, if time permits, in a general discussion of the topic.

DECs can be used as ongoing assignments over the course of a semester to ensure mastery of the course material. Students who have read two essays and written two essays on each chapter in an ongoing series retain far more material than those who have merely heard a lecturer expound on them. With their versatility, DECs can promote higher-order thinking skills; focus students on outside assignments so that time is available for interactive group work rather than for lectures designed to cover the content; foster student-student interdependence resulting in respect for diverse opinions; and reinforce the value of peer learning. They also complement writing-across-the-curriculum efforts.

DEC can be used in virtually any discipline. Instructors in three different disciplines, English, accounting, and psychology—have effectively adapted the DEC structure to their university classes (Millis, Cottell, and Sherman, 1993).

Sherman uses it in educational psychology classes focused on social and developmental psychology theories. To evaluate the essays, he uses a combination of peer and instructor evaluation, assessing both the questions and the answers on the basis of five attributes: (1) an overall general impression; (2)

importance; (3) clarity; (4) integration; and (5) creativity. He and the students use a five-point scale ranging from 0 (poor) to 4 (excellent) to rate each of the five attributes. They then evaluate the question and both answers—the out-of-class carefully prepared answer and the in-class spontaneous answer—using these criteria and scales. The total possible score is 120 (4 possible points for each of the five attributes as rated by the instructor and the peer/student evaluator).

In Modern Children's Literature, an upper-level English elective in an adult education setting, Millis must cover an enormous amount of content, packaged in a huge, but readable, text organized around eight different genres. The DEC process gives students learning incentives. She prefers to mark DEC-generated essays by emphasizing responses rather than grades. She thus uses a criterion-referenced grading scheme combined with mastery learning, allowing her to write frequent comments on student work, without, however, having to attach a specific grade to each piece. Ten points for each essay, the one prepared at home and the one written in class, if they are of sufficient depth and quality, count toward the total number of points students acquire for the course grade.

Cottell uses DEC in two accounting courses, an honors seminar focused on accounting ethics and an advanced financial accounting seminar offered as an elective to students pursuing a masters degree in accounting. In the latter course, the primary texts are Financial Accounting Standards Board (FASB) Discussion Memoranda which present alternative points of view on recommended accounting treatments of issues currently before them. Each day, students read a portion of the FASB Discussion Memorandum and write a question and response about that section. In this class, the DEC essays are not individually graded: the class grade is based solely upon a paper on the accounting issues addressed by the FASB Discussion Memoranda.

Although such instances are thankfully rare, even well-motivated students sometimes come to class unprepared. Front-loading activities such as DEC mean that the nonparticipation of such students does not hinder the class's progress, and that their time in class is still academically directed. Unprepared students can spend the class time productively by completing the assignment they should have done at home, while their peers engage in creative pair work. They will lose some points, of course—they receive credit for only one essay, not two—but such results emphasize the importance of individual accountability. (Figures 8.4 and 8.5 offer some forms useful for DEC activities.)

FORM A

Name: _____ Team: _____

Assigned Reading: _____

Your Question: _____

_____

_____

Answer to the question (one page, single-spaced.)

FORM B

Name: _____ Team: _____

Assigned Reading: _____

Your Question: _____

_____

_____

DYADIC ESSAY CONFRONTATION — TWO FORMS FOR STUDENTS TO COMPLETE AT HOME

FIGURE 8.4

Your Name: _____ Your Team: _____
Name of Peer Partner: _____ Team: _____

Student Evaluation of Peer Partner

Evaluate your peer partner on the three attributes in the table below. Use the following guidelines. Exceptional—10; Good—9; Competent—8; Deficient—7; Failure—6.

Quality of the question you posed	
Quality of your proposed answer to posed question	
Quality of in-class response to your question	

Instructor's Evaluation of Peer Partner

Quality of question posed	
Quality of your proposed answer to posed question	
Quality of your in-class response to peer's question	
Overall writing ability	
Ability to evaluate another student's work	

Grade for the DEC: _____

DYADIC ESSAY CONFRONTATION — EVALUATION FORM FOR STUDENTS AND INSTRUCTOR

FIGURE 8.5

Generic Questions	Specific Thinking Processes Induced
Explain why ____. (Explain how ____.)	analysis
What would happen if ____?	prediction / hypothesizing
What is the nature of ____?	analysis
What are the strengths and weaknesses of ____?	analysis / inferencing
What is the difference between ____ and ____?	comparison-contrast
Why is ____ happening?	analysis / inferencing
What is a new example of ____?	application
How could ____ be used to ____?	application
What are the implications of ____?	analysis / inferencing
What is ____ analogous to?	identification / creation of analogies and metaphors
How does ____ effect ____?	analysis of relationship (cause-effect)
How does ____ tie in with what we learned before?	activation of prior knowledge
Why is ____ important?	analysis of significance
How are ____ and ____ similar?	comparison-contrast
How does ____ apply to everyday life?	application to the real world
What is a counter-argument for ____?	rebuttal to argument
What is the best ____, and why?	evaluation and provision of evidence
What is the solution to the problem of ____?	synthesis of ideas
Compare ____ and ____ with regard to.	comparison-contrast & evaluation based on criteria
What do you think causes ____? Why?	analysis of relationship (cause-effect)
Do you agree or disagree with this statement: ____?	evaluation and provision of evidence
What evidence is there to support your answer?	
What is another way to look at ____?	taking other perspectives
What does ____ mean?	comprehension
Describe ____ in your own words.	comprehension
Summarize ____ in your own words.	comprehension

Adapted from King, 1989, 1992, & 1994.

GUIDING CRITICAL THINKING

FIGURE 8.6

GUIDED RECIPROCAL PEER QUESTIONING

"Isidor Rabi, a Nobel prize-winning physicist, tells a story of when he was growing up in the Jewish ghetto of New York. When the children came home from school, their mothers would ask them, 'What did you learn in school today?' But Isidor's mother would ask him, 'What good questions did you ask today?' Dr. Rabi suggests he became a physicist and won the Nobel Prize because he was valued more for the questions he was asking than the answers he was giving" (Barell, 1988).

Instructors wishing to encourage critical thinking skills and relativistic conceptualizing will find Guided Reciprocal Peer Questioning a particularly apt structure. Developed and researched by King (1990; 1992; 1995), this structure helps students to generate task-specific questions which can then be answered within the structured-learning team. The activity can be used as a front-loading device to ensure that students read assigned materials, with the processing done in class, or it can be used in-class only.

To initiate this activity, instructors assign outside reading or conduct a short lecture on a course-related topic. Students use a set of generic question stems, or prompts, as a guide for formulating their own specific questions about the content of the material. This list (Figure 8.6) contains some questions more appropriate and challenging to dualistic thinkers, such as What is the difference between ___ and ___? Other questions are more appropriate for the more advanced relativistic thinkers, such as What are the strengths and weaknesses of ___?

Students bring their questions to class or instructors provide students with classroom time to use the generic stems to write two or three specific, thought-provoking questions about the lecture they have just heard. During the latter model, students should be given several minutes to review their lecture notes, to rehash the key points and their relevance to other knowledge or first-hand experiences, and to formulate their specific questions.

The first time this structure is used, instructors should provide specific examples to help students understand the process of generating effective questions. Students do not need to be able to answer the questions they formulate: their purpose is to stimulate discussion. This step results in relevant questions, not meaningless ones for which students already hold canned responses. It also encourages students to identify important concepts, to elaborate on those ideas in their minds, and to think about how the ideas are connected to each other and to their own prior knowledge and experiences.

The students now put these questions to use in their structured-learning teams. The team leader poses one of the specific questions he or she has written and the other team members respond. Since the questions have no single right answer, reflective discussion follows. Each student, in turn, offers a question for the team to discuss, preferably using a different stem. Everyone should have an opportunity to pose at least one question: the team leader should be careful that there is equitable participation both in the discussion and in the questions shared.

The instructor should design the time element carfully. Because students often welcome closure and worry that their team discussion may not have covered all the salient points, a whole-class discussion is useful. Here students can share insights, concrete examples, and particularly cogent explanations that arose in their group work. The instructor, using specific examples gleaned from monitoring teams, can provide a succinct summary, inviting contributions, or she might ask a particular team to summarize. Because she will have moved among the groups during their discussion period, she also has the opportunity to elaborate on any cloudy points or clear up any misconceptions. The questions can be taken up and reviewed later to provide feedback for both the instructor and the students.

Guided Reciprocal Peer Questioning lends itself to virtually any discipline. The possibilities are endless. King (1995) notes that she and her colleagues throughout California have used the question stems with subjects as diverse as anthropology, biology, business accounting, history, mathematics, psychology, research methods, and teacher education. Millis has used them in composition and literature courses. The more often students practice this activity, the higher the quality of the questions. This is particularly true if the instructor conscientiously provides feedback on the value of the questions that summarize relevant points and lead to higher-order thinking skills. Davis (1993) reminds us that:

> [Good thinking] is learned by practice—by thinking—under the guidance and criticism of an effective mentor, presumably a teacher who is also a "good thinker" and who understands thinking processes. Above all, thinking involves asking questions—sometimes new questions about old questions in the search for new answers (p. 234).

Guided Reciprocal Peer Questioning empowers students to take charge of their own learning and to generate their own critical questions through structured practice.

STRUCTURED CONTROVERSY

Structured Controversy, sometimes called academic controversy (Johnson, Johnson, and Smith, 1991 and Johnson and Johnson, 1995), develops critical-thinking skills by compelling students to examine issues for which there are no "right answers." Conflict has value only when it is managed constructively. The Cooperative Learning Center at the University of Minnesota identifies these positive outcomes of well-structured, well-monitored conflict:

- greater quantity and quality of achievement, complex reasoning, and creative problem solving;
- higher-quality decision making;
- healthier cognitive, social, and psychological development by being better able to deal with more stress and cope with unforeseen adversities;
- increased motivation and energy to take action; higher-quality relationships with friends, co-workers, and family members;
- a greater sense of caring, commitment, joint identity, and cohesiveness with an emphasis on increased liking, respect, and trust;
- heightened awareness that a problem exists that needs to be solved; and increased incentive to change. (Cooperative Learning Center, n. d.)

As in Within-Team Jigsaw, students initially work with partners in their structured-learning teams. Instructors identify a controversial topic that lends itself well to two opposing viewpoints, and gather material, such as articles, monographs, or book chapters, that support either or both sides. If this structure is to be used for a long-range project, then the students themselves can identify and accumulate the material. Each pair within the team takes one side of the issue. In the first of five phases of Structured Controversy, students research and review the materials and discuss their side of the issue. They synthesize and organize their findings and prepare to advocate and defend their positions.

In the second phase, the two pairs alternately present their side of the issue, giving full rationales and explanations for their stance. The other pair listens attentively, keeping in mind that during the next phase they will be challenging the points they hear and defending their own positions.

During a general discussion in the third phase, all four students seek to become fully informed about both sides of the issue and begin to weigh critical arguments in favor of each. Instructors should stress that the students' purpose should be to become more informed about the issue rather than to win debates. They should use skillful questioning techniques to draw out their fellow teammates and to encourage everyone to examine deeply all sides of the issue. The result of the discussion, which must be conducted and carefully monitored according to the established group or class norms for productive behavior and interaction, is often intellectual disequilibrium and uncertainty. This phase of the activity is particularly important because Brookfield (1987) and others have emphasized that critical thinking depends on identifying and challenging assumptions and subsequently exploring and conceptualizing alternatives. Curiosity prompted by this discussion often leads to a search for additional information.

During the next step, students reverse their positions and each pair argues forcefully for the opposing viewpoint. Building on what they have heard earlier and what they have come to learn through their own research and the subsequent team discussion, each pair should present their best possible case.

In the fifth and final phase, the team works together to synthesize their findings and prepare a group report. This final review should reflect the best information and critical reasoning from both sides. All four students must agree with this joint summary. Following this stage, the team may make a whole-class presentation. If so, then the instructor evaluates the report based on the quality of the writing, the logic and development of the accumulated evidence, and the caliber of the oral presentation. To ensure individual accountability, the instructor may wish to administer an issue-related examination that students will take independently. Group processing should occur so that each team member, and the team as a whole, can evaluate their contributions and resolve to do better in the future.

Structured Controversy Topics

Because almost every discipline offers opportunities for controversial debate, the topics for Structured Controversy are virtually limitless. Johnson and Johnson (1997), for example, suggest that students in an English class debate the constructiveness or the destructiveness of civil disobedience in a democracy. This structured debate would ensue after students had studied literary works, such as Mark Twain's *The Adventures of Huckleberry Finn* and would encourage them to draw on a variety of sources, such as the *Declaration of Independence*, "Civil Disobedience" by Henry David Thoreau, and "Letter from Birmingham Jail" by Martin Luther King Jr. Following are some topics in a variety of disciplines suitable for Structured Controversy, including the following identified by Bredehoft (1991).

- *Anthropology:* Was the discovery of the Philippine Tasaday tribe in 1991 an elaborate hoax or are the Tasaday people truly living remnants from the Stone Age? Were white settlers justified in retaliating against Native Americans who attacked settlements on their hunting grounds?
- *Art:* Should taxpayers support art exhibits by controversial artists, such as Robert Mapplethorpe?
- *Economics:* Should new laws be enacted to limit foreign countries' buying of U.S. properties? Should the flat income tax be adopted?
- *Education:* Should Ebonics be taught in the public schools? Do HIV-positive children have the right to attend public school?
- *Environmental Sciences:* Is the greenhouse effect fact or science fiction?

- *Government and Politics:* Should the U.S. support a Palestinian state within the nation of Israel? Should the I.R.S. be abolished? Should the U.S. Postal Service be privatized?
- *Psychology:* Should the insanity plea be abolished?
- *Criminology:* Should individuals found not guilty of criminal acts be retried under civil lawsuits?
- *Religious studies:* Does religion belong in the public schools?
- *Sociology:* Should assisted suicide be lawful for terminally-ill adults who choose it?

GROUP INVESTIGATION

Sharan and Sharan (1992; 1994) have developed an extensive model for progressive research and problem solving. Students work in teams to investigate a complex, challenging problem, one usually identified by the instructor. They follow a systematic approach to explore the problem, which results in "constructed" knowledge, with students taking the initiative as to what questions are posed, what sources they consult, and what answers they derive. The students actively share their knowledge, ideas, and interpretations in a series of meetings and presentations that involve reciprocal teaching. The investigation is carried out in six systematic stages.

In Stage One, the instructor introduces the problem to the students and shares with them a variety of resources, such as films, books, lectures, maps, or stamps, intended to arouse their curiosity. The students then generate through individual and cooperative activities, such as pairs or brainstorming groups, the relevant questions that will guide the investigation. Their goal is to create a series of lists based on input from all students. The teacher then collects all the questions and develops a composite list which reflects questions from the entire class.

The students then combine these ideas to determine major subcategories. These subtopics become the exploratory topics each group will subsequently investigate. The new groups are formed based on student interest. If more than five or six students sign up for a specific subtopic, then the teacher might form several groups to investigate it, so long as all the major topics are assigned to at least one team.

In Stage Two, the groups plan their investigations. They choose the questions for which they will seek solutions. They identify the resources they have at hand and the resources they will need. During this stage of the investigation, they remain creative about potential resources, which could be people to interview, books and articles to consult, Web sites to "surf," or archives to explore. After the groups decide what to investigate, tasks are assigned, based on students' interests and talents.

Stage Three may last several class periods as the students carry out their investigations. Working independently or in pairs, they locate information, evaluate it, organize and record relevant data, share their findings with teammates, determine what information is missing, and finally analyze and integrate their pooled knowledge. Typically, students work independently outside of class but share information, observations, and interpretations during in-class hours.

In Stage Four, the groups plan their presentations to maximize learning for the rest of the class. Sharan and Sharan (1994) suggest these guidelines:

- Emphasize the main ideas and conclusions of the inquiry.
- Make sure everyone in the group takes an active part in the presentation.
- Set and observe time limits for the duration of the presentation.
- Plan to involve classmates from the "audience" as much as possible by giving them roles to perform or otherwise having them be active during the presentation.
- Allow time for questions.
- Make sure all necessary equipment and materials are available (pp. 107–108).

Usually, the teacher will conduct a joint meeting with representatives from all groups to review their plans and to determine audiovisual and other equipment needs.

During Stage Five, the presentations are given and the students in the audience fill out a feedback form with prompts such as: What was the main idea of the presentation? How did each group member contribute to the presentation? Give examples of how the group used resources well or could have used them better. What did you like best about the presentation? The teacher can summarize the presentations through a whole-class discussion that focuses on the integration of subtopics to illuminate the problem the class addressed.

Stage Six involves an assessment of the learning fostered through the investigation. Students can take a test based on questions submitted by all the groups and supplemented by the teacher's questions. They can create a composite report or undertake other projects that emphasize integration and reflection.

Group Investigation, like most cooperative structures, requires teachers to become facilitators who guide students through the learning process. They serve as monitors and resources, but the students themselves collaborate to achieve their own identified academic and personal goals. The classroom management strategies relevant in all cooperative-learning activities are important here. Students learn how to learn by tackling problems central to virtually every discipline.

SUMMARY

Educators in every subject area value critical thinking. Kurfiss (1988) has identified eight teaching principles that support critical thinking across the curriculum. All of them can be "operationalized" by the cooperative structures discussed in this chapter:

1. "Critical thinking is a learnable skill; the instructor and peers are resources in developing critical-thinking skills."

    In Jigsaws, Within-Team Jigsaws, Dyadic Essay Confrontations, Structured Controversies, and Guided Reciprocal Peer Questioning, students teach one another as a teacher/mentor monitors their progress. Peers in particular help one another by challenging assumptions and questioning premises within the confines of clearly defined social and academic perimeters.

2. "Problems, questions, or issues are the point of entry into the subject and the source of motivation for sustained inquiry."

    The structures themselves do not generate the cooperative activities, they merely provide a framework to explore the topic. Students identify the problems, questions, or issues within the framework of the structure.

3. "Successful courses balance challenges to think critically with support tailored to students' developmental needs."

    One of the strengths of a cooperative classroom is the peer support available in a well-monitored structured-learning team where students can stretch their minds without fear of "put-downs."

4. "Courses are assignment centered rather than text-and-lecture centered. Goals, methods, and evaluation emphasize using content rather than acquiring it."

    All of the structures discussed in this chapter are process-oriented. Students are not handed the correct answers; instead they reach conclusions collectively by formulating problems, identifying issues, challenging assumptions, and weighing evidence.

5. "Students are required to formulate and justify their ideas in writing or other appropriate modes."

    These structures encourage students to express themselves in a variety of modes. Jigsaw and Within-Team Jigsaw allow students a gamut of creative approaches to teaching, including visual aids. Dyadic Essay Confrontations and Structured Controversies emphasize writing, with the latter providing opportunities for constructive public debates. Guided

Reciprocal Peer Questioning combines both writing and creative questioning.

6. "Students collaborate to learn and to stretch their thinking, for example, in pair problem solving and small-group work."

   All these structures and many other others discussed in this book produce these desired results.

7. "Several courses, particularly those that teach problem-solving skills, nurture students' metacognitive abilities."

   Because all of these cooperative structures involve group processing and individual feedback, metacognitive skills-building emerges naturally.

8. "The developmental needs of students are acknowledged and used as information in the design of the course. Teachers in these courses make standards explicit and then help students learn how to achieve them" (pp. 88–89). As all the chapters have emphasized, cooperative learning is not a pedagogy where teachers or students "wing it." Teachers identify learning objectives and carefully structure the avenues their students will travel to achieve those goals. Because teams are heterogeneous and because group work constitutes only a percentage of students' learning experiences, students can reach their fullest potential. The variety of teaching approaches appeals to various learning styles.

The critical-thinking skills fostered by the structures discussed in this chapter are essential. We will do our students a disservice if we failed to teach them the skills needed for success in the 21st century. As Ventimiglia (1994) suggests: "The two skills we will all need to be successful in the workforce 2000—neither of which is taught as the content of a course or from a textbook—are the ability to work together cooperatively and the ability to be a life long learner" (p. 6). Regurgitation of information will not suffice in a world where computers can perform this task far more efficiently. Rather, our citizens and leaders must learn to construct knowledge instead of merely reproducing it. Furthermore, as the world grows increasingly complex, effective teamwork will become an increasingly valued skill.

REFERENCES

Aronson, E., Stephan, C., Sikes, J., and Snapp, M. (1978). *The Jigsaw Classroom*. Beverly Hills, CA: Sage.

Barell, J. (1988). cited (p. 59) in Costa and O'Leary, "Co-cognition: The Cooperative Development of the Intellect." In J. Davidson and T. Worsham (Eds.), *Enhancing Thinking through Cooperative Learning*. (1988, Apr.).

Bredehoft, D.J. (1991). "Cooperative Controversies in the Classroom." *College Teaching*, 39(3), 122–25.

Brookfield, S.D. (1987). *Developing Critical Thinkers: Challenging Adults to Explore Alternative Ways of Thinking and Acting.* San Francisco: Jossey-Bass.

Clarke, J. (1994). "Pieces of the Puzzle: The Jigsaw Method." In S. Sharan (Ed.). *Handbook of Cooperative Learning Methods* (pp. 34–50). Westport, CT: Greenwood Press.

Cooperative Learning Center, University of Minnesota, College of Education & Human Development. Online at <http://134.84.183.54/pages/conflict.html>. Downloaded 10 Feb. 1997. No longer available.

Cuseo, J.B. (1994). "Critical Thinking and Cooperative Learning: A Natural Marriage." *Cooperative Learning and College Teaching,* 4(2), 2-5.

Davis, J.R. (1993). *Better Teaching, More Learning: Strategies for Success in Postsecondary Settings.* Phoenix, AZ: Oryx Press.

Gartner, A., Kohler, M., and Riessmann, F. (1971). *Children Teach Children: Learning by Teaching.* New York: Harper & Row.

Gere, A.R. (1987). *Writing Groups: History, Theory, and Implications.* Carbondale and Edwardsville: Southern Illinois University Press.

Gibsen, J. (1995). "Protein Model Lab ala Rand." In S.C. Nurrenbern (Ed.). *Experiences in Cooperative Learning: A Collection for Chemistry Teachers* (p. 62). Madison, WI: Institute for Chemical Education.

Johnson, D.W. and Johnson, R.T. (1995). *Creative Conflict: Intellectual Challenges in the Classroom.* Edina, MN: Interaction Book Company.

Johnson, D.W. and Johnson, R.T. (1997). "Academic Controversy: Increase Intellectual Conflict and Increase the Quality of Learning." In W.E. Campbell and K.A. Smith (Eds.), *New Paradigms for College Teaching.* Edina, MN: Interaction Book Company.

Johnson, D.W. , Johnson, R.T., and Smith, K.A. (1991). *Active Learning: Cooperation in the College Classroom.* Edina, MN: Interaction Book Company.

Jones, P. (1991, Apr.). *You Be the Judge: A Series of Cooperative Learning Activities Based on Three Fairytales.* Unpublished manuscript, Modern Languages, Donevan Collegiate, Oshawa.

Kagan, S. (1989). *Cooperative Learning Resources for Teachers.* San Juan Capistrano, CA: Resources for Teachers, Inc.

King, A. (1990). "Enhancing Peer Interaction and Learning in the Classroom through Reciprocal Questioning." *American Educational Research Journal,* 27(4), 664–87.

King, A. (1992). "Promoting Active Learning and Collaborative Learning in Business Administration Classes." In T. J. Frecka (Ed.), *Critical Thinking, Interactive Learning and Technology: Reaching for Excellence in Business Education* (pp. 158–73). Arthur Andersen Foundation.

King, A. (1995, Winter). "Guided Peer Questioning: A Cooperative Learning Approach to Critical Thinking." *Cooperative Learning and College Teaching,* 5(2), 15-19.

Kurfiss, J.G. (1988). *Critical Thinking: Theory, Research, Practice, and Possibilities.* ASHE-ERIC Higher Education Report No. 2. Washington, DC: Association for the Study of Higher Education.

Millis, B.J., Cottell, P., and Sherman, L. (1993, Spring). "Stacking the DEC to Promote Critical Thinking: Applications in Three Disciplines." *Cooperative Learning and College Teaching,* 3(3), 12–14.

Newmann, F.M. and Wehlage, G.G. (1993, Apr.). "Five Standards for Authentic Instruction." *Educational Leadership,* 50(7), 8–12.

Presselsen, B.Z. (1992). "A Perspective on the Evolution of Cooperative Thinking." In N. Davidson and T. Worsham (Eds.), *Enhancing Thinking through Cooperative Learning,* (pp. 1–6) New York: Teachers College Press.

Rivkin, M.S. (1994). "Using Jigsaw for Perspective-taking." In S. Kadel and J.A. Keehner (Eds.), *Collaborative Learning: A Sourcebook for Higher Education*, Vol. II (p. 143). University Park, PA: National Center on Postsecondary Teaching, Learning, and Assessment.

Semb, G.B. and Ellis, J.A. (Summer 1994). "Knowledge Taught in School: What is Remembered?" *Review of Educational Research*, 64(2), 253–86.

Sharan, Y. and Sharan, S. (1992). *Expanding Cooperative Learning through Group Investigation.* New York: Teachers College Press.

Sharan, Y. and Sharan, S. (1994). "Group Investigation in the Cooperative Classroom." In S. Sharan (Ed.). *Handbook of Cooperative Learning Methods.* (pp. 97–114) Westport, CT: Greenwood Press.

Sherman, L.W. (1991). *Cooperative Learning in Postsecondary Education: Implications from Social Psychology for Active Learning Experiences.* Presentation at the American Educational Research Association, Chicago.

Slavin, R.E. (1986). *Using Student Team Learning: The Johns Hopkins Team Learning Project.* Baltimore, MD: The Johns Hopkins University Press.

Ventimiglia, L.M. (1994, Winter). "Cooperative Learning at the College Level." *Thought and Action: The NEA Almanac of Higher Education,* 9(2), 5–30.

Webb, N. (1983). "Predicting Learning from Student Interaction: Defining the Interaction Variable." *Educational Psychologist*, 18, 33–41.

Webb, N. (1991). "Task-related Verbal Interaction and Mathematics Learning in Small Groups." *Journal of Research in Mathematics Education*, 22, 366–89.

Whitman, N. A. (1988). *Peer Teaching: To Teach Is To Learn Twice.* ASHE-ERIC Higher Education Report No. 4. Washington, DC: Association for the Study of Higher Education.

CHAPTER 9

Specialized Uses of Cooperative-Learning Principles

"What I hear, I forget; What I see I remember; What I do, I understand."

Chinese Proverb

Because of their versatility, cooperative-learning techniques can be adapted for a number of different applications. Instructors need to keep in mind the principles behind cooperative learning, including individual accountability, positive interdependence, and the need for group processing and feedback. Additionally, teachers will want to place these activities in the context of sequenced learning: students should be responsible for learning material on their own so that class time can be used beneficially for student interactions and active-learning techniques that provide feedback on how well the material has been mastered. This approach fosters a deep learning approach. Games and simulations are one way to achieve these goals.

INSTRUCTIONAL GAMES

Popular in corporations and training settings, games and simulations can occupy an important place in the classroom. Although discipline-specific commercial games such as B'ha, B'ha (anthropology) are available and electronic games now proliferate, most of dubious educational value, this chapter will focus on instructor-produced and instructor-monitored collaborative games. The word "game" carries with it a certain amount of "baggage" for many educators who may echo Ms. Trunchbull's credo in the movie *Matilda*: "If you are having fun, you are not learning." Many instructors, on the contrary, have found that students become engaged in learning through carefully structured, highly interactive game formats.

Games can play a significant role in the cooperative classroom. For one thing, they invariably involve all students in active learning. This learning can enliven rote memorization, making it more appealing to students, or at the other end of the spectrum, the learning can involve problem solving in real-life simulations. Typically, instructors will assign specific material to be mastered prior to the game and then use the in-class game activity as a means of processing the information and providing feedback on whether or not it has been mastered. Occasionally, a game will precede formal instruction. Games can provide motivation for students to learn. Lepper and Malone (1985), for example, found that students involved with computer games experience challenge, self-competence, curiosity, personal control, and fantasy.

In designing an effective classroom game, instructors must keep in mind the learning objectives, the time constraints of the class sessions, and the importance of "debriefing" the game. Much learning will be lost if the game dynamics and excitement overshadow the information to be mastered or the skills to be developed. Furthermore, any game should foster the cooperative principles guiding the course. Therefore, instructors will want to select or develop games that promote cooperation, at least among teammates. Some basic premises should be carefully applied.

Principles Underlying Effective Game Use

Students must understand the relevance of any games to the course objectives. Adult learners, in particular, may find games a waste of their time and money if they perceive them to be frivolous. Any game activity must be preceded by clear explanations, including a careful rationale linked to course goals.

One way to ensure the educational value of games is to match the level of challenge to students' skills. Thus, games should offer challenges to all students, but the material should not be so complex that students feel overwhelmed and give up, or so simple that they lose interest in participating.

To ensure continuing interest, games should be designed so that they are predicated on a combination of knowledge and luck. This premise is extremely important; otherwise one or two dominant teams could discourage other teams from contributing their best efforts. If only knowledge is involved, then the same teams will repeatedly win, a disincentive for other teams to master the material prior to play or to continue trying to score if they fall behind. If the game is predicated only on luck, then obviously students have no incentive to study the material prior to play. The structure of a game such as "Bingo" will incorporate this design plan, since the luck of the draw determines the placement of markers. (Other games, however, do not guarantee this element of luck, so teachers will want to be certain that students are operating on a level playing field, even if this means switching team members, a practice not recommended in more traditional cooperative activities.)

To maximize learning, games should be structured cooperatively. There can be competition between teams, but optimum learning will take place during the independent learning accomplished prior to the game and the peer coaching that occurs as the team players agree on a response. Peer consultations reinforce learning or provide instantaneous feedback that learning was either nonexistent, incomplete, or misguided.

Instructors and students must both recognize that the genuine learning occurs during these "processing " periods. The processing also includes the post-game instructor "debrief" where students learn what they have mastered or should have mastered. Too often, instructors tend to gloss over this final critical "teachable moment" in the spirit of fun. This is a serious mistake, however unconscious, because the game then loses its relevance. Cheryl Keen, dean of the faculty of Antioch College, states that the research on whether games promote learning is still mixed: "It depends on whether you're savvy about why you are doing it and if you take the time to work up to it and to debrief. The rule is to spend at least as much time debriefing as you spend playing the game; otherwise, what did you do it for?" (quoted in Rhem, 1996).

Any classroom games must be well-organized and well-structured so that class time is not wasted on vague instructions and confusion. Obviously, the game-playing period must be appropriate for the length of the class and the physical environment must allow teams to work together. There should be an intriguing blend of novelty and familiarity. That is why well-known formats such as Bingo or Jeopardy are particularly effective. Instructors can add their own creative touches by using small Tootsie Rolls, M&Ms, or Skittles for Bingo markers or by adding a course-specific banner to the classroom to announce the latest Jeopardy round.

Two Game Structures to Encourage Cooperative Learning

Bingo Games

Ideally, games should be predicated on sequenced learning. Bingo offers a game format easy to adapt to virtually any discipline. It can be used, for example, in foreign language or English as a Second Language (ESL) classrooms, where word or sentence translations provide the content for rapid scoring. Two extended examples, from two different disciplines, offer insights into developing and conducting a game based on Bingo.

Brain Bingo

Brain Bingo was designed by Boyce (1996) to help students identify the major regions of the brain and their primary structures and functions. The game is also used as a tool to review the structures and communication processes of the nervous system.

During the lesson prior to Brain Bingo, each student receives the Brain Bingo Worksheet (Figure 9.1), which all students complete. Additionally, each individual student is assigned specific brain part term(s) they are to teach to their classmates. These twenty terms can be divided up according to class size. In smaller classes, students might research two terms; in larger classes, several students might prepare a lesson on the same term. Working independently, students create a mnemonic (technique to enhance memory) for their assigned term that includes its location, function, and lesions. A student presentation for the amygdala might be: "The Amygdala is located in the limbic system and plays an important role in regulating emotions. One way to remember this is "Amy G. Dala is an emotional girl I knew in high school." Because the lesson is only 30 seconds long, students must understand their information enough to impart it succinctly. This focus allows their classmates to take concise notes and minimizes the class time spent on pre-game activities.

BRAIN BINGO WORKSHEET

BRAIN PART	LOCATION	FUNCTION	MNEMONIC	NOTES
Amygdala				
Hippocampus				
Hypothalmus				

Source: Cooperative Learning and College Teaching. (Reprinted with permission.)

BRAIN BINGO WORKSHEET

FIGURE 9.1

After the students review the key terms, they form teams of two. Each pair receives the playing boards (Figure 9.2) and game pieces or markers.

The rules of play are similar to Bingo. Instructors randomly draw pre-prepared index cards which offer a clue based on location, function, and lesions. Location clues are given by pointing to a location on an overhead transparency or a model brain. Function clues are provided by explaining a particular structure's function. Lesion clues are given by either acting out the effect of a lesion on a particular brain structure or by describing the disability or change in a lesioned patient. Each team, after discussion, identifies the brain part and covers the appropriate term. If they are correct, the marker remains. After a team covers five diagonal, horizontal or vertical squares, they

BRAIN BINGO				
FRONTAL LOBE	PARIETAL LOBE	TEMPORAL LOBE	OCCIPITAL LOBE	SOMATO-SENSORY CORTEX
MOTOR CORTEX	CEREBRAL CORTEX	CEREBELLUM	MIDBRAIN	PONS
MEDULLA	RETICULAR FORMATION	PITUITARY	CORPUS CALLOSUM	CAUDATE NUCLEUS
THALAMUS	HYPO-THALAMUS	HIPPO-CAMPUS	AMYGDALA	OLFACTORY BULB
OPTIC CHIASM	ANTERIOR COMMISSURE	DENDRITE	AXON	CELL BODY

Source: Cooperative Learning and College Teaching. (Reprinted with permission.)

BRAIN BINGO BOARD

FIGURE 9.2

yell "Brain Bingo." To ensure they have covered the appropriate terms for the correct clues, the team must state the term and clue back to the class. Their classmates verify their accuracy.

Typically, students want to continue play even after one or more teams have yelled "Brain Bingo." Thus, the learning cycle continues. At the conclusion of the class session, it is important to allow time for questions and clarification.

Like other activities described in this book, Brain Bingo contains the main elements of sequenced learning. Students receive material they are expected to master on their own. They turn in the Brain Bingo Worksheet for individual credit. They have an incentive, however, beyond the individual points they will acquire, because they know that knowledge will be "processed" during the Brain Bingo activity. Students typically prepare the mnemonic because failure to do so would be a public acknowledgment that they are not contributing toward the class's learning achievements. Peer pressure to learn the material also arises because no one knows beforehand with whom they will be paired. Thus, students are motivated to master an integrated body of knowledge and receive further reinforcement through dynamic student-student interactions during the class period. Feedback is immediate; students learn through the game whether they have previously mastered the material or not.

Research Methods Bingo

Millis uses another variation of Bingo, called QUIZO (Sugar, 1994) to help first-year composition students master important elements of research. She uses candy for markers, and, as in traditional Bingo, she uses cards covered with numbers rather than course-related terms. The cards have the letters QUIZO at the top.

To prepare for the game, students study chapters in a research manual, material they often find dry. They know that their learning will be processed through a class Bingo game, but they are not assigned time-consuming questions or exercises to prepare individually, which is a more traditional approach.

The teacher pairs students when they come to class and distributes the game sheets and markers. Two students assist: one draws a scrabble letter corresponding to the QUIZO letters at the top of the card, and the second rolls a die to determine the number under the letter which may be covered if the team-pair has answered correctly. (Because the card contains only five numbers, the student rethrows the die if a six emerges.)

The questions in this Bingo variation can range from simple recall ("What system of classification is used in our library?") to the more complex ("Prepare a bibliography card for this research information"). Each paired team receives a copy of the questions, which are also displayed on an overhead projector. To save time and facilitate learning, a series of three to five simple questions appear on one worksheet. There must, of course, be adequate time for discussion and marker placement. For example, a worksheet might include a library reference card with the following questions underneath: "What is the call number? Who is the author? Who is the publisher? Under what heading will the subject card be found? What is the book's title?" Another worksheet might ask students to punctuate and document three quotations. To be eligible to place a marker on their QUIZO card, the students must correctly answer all, or a designated percentage, of the questions.

The learning occurs when the instructor provides the answer. Processing time is essential. For less-complex questions, the answer and a brief explanation will suffice. For more-complex questions, such as the bibliography entry, the teacher takes this opportunity to teach a mini-lesson on the proper elements of documentation.

As with Brain Bingo, the students are expected to master material individually outside of class; the game with its active peer discussion provides in-class processing to reinforce or challenge the learning; and the teacher-directed discussion of answers offers immediate feedback as to actual learning. Thus, learning in a logical sequence occurs, with a cycle of independent learning, processing, and feedback.

Jeopardy

As a review prior to examinations, a psychologist (Gibson, 1991) divides the material into six categories, such as "reliability of the scientific method." The students are divided into teams. During the day of the review, the instructor, serving as the emcee, provides the teams with "answers of increasing difficulty, allowing students to accumulate points as they confer on the proper responses. As in the TV show, the game includes daily doubles and a final jeopardy."

Gray-Shellberg (1994) devised an ingenious ongoing Jeopardy game combining the well-known quiz-show format with the cooperative Jigsaw technique. On index cards, students submitted ten Jeopardy questions for each chapter, rated on five levels of difficulty. Each team assigned one student to a particular subtopic in the chapter. The students then met in expert teams where they discussed the topic in depth, determining that each expert had not only mastered the materials, but was capable of teaching it in the same depth to the other team members prior to the Jeopardy competition. In preparation for the game, the home teams reassembled and each team member coached the other students on their portion of the chapter. Meanwhile, the instructor selected student-generated questions of various difficulty levels from each section of the chapter. During play, designated players, rotating systematically, responded from each team, ensuring that no one student could dominate. The teams indicated their readiness to respond with a noisemaker, and the instructor, serving as emcee, assigned points based on difficulty. To facilitate play, a student assistant distributed point/money cards to the teams that responded correctly.

Course grades were not based on student performance during the Jeopardy game. To emphasize individual accountability, the following percentages were used:

- Quality and quantity of the Jeopardy questions: 25%
- Scores on three class examinations   55%
- Attendance   10%
- Participation   10%

Although Gray-Shellberg conceded that this ongoing class format was time-consuming, she felt students' positive attitudes toward the course and their documented learning made the effort worthwhile.

PROBLEM-BASED LEARNING

Problems motivate. Meyers (1986), in fact, suggests that teachers should begin every class session with "something that is a problem or a cause for wonder" (p. 44).

Problem-Based Learning (PBL) is an instructional, student-centered strategy that uses a problem situation to drive the learning activities on a need-to-know basis. Working in groups, students explore a problem by first identifying the relevant knowledge they can apply and then pinpointing the knowledge they must acquire. Students then prioritize the learning needs by setting goals and objectives and determining a feasible learning plan. Such plans often require them to tackle different learning tasks. They then work independently, researching and preparing for a group meeting where they will share their new knowledge. The pooled knowledge is then applied to solve the problem. As a final step, students assess their team skills and their success in solving the problem. Arambula-Greenfield (1996) characterizes PBL as "an instructional format requiring students to participate actively in their own learning by researching and working through a series of real-life problems to arrive at a 'best' solution" (p. 26). Savery and Duffy (1995) find that it is based on a constructivist framework with "constructivism" defined as "a philosophical view on how we come to understand or know" (p. 143).

PBL originated in 1969 with the establishment of the new Faculty of Medicine at McMaster University, Hamilton, Ontario and gained impetus in 1984 when the Report of the Project Panel on the General Professional Education of the Physician (GPEP Report) recommended less emphasis on lecture-based instruction and more on independent and problem-centered learning. The Harvard Medical School's successful "New Pathway" track, begun in 1985, encouraged other medical institutions to initiate programs emphasizing individual skills and capabilities rather than a static body of knowledge. (Davis, 1994, pp. 18–19). Today PBL is used in a variety of institutions and disciplines (Boud and Feletti, 1991). It is used, for example, in business schools (Milter and Stinson, 1994), schools of education (Bridges and Hallinger, 1992; Duffy, 1994) and high schools (Barrows and Myers, 1993).

Because the problems are intrinsically interesting and because students choose their own topics and learning strategies, Problem-Based Learning tends to motivate students. The concrete applications give students a specific context in which to embed knowledge. Furthermore, since reciprocal teaching and peer tutoring are involved, students have an opportunity for deep, not surface, learning.

Woods (1994) has been using PBL in engineering courses at McMaster for over 25 years. Under Woods's guidance, faculty participants at a USAF Academy workshop explored topics such as how to help students frame and resolve ill-defined problems and how to integrate peer and self-assessment into all classrooms that are using small-group learning. Woods emphasized, for example, that assessment that makes students accountable for their own learning (an independent approach) and the learning of peers (a cooperative approach) must include instruments to evaluate both content mastery and group contributions. Sessions dealt with setting measurable objectives. "Assessment is vital for growth, motivation, and progress," noted Woods. He shared the following guidelines:

- Set explicit goals; you will perform better because of them. Goals help focus your energies. Goals motivate us.

- Include measurable criteria.
- The goal and the criteria should be achievable with the resources available.
- There must be agreement as to what constitutes evidence and an effort to collect evidence that satisfies the goal and the criteria.

A key aspect of Woods's approach is deliberate skill building. Students are not thrown cold into group-based problem solving without mini-workshops on topics such as stress management, group skills, critical thinking, becoming independent learners, providing constructive feedback, and so forth. Interested faculty will want to consult Woods's detailed WWW page: <http://chemeng.mcmaster.ca/pbl/pbl.html>.

Duch (1996) offers these guidelines for developing PBL problems and cases:

1. An effective problem must first engage students' interest and motivate them to probe for deeper understanding of the concepts being introduced. It should relate the subject to the real world, so that students have a stake in solving the problem.

2. Good problems require students to make decisions or judgments based on facts, information, logic and/or rationalization. Students should be required to justify all decisions and reasoning based on the principles being learned. Problems should require students to define what assumptions are needed (and why), what information is relevant, and/or what steps or procedures are required in order to solve them.

3. Cooperation from all members of the student group should be necessary in order to effectively work through a good problem. The length and complexity of the problem or case must be controlled so that students realize that a "divide and conquer" effort will not be an effective problem-solving strategy. For example, a problem that consists of a series of straight-forward "end of chapter" questions will be divided by the group and assigned to individuals and then reassembled for the assignment submission. In this case, students end up learning less, not more.

4. The initial questions in the problem should have one or more of the following characteristics so that all students in the groups are initially drawn into a discussion of the topic: open-ended, not limited to one correct answer; connected to previously learned knowledge; [confronting] controversial issues that will elicit diverse opinions. This strategy keeps the students functioning as a group [and] drawing on each other's knowledge and ideas, rather than encouraging them to work individually at the outset of the problem.

5. The content objectives of the course should be incorporated into the problems, connecting previous knowledge to new concepts, and connecting new knowledge to concepts in other courses and/or disciplines.

In addition to these characteristics, good problems should challenge students to achieve higher-level critical thinking. Too often, students view learning as remembering facts, terms, and definitions in order to answer questions on tests. Many students seem to lack the ability or motivation to go beyond factual material to a deeper understanding of course material (p. 7).

Burch (1995) found PBL approaches effective in a Contemporary Problems in World Politics course where he used films and brief novels to provoke discussions and debates on current issues: "As educators, we can easily convey information. We then become mobile, vocal encyclopedia. Yet [it] is when we develop skills and foster learning, [that] we become effective teachers. Many students think that "knowledge" means "information." As faculty, we realize that true knowledge implies understanding. Therefore, we need to provide opportunities for our students to foster understanding. PBL provides such opportunities. It may be adapted for myriad subjects, grade levels, or course structures. It can be used throughout a course or as a model for a single unit. Both teachers and students will be pleasantly startled by the results" (p. 2).

Miller (1996) offered this scenario to students enrolled in his course, Myth, Religion and Art:

> You have been hired as consultants for a major motion picture. Although the story, set in ancient Greece (c. 425 BC), is fictional, the director wants every detail in the film to be as historically accurate as possible. Part of the action will take place around a temple. Your task is to determine what this temple should look like—including the interior, the exterior, the immediate vicinity, and the activities in and around the temple. If possible, recommend a location (or locations) where the filming of the temple scenes could take place. Include notes about what, if any, aspects of the setting would need to be altered—either physically or through special effects—in order to be accurate (p. 3).

At the USAF Academy, the ENGR 110-Z course uses a Problem-Based Learning approach, with students working in groups responsible for the design and deployment of a manned research base on Mars. Using a Socratic method, the course instructors (mentors) guide students as they identify the relevant tasks and pertinent engineering requirements. Students are coached in group skills, problem-solving approaches, and other learning tools.

CASE STUDIES

The case study method is becoming more widely known and used by innovative classroom instructors. Silverman and Welty (1994) describe a case as "a real-life problem or dilemma which has no immediate, obvious, single or correct solution" (p. 1). Cases are effective learning tools because they bring immediacy and relevance to discussion topics. They also encourage active learning by engaging students in stimulating, experiential, real-world scenarios. Such scenarios promote active problem solving and enhance critical-thinking skills. Wilkerson and Boehrer (1992) conclude that cases can be used effectively "to introduce new educational concepts, provoke attitudinal changes, provide practice in solving . . . problems, and stimulate the desire to acquire new skills" (p. 253). Most cases provide students with written scenarios, However, Tower (1995) emphasizes that a case can actually be any subject matter—a diseased organ, a malfunctioning engine, historical documents— "about which students are required to make a decision in a group or collaborative environment" (p. 4). The group or collaborative environment contributes to the power of cases.

Rationale for a Cooperative Approach

The most commonly used case discussion format is the whole-group case method developed by the Harvard Business School (Christensen and Hansen, 1987). This method, used effectively with groups as large as 30, engages participants in an active, stimulating teacher-directed discussion. It elicits multiple viewpoints and draws on a wide range of experiences. It also results in a shared experience, with all participants exposed to the same ideas. The facilitators, too, have ample opportunities to offer summaries, to redirect misunderstandings, and to provide both guidance and a sense of closure. Sometimes, however, cooperative-learning approaches, where students work in structured small groups, can offer a valuable alternative or supplement to the whole-group approach. Cooperative-learning discussion methods are effective for a number of reasons: (1) the large-group format promotes interactions where usually only one individual at a time is center stage; in cooperative-learning teams participants experience not this sequential participation, but simultaneous exchanges actively involving one-fourth of the students at any given moment; (2) whole-group formats—particularly if the exchanges are dynamic and thought-provoking—can prove to be risky arenas where less vocal members are unlikely to speak up; (3) whole-group exchanges, while intellectually stimulating, may not offer most individuals the opportunity to test their ideas and receive peer feedback within a relatively safe environment; and finally, (4) unlike whole-group discussions, a cooperative-learning format, where large groups are broken down into smaller units, allows for any number of student participants. Often the best approach will be a combination of the two models, with teachers (case facilitators) using both structured small-group work and whole-group discussion. Such approaches require careful planning.

Planning Cooperative Cases

No effective case facilitator ever wings it. Cooperative cases, like all coopera-tive-learning activities, require extensive upfront planning. Instructors must first select or prepare an appropriate case with a list of focus questions that challenge students to move beyond obvious conclusions. Questions should stimulate and deepen the learning process as they demand a creative diversity of opinion. Cases should be, according to Tower (1995), "self-contained, self-explanatory, and appropriate to the level of the student being taught." Fur-thermore, although teachers can encourage research after the case discussion, it should not be required beforehand (p. 5). Students usually receive the case about a week before the scheduled discussion. Shorter, less-complex cases will need less preparation time. Instructors should emphasize to students the importance of in-depth preparation: they must take responsibility for their own learning and for their classmates' learning. Teachers presenting coopera-tive cases must pay particular attention to four important factors: (1) forming groups; (2) establishing classroom norms for discussion; (3) conducting the case; and (4) providing closure.

Forming Groups

Group formation techniques will depend on variables such as the size and layout of the classroom and the students' and instructor's familiarity with cooperative-learning techniques. The teacher should determine the optimum size of the groups or teams. Three to six participants can work efficiently and effectively. The larger the size of the group, the less opportunity for individual participation. Many cooperative-learning practitioners prefer quads, formed prior to the case discussion. Teachers typically balance personalities, learning styles, academic levels, and any other relevant variables. In some instances, however, teachers may prefer to place students in teams on the day of the discussion. This approach emphasizes the importance of individual account-ability (the students' at-home preparation) as well as positive interdependence (students' reliance on group interactions while the case is processed). Teach-ers can use any of the team formation approaches discussed in chapter 4. They may also use cooperative-learning structures such as structured problem solving (chapter 6).

Before the groups begin any discussion, the teacher must establish class-room norms. These norms, which build community and allow for a free, but respectful exchange of ideas, can be as simple as listening attentively until each person has finished speaking, asking probing questions, and encouraging all group members to participate. If the students are accustomed to case discussions, a simple reminder of pre-established guidelines such as Tower's "Nine Rules of Engagement (ROE)" (Appendix A) may suffice. Teachers accustomed to cooperative-learning approaches may wish to conduct a norm-setting discussion. Establishing such norms upfront empowers students to constructively confront any members who are not contributing productively or permitting others to do so.

Conducting the Cooperative Case

Cases suitable for a cooperative approach must have a number of probing focus questions, preferably ones reflecting the range of Bloom's well-known taxonomy (application, evaluation, and synthesis questions are particularly important). Questions can be action-oriented ("What needs to be done?" or "What should X do?"), hypothetical ("What would happen if?"), challenging ("Why do you believe that?"), or diagnostic ("What is your analysis of?") (Drohan, 1994). Usually, the teacher will begin the case discussion with one or two open-ended questions to be explored in a whole-group format. Reaction questions ("What was your impression of?") work well. This warm-up exercise helps sets the tone for open, interactive discussion and builds student camaraderie.

To encourage in-depth discussion, each group should be assigned one or two specific focus questions. If five focus questions remain after the opening discussion and there are more than five groups, then two groups can work on the same question. This approach is often desirable because the subsequent report-outs reveal alternate viewpoints and solutions, reinforcing the value of divergent opinions in a critical-thinking setting. Students must be given specific instructions and timelines. It is useful, also, to establish a quiet signal to call the class to attention. The responsibilities of each team member should be clearly delineated, whether they are general group responsibilities or specific role-related ones, such as serving as a leader or reporter. As with other cooperative-learning tasks, it is always important to assign a sponge, or extension activity, for groups that work more rapidly than others. Thus, after each group prepares a report-out on their own focus question, they have a responsibility to explore other focus questions, as time permits.

During cooperative cases, teachers must rethink their roles. In a traditional whole-group case study discussion, the instructor is centerstage, visibly controlling the flow and content of the discussion. Although good facilitators always encourage participant interactions, often by deliberately asking for responses to specific comments, their presence tends to dominate. Sometimes participants recall, "Wow! What a great discussion that was! What a great case teacher Dr. X is!" Unfortunately, they sometimes forget the content and specific points of the discussion. With a cooperative case approach, the instructor's role is no less important, but it is often less obvious. The participants play a more direct, interactive role within their structured small groups. They are therefore more likely to remember what transpires, particularly their own ideas. The instructor moves among the groups, prepared to contribute if students have questions or if the discussion takes a counterproductive turn.

The value of case studies lies in their authenticity and in the fact that they frequently have no right or wrong solutions. Boehrer (1990–91) reminds us that "The irony of schooling . . . is that it often separates students from the experience of striving to resolve a problem for an intrinsically meaningful purpose. By focusing on solutions and answers already known, it abstracts the process of learning from the individual drive to overcome obstacles" (p. 1). This strength of the case study method, however, makes closure particularly important. Teachers need to monitor their time carefully so that this crucial segment of the case discussion is lively, but unhurried. Closure involves, typically, both student reports and the instructor's summation.

Three procedures work well for closing oral report-outs. If the overall class is small, then the reporters can simply rise and give a summary of their team's deliberations. Generally, faculty should allow about five minutes per report-out, less if the groups are highly focused and well-prepared. Report-outs may be submitted in writing as well. With larger groups, instructors give each team a clean sheet of acetate and a transparency marking pen and encourage the reporters to use visual prompts from the front of the room. Or, they distribute flip chart paper and large markers for the final report-outs. This practice has the advantage of fostering team cohesion, because it usually takes at least two people to hold up the flip chart paper or tape it to a wall.

In a closing summary instructors should provide official validation for the content and the process of the teams' work. It is a good practice to repeat, preferably in a congratulatory or even humorous format, the points made by various teams. The summary need not be long, and it need not provide definitive answers (often there are none), but students should leave class with a sense of accomplishment and closure.

The power of cases, like the power of "stories," is well known. They bring immediacy and reality to potentially theoretical material. They stimulate in-depth collaborative problem solving and thought-provoking, context-specific discussions. Perhaps best of all, they offer opportunities for active, experiential learning.

TEAM LEARNING

Team Learning, a challenging teaching method closely related to cooperative-learning, was developed by Michaelsen (1992; 1996; Michaelsen, Fink and Black, 1996) as a way of coping with large classes. It places upon students much of the responsibility for their own learning and enables instructors to focus less class time on basic concepts and more on higher-order applications. Team Learning departs from one cooperative-learning principle in that a large component of the students' grade is group based, a practice not recommended by cooperative-learning researchers such as Spencer Kagan. On the other hand, Team Learning reinforces the group processing function of cooperative-learning by highlighting the benefits of working together in a practical way. Team Learning relies on structured-learning teams kept in place throughout the term.

Team Learning occurs in four phases. First, prior to coming to class, the students study an assignment, such as a chapter, a text, or a journal article. The second phase occurs during class, when the instructor administers a short closed-book quiz which students take individually. In the third phase, after students have finished the individual quiz, the instructor administers an identical quiz, which the students now complete as a closed-book group test within their teams.

During this third phase, students must come to consensus, since only one quiz is completed for the group. Much learning occurs as students attempt to maximize their group score; the individual quiz and the group quiz weigh equally in the determination of their final course grade. Since the group grades are almost without exception higher than the individual scores, students quickly learn to value their peers as sources of learning and knowledge.

In the fourth and final phase, during which the students may open their books, the instructor announces the suggested correct answers for the quiz and gives the students an opportunity to appeal, using a form such as the one shown in Figure 9.3. The appeal process prompts students to delve deeply and energetically into their texts, focusing on the most relevant quiz-related material. Since learning occurs, and is reinforced, during this phase, instructors should be quite liberal in granting appeals. They may even wish to announce occasionally that, because of the number and caliber of the appeals, an incorrect answer will receive credit. Credit is given, however, only to teams that appeal or challenge, thereby motivating students to work actively with their teams and to pore over the text in an attempt to verify or refute the announced answers. Students cannot rely upon the work accomplished by other groups.

To maximize the utility of Team Learning, instructors should count the individual quizzes and group quizzes heavily in the determination of the course grade. The remainder of the grade may rest on traditional assessment measures, such as midterm exams, papers, projects and/or final exams.

Team Learning quizzes are not given every class period. The value of the team learning process lies in the assurance that students will learn the foundational material. Having mastered the "basics," students may then move on to higher-order skills such as structured problem solving and the students, not the instructor, now have the responsibility to get "up to speed." Experienced cooperative-learning instructors are able to "front-load" much of the

Group: _____

Question Number: _____

Proposed Correct Answer: _____

Rationale for your Appeal: _____

Supporting Evidence: _____

Instructor Decision: _____

TEST AND QUIZ APPEAL FOR TEAM LEARNING

FIGURE 9.3

student learning, thereby freeing class time for student information-processing activities in deep learning situations, rather than instructor-dominated information giving.

SUMMARY

All of the activities described in this chapter—educational games, Problem-Based Learning, cooperative case studies, and Team Learning—promote active, experiential learning. They all involve an investment on the students' part (individual accountability) in independent study. But, the nature of the activities themselves require that students cooperate (positive interdependence). As students interact, the instructor carefully monitors their progress. Ideally, too, the students perform self-assessments and peer assessments. Thus, cooperative-learning characteristics support and inform these specialized approaches to learning. In all cases, the learning itself is tied directly to the course goals.

APPENDIX A

The Case Method's Nine Rules of Engagement (ROE)*

The following guidelines give students an overview of their responsibilities during a case discussion.

1. PREPARE THOROUGHLY. Read the case, reflect on its content, and discuss it with others before coming to class.

---

*Handout developed by Lt Col "Pat" Tower, U.S. Air Force Academy, for Philosophy 310 course, September 1995.

2. TAKE "FREEFALL" RISKS. Express your views without prejudging them. We want to hear what you have to say because you may have that golden angle or perspective that helps us to break through confusion and ignorance.

3. LISTEN CAREFULLY. Focus on the other person's thoughts, not his/her efforts to express them. Ask questions to clarify what is said. Restate the person's remarks to be sure you understand the point.

4. PROMOTE DEMOCRACY. Become suspicious whenever everyone agrees that a judgment is true or an argument successful. Encourage a wide variety of viewpoints and opinions. Avoid "group think," peer pressure, and the convergence of opinion. (The more views that you entertain, the more likely it is that you will discover the internal logic of the situation you are assessing and find the best available course of action.)

5. EXTEND CHARITY. Always give your colleagues the benefit of the doubt.

6. PRACTICE CIVILITY. Never forget that your colleagues have a fundamental, inviolable worth as human beings and always must be respected as such. Avoid dealing in personalities or making personal attacks. Leave your ego in a box in your room. The case discussion classroom is a forum and a laboratory, not an arena. We are here to hammer out new levels of understanding, new agendas for investigation, and tentative solutions, we are not here to hammer on each other. Encourage others to take part and applaud the efforts of those who do.

7. EMBRACE AMBIGUITY. There is very little "closure" in life. Learn to live with it. Most of the "solutions" we discover are, at best, tentative and hypothetical. What we must do is use the best available means to reach the best working hypotheses, and that means drawing upon the strengths of the Learning Community.

8. BUILD COMMUNITY. Faithfully observe the ROE and gently remind others that they should do the same. Constantly seek new ways to perpetuate and expand the community.

9. TAKE RESPONSIBILITY. Someone once said that the 10 most important words in life are, "If it is to be, it is up to me." Believe it.

REFERENCES

Angelo, T.A. and Cross, K.P. (1993). *Classroom Assessment Techniques: A Handbook for college Teachers.* 2d Ed. San Francisco: Jossey-Bass.

Arambula-Greenfield, T. (1996). "Implementing Problem-based Learning in a College Science Class." *Journal of College Science Teaching,* 26(1), 26–30.

Barrows, H.S. and Myers, A.C. (1993). *Problem-Based Learning in Secondary Schools.* Unpublished monograph, Springfield, IL: Problem Based Learning Institute, Lanphier High School, and Southern Illinois University Medical School.

Boehrer, John. (1990-1991). "Spectators and Gladiators: Reconnecting the Students with the Problem." *Teaching Excellence,* 2(7), The Professional and Organizational Development Network in Higher Education. Stillwater, OK: New Forums Press, Inc.

Boud, D. and Feletti, G. (Eds.), (1991). *The Challenge of Problem Based Learning.* New York: St. Martin's Press.

Boyce, L.A. (1996, Spring). "Brain Bingo: Using an Old Game to Help Students Learn New Material." *Cooperative Learning and College Teaching,* 6(3), 11–12.

Bridges, E. and Hallinger, P. (1992). *Problem Based Learning for Administrators.* ERIC Clearinghouse on Educational Management, University of Oregon.

Burch, K. (1995). "PBL and the Lively Classroom." *About Teaching,* 47, University of Delaware: A Newsletter of the Center for Teaching Effectiveness. Online at <http://www.physics.udel.edu/~pbl/cte/jan95-posc.html>. Downloaded 18 Feb 1997.

Christensen, C.R. and Hansen, A.J. (1987). *Teaching and the Case Method.* Boston: Harvard Business School.

Davis, S.S. (1994). *Problem Based Learning in Medical Education: A Qualitative Study of Curriculum Design and Students' Experience in an Experimental Program.* Unpublished dissertation. The Ohio State University.

Drohan, T. (1994, Nov.). *Teaching with Cases at the Academy.* Workshop at the United States Air Force Academy.

Duch, B.J. (1996). "Problems: A Key Factor in PBL." *About Teaching: A Newsletter of the Center for Teaching Effectiveness,* 50, 7–8, University of Delaware.

Duffy, T.M. (1994). *Corporate and Community Education: Achieving Success in the Information Society.* Unpublished paper. Bloomington: Indiana University.

Gibson, B. (1991). "Research Methods Jeopardy: A Tool for Involving Students and Organizing the Study Session." *Teaching of Psychology,* 18(3), 176–77.

Gray-Shellberg, L. (1994). "Jeopardy 305: A Cooperative Learning Method for Teaching History and Systems of Psychology." *Cooperative Learning and College Teaching,* 5(1), 12–14.

Lepper, M.R. and Malone, T.W. (1985). "Intrinsic Motivation and Instructional Effectiveness in Computer-based Education." In R.E. Snow and M.J. Farr (Eds.), *Aptitude, Learning, and Instruction: III. Conative and Affective Process Analysis.* (pp. 255–83). Hillsdale, NJ: Erlbaum.

Meyers, C. (1986). *Teaching Students to Think Critically: A Guide for Faculty in All Disciplines.* San Francisco: Jossey-Bass.

Michaelsen, L. (1996). *Problems with Learning Groups: An Ounce of Prevention.* Preconference Workshop. Annual Conference of the Professional and Organizational Development Network in Higher Education. Snowbird Resort and Conference Center, Salt Lake City, UT.

Michaelsen, L.K. (1992). "Team Learning: A Comprehensive Approach for Harnessing the Power of Small Groups in Higher Education." In D.H. Wulff and J.D. Nyquist (Eds.), *To Improve the Academy: Resources for Faculty, Instructional, and Organizational Development,* Vol. 11 (pp. 107–22). The Professional and Organizational Development Network in Higher Education. Stillwater, OK: New Forums Press, Inc.

Michaelsen, L.K., Fink, D.L., and Black, R.H. (1996). "What Every Faculty Developer Needs to Know about Learning Groups." In L. Richlin (Ed.), *To Improve the Academy: Resources for Faculty, Instructional, and Organizational Development,* Vol. 15 (pp. 31–57). The Professional and Organizational Development Network in Higher Education. Stillwater, OK: New Forums Press, Inc.

Miller, M.P. (1996). "Introducing Art History through Problem-based Learning." *About Teaching: A Newsletter of the Center for Teaching Effectiveness*, 50, 3. University of Delaware.

Milter, R.G. and Stinson, J.E. (1994). "Educating Leaders for the New Competitive Environment." In G. Gijselaers, S. Tempelaar, and S. Keizer (Eds.), *Education Innovation in Economics and Business Administration: The Case of Problem-based Learning*. London: Kluwer Academic Publishers.

Nuhfer, E.B. (1997). "Student Management Teams—the Heretic's Path to Teaching Success." In W.E. Campbell and K.A. Smith (Eds.), *New Paradigms for College Teaching* (pp. 103–25). Edina, MN: Interaction Book Company.

Rhem, J. (1996). "Urgings and Cautions in Student-centered Teaching." *The National Teaching and Learning Forum*, 5(4), 1–5.

Savery, J.R. and Duffy, T.M. (1995, Sept./Oct.). "Problem-based Learning: An Instructional Model and its Constructivist Framework." *Educational Technology*. 31–38. Reprinted in *Educational Psychology 97/98 Annual Editions* (pp. 143–51). Guilford, CT: Duskin/McGraw-Hill.

Silverman, R. and Welty, W. (1994, Winter). "Case Studies to Promote Active Learning in the Classroom," Chalkboard, No. 9. University of Missouri-Columbia, 1–2. Adapted with permission from "Case Studies in Diversity for University Faculty Development," Rita Silverman and William Welty, 1993, Center for Case Studies in Education, Pace University.

Sugar, S. (1994). Workshop at the University of Maryland. College Park, MD.

Tower, P. (1995). "Teaching with Cases: The Tao of the Classroom." *USAFA Educator*, 4(1), 1; 4–6.

Wilkerson, L. and Boehrer, J. (1992). "Using Cases about Teaching for Faculty Development." In D.H. Wulff and J.D. Nyquist (Eds.), *To Improve the Academy: Resources for Faculty, Instructional, and Organizational Development*, 11 (pp. 253–62). The Professional and Organizational Development Network in Higher Education, Stillwater, OK: New Forums Press, Inc.

Woods, D.R. (1994). *Problem-based Learning: How to Gain the Most from PBL*. Waterdown, ON: Donald R. Woods.

CHAPTER 10

Using Cooperative Technology to Enhance Learning

"There is a growing recognition of the power of information technology to help improve the quality of teaching and learning, improve the motivation and attention of students, and improve students' career preparation."

Steve Gilbert

With the advent of e-mail, networked classrooms, satellite communications, interactive television, and the Internet, information technology is having a sweeping impact on all areas of academia. Faculty looking toward the 21st century must contemplate appropriate educational responses in an uncertain and unsettling future, where traditional "assembly line" models of teaching and learning may no longer have relevance. Many questions are pertinent: What are the promises of technology? What will education be like? What will teachers do in the future, including those things they are doing now? What will they need to do these things well? And, what issues and concerns affect teachers now or will affect teachers in the future? As Green and Gilbert (1995) remind us, "The key issue, of course, is the effective use of information technology resources as **tools** to support instruction and learning outcomes" (p. 13).

THE INFORMATION TECHNOLOGY EXPLOSION AND ITS IMPACT ON HIGHER EDUCATION

There is no doubt that technology is now a permanent part of the academic landscape, as Green (1996) documents:

Fueled by more than four decades of aspirations and a dozen years of sustained (if often ad hoc) experimentation, information technology has finally emerged as a permanent, respected, and increasingly essential component of the college experience. . . . A rapidly rising minority of **all** of college students and faculty—some 16 million people—now have some sort of recurring instructional experience with information technology resources and technology-based learning activities. These are technology activities that go beyond the broad use of word processing (at one end of the continuum) and the technical skill of computer programming (at the other); rather, these are experiences that extend the content of the curriculum, enrich the classroom discourse, and enhance learning opportunities (p. 24).

Schmidt (1996) notes that in January 1996 there were one hundred million URLs and one hundred thousand World Wide Web servers. Furthermore, he thinks the number of users on Internet/WWW will double each year for at least the next two years. He labels the "Netscape Era" as the "era of infinite variety." There is no question that these changes are having, or will have, a significant impact on higher education worldwide.

Rather than isolating students, as once was feared, the most compelling results of the information technology explosion have been "connection" and "communication." In fact, Williamson (1996) cogently suggests that any paradigm shift focuses less on learning and education and more on a "shift in communication and sharing, manipulation and dissemination of information." This change, however, enables educators to enhance the "skills, concepts, approaches, [and] critical thinking" that have defined liberal arts institutions for decades" (pp. 39–40). O'Donnell (1995) reminds us, "What has changed now, and what marks the decisive turning, is the degree of interconnection between people that networked information brings. For the most part, there's no question of replacing the tried and true with the novel, but rather an explosion of opportunities for making links of one kind or another" (p. 1). Because of this emphasis on interconnectivity—often at a distance—scholars are reassessing the roles communication and cooperation play in education.

Collins (1991) has identified several effects of technology on K–12 education, effects that are evident as well in higher education. These student-centered shifts emphasize the important role cooperative learning will play in the electronic/information age.

Increased technology will result, he postulates, in a shift from recitation to coaching, which will engender more-engaged students. As indicated earlier, teachers committed to cooperative-learning approaches have already discarded the podium in favor of student-directed classrooms. Living in the information age requires new values, attitudes, and behaviors. Students with worldwide access to information will discover far too many ideas to effectively evaluate and assimilate them. Instructors must coach students to integrate numerous ideas into a productive framework. Menges (1994) sees teachers working with students to identify, often without contextual clues, what is essential within each discipline. Despite its educational potential, Peters (1996) equates web surfing to channel hopping on a television, but instead of 57 channels, there are 57,000 channels. He compares the dark side of the Internet to a boom town complete with "honky tonks and hucksters." Mentoring teachers can rescue students from the seductions of the "dark side." Green and Gilbert (1995) predict that "in the near term . . . the demand for faculty guidance and intervention—**for faculty mentoring**—is much more likely to increase than to decrease" (p. 17).

At the same time, however, teachers will not stifle students' natural curiosity. Students tend to be motivated to learn, according to McMillan and Forsyth (1991), "if their needs are being met, if they see value in what they are learning, and if they believe that they are able to succeed with reasonable effort" (p. 50). Allowing students some choice in content, approaches of study, and even evaluation will help them become more autonomous as learners. As they become more adept at using electronic sources, they will experience even more diverse media.

Collins also postulates that increased technology and the change in teach-ers' delivery modes will result in a shift from whole-class instruction to small-group instruction, where students work at their own level and pace and where attention can be directed to those students needing the most help. Because students will have access to a variety of resources, including teacher-selected compact discs or computer-mediated instruction, there is no reason for students to learn lock-step fashion as they have been expected to do in traditional classrooms. Teachers and peer mentors will work more with individuals and with small groups. Within these small groups, students will need to know how to be self-directed learners, processes emphasized in the cooperative-learning literature. The power of groups has been well documented, but groups function well only under structured conditions where there is a clear, compelling task and where, according to Katzenbach and Smith (1993) the "team performance requires **both** individual accountability **and** mutual accountability. The members **hold themselves accountable** for their individual contributions to the team, their collective contributions to the team, and the team's overall result" (p. 277). The challenge, as Salomon (1995) points out, is to create electronically genuine interdependence:

> For genuine collaboration to take place, you need genuine interdependence. In its absence, teams do not function the way they ought to, regardless of how wonderful the computer tools they are given to work with are. In other words, computers can support collaboration provided it entails interdependence, but the computer is not likely to produce this interdependence all on its own (p. 3).

Hooper (1992) emphasizes that "it is important to distinguish between cooperative-learning and other small-group learning methods" because without the careful attention to effective student interaction, which is a hallmark of cooperative learning, cognitive and affective gains may be negligible" (p. 22).

The talent development model of student achievement, advocated by Astin (1985), allows faculty to target their efforts to maximize learning for all students regardless of their starting point. Astin (1988) feels that "the talent development view symbolizes a cooperative value system by emphasizing the need to focus institutional energies on the task of helping students develop to their maximum potential" (p. 15). Technology will enable teachers to work with individuals and small groups who need the most attention. Peer tutoring in a cooperative setting will further unshackle teachers from the tyranny of uniform instruction.

As Collins further notes, because student learning will not be lock step, teachers must adjust their assessment efforts as well, moving away from test performance and toward authentic evaluation of processes and products. Such criterion-referenced, often individualistic, assessment will result in a shift from a competitive to a cooperative goal structure. With access to extensive databases and networking opportunities, more projects will become collaborative, as they are in the workplace. The final shift, according to Collins, will be toward an appreciation for both visual and verbal thinking. As chapter 11 suggests, cooperative learning can provide answers for grading issues such as peer assessment and the determination of individual contributions.

Cooperative learning cannot address all of the issues facing instructors and students who must deal with these significant shifts, but it does offer guidelines, resting on solid pedagogical practices, that can provide a reassuring anchor as we address the key issue of using technology as a tool to further learning. O'Donnell(1994) reminds us that "We do not need specific technology so much as we need resourceful adaptations of technology and of the social, intellectual, and cultural systems that we find ourselves managing. It is a challenge to institutional evolution."

The connection between cooperative learning and technology is longstanding. Light and Mevarech (1992) point out that

> Since the early 1980s there has been a growing interest in the potentialities of both **cooperative learning** and of **computers** as facilitators of student learning. In some respects, the claims made for each are rather similar. They are both based on theories in the area of social cognition and they both emphasize the role of student interactions in enhancing a wide range of school outcomes, including academic achievement, cognitive processes, metacognitive skills, motivation toward learning, self-esteem, and social development (p. 155).

In a number of ways, cooperative learning in conjunction with technology can promote the deep learning that has been the focus of this book. Based on the literature on deep learning, Woods (1994) recommends that instructors "create an environment that encourages and rewards, and allows sufficient time for 'deep processing.' Another way of viewing 'deep processing' is: "Don't try to learn everything from the first activity. Build up your subject knowledge successively" (p. 7.)." This progression by "deep versatile" learners cannot occur, according to Entwistle, (1981) when surface learning is encouraged by: (1) work overload; (2) stress; (3) examinations that emphasize memorization and "regurgitation"; (4) an environment that rewards surface learning. Using technology in ways that promote sequenced learning within groups can lead to more in-depth processing of course content and, hence, more retention of information, whether students are interacting within a classroom setting or interacting through out-of-class electronic networks.

TECHNOLOGY-ENHANCED, CLASSROOM-BASED COOPERATIVE LEARNING

Technology offers far more creative teaching options than the simple "chalk and talk" approaches of times past. Independent learning, including distance education, is beyond the scope of this chapter, but even in classes where students routinely meet face-to-face, technology can play a vital educational role by extending the classroom walls. As Figure 10.1 suggests, it enables faculty to double the opportunities for student interactions and student-teacher interactions.

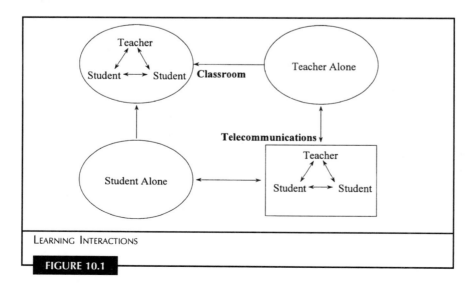

LEARNING INTERACTIONS

FIGURE 10.1

This chapter will thus focus on what Dorwick (1996) calls the Transitional Model, where the basic classroom setting is augmented by visits to a computer lab or a computerized classroom, and the Internet and e-mail are used as alternate delivery modes for instruction and collaboration. "Instructors in the Transitional model may post course materials to a syllaweb or to a class listserv and may also allow students to submit assignments over electronic mail or to collaborate with each other through synchronous conference software" (p. 1). Gilbert (1996), in fact, sees "distance education" and this transitional, class-room-based model as operating under two separate paradigms. The first focuses on "Improving Institutional Productivity and Extending Access to Education"; the second, which shapes this chapter, focuses on "Enhancing or Changing Teaching and Learning; Extending Content." Some of the goals of this latter paradigm are to promote "deep learning," to increase and enhance student-student and student-teacher communications, to offer teaching/learning options that are responsive to individual preferences, styles, and capabilities, and to create learning communities which foster both collegiality and shared responsibility for learning outcomes (p. 9).

We will not delve into the intricacies of specialized definitions and concepts, but will try, instead, to focus on the philosophical and practical assumptions behind technological options, keeping in mind the nature of the electronic media and the nature of human learning. Technology in current classrooms is used in a variety of ways. The most obvious, but least interesting, is the use of presentation software, such as PowerPoint slides, to enhance lectures. Cooperatively, students and teachers are experimenting with learning through networked multimedia labs, through computer-assisted learning, and, most fruitfully, through Internet and e-mail extensions of the classroom walls.

Networked Classrooms

Networked multimedia computer labs are common on many campuses. They offer faculty and students a wide range of teaching and learning tools. In such labs, students can use interactive CD-ROM-based presentations, such as A.D.A.M, a set of programs in human anatomy and physiology. They can solve problems using software packages such as Mathematica, a technical computing environment for applications ranging from simple calculations, complex programming, advanced computations, data analysis, and graphic modeling to sharing and publishing documents on the Web. Film clips appear with the click of a switch: first-year engineering students studying trusses, for example, can watch James Bond leap about the Eiffel Tower. Through technology, philosophy students can interact live with Jorge Garcia, a noted African-American philosopher, about a work in progress, "Reconceiving Moral Rights." (Degnan, 1997). So-called Groupware, such as Lotus Notes, Firstclass, and CommonSpace, enables students to work collaboratively on various projects, including peer editing of papers. In fact, networked writing classrooms are becoming more and more common. Gallaudent University's pioneering work in this area, for example, is well known. Another interesting experiment, the AT&T Learning Network, is directly based on cooperative learning. Riel (1995) notes that the Learning Circle design of the AT&T Learning Network is based on the group investigation model developed by Sharan (chapter 8). In this case, a small number of classrooms are linked electronically, enabling students in each class to contribute toward the final product using asynchronous communication.

In a networked classroom that is primarily lecture-based, collaborative activities typically occur after a lecture or demonstration. In the case of computer-assisted learning in pairs, however, students may be working collaboratively during a regularly scheduled time period, but without the presence of the teacher.

Independent/Paired Learning Through Technology

Computer-assisted instruction (CAI), which originated in the 1960s, was originally intended to promote independent learning. Its value, particularly in self-paced programs such as mathematics or grammar, where answers are right and wrong has been well-documented through research. Ehrmann (1995) cites a summary by Kulik, Chen-Lin, and Kulik (1991) that finds: "This method results in substantial improvement in learning outcomes and speed, perhaps around 20 percent or more on average" (p. 24). However, CAI software is expensive and quickly becomes obsolete. Thus, CAI—once expected to revolutionize human learning—remains only an unfulfilled promise.

Recognizing this promise, however, particularly as software becomes more and more sophisticated, educators are looking for ways to lower costs and to eliminate the isolating effects of self-paced instruction. Light and Mevarech (1992) state: "Current trends are throwing the spotlight on the embedding of CAL [Computer-Assisted Learning] in cooperative-learning environments. At the intersection of these two domains, cooperative learning and CAL, a body of research has emerged which has examined peer interaction in relation to computer-based learning" (p. 156–57). Such research efforts involve a number of variables including task design, size and dynamics of learning groups, age, gender, and time on task. Many studies, such as those by Dalton, Hannafin, and Hooper (1989), seek to measure both performance and attitudes.

The medium of interactive video, Supinski (1996) postulates, may be even more effective than CAI when students also interact, often in pairs. In fact, his research has affected practice in the Department of Foreign Languages at the U.S. Air Force Academy. Many instructors there use cooperative-learning techniques in both the Language Learning Center (LLC) and in the classroom. The departmental guidelines for teaching in the LCC (Department of Foreign Languages, USAFA, 1996) recommend scheduled interactions between students, with the stipulation that "interactions should be between group members as well as between group members and the technology: ensure that there is time for both." The amount of time spent on each segment should be timed with recommended splits of 30/20 (thirty minutes of video-watching followed by 20 minutes of student-student interaction) or 15/10. During the human-interaction time, the students are directed to perform various tasks for which they are held accountable. They can

- orally summarize the events of the video;
- describe some of the characters or scenes;
- construct a dialog or conversation using the vocabulary they learned (this can be oral or written);
- complete a worksheet together.

Because most faculty do not have the luxury of CAI software or interactive video discs, they have tended to harness tools, such as electronic mail and the Internet, which were not specifically designed for teaching and learning. Many educators see these tools as ways to "extend the classroom walls."

Extending the Classroom Walls

The use of multimedia and electronic options during regular classroom sessions can be beneficial or not, depending on a number of factors, including the quality of any software employed, the logistics of the interactive process, and the purpose and use of the assignment. Creed (1997) states, "Technology amplifies bad pedagogy." Knowing how to use technology does not necessarily lead to effective teaching and learning: "If its use is not grounded in a thorough understanding of cognitive development and a pedagogy that is driven by this understanding, the use of the technology will be frustrating to both instructor and students, will impede rather than enhance student learning, and will distance us from each other" (p. 182).

For example, if technology is to be seen as a tool rather than as a driver or an "add-on," then it must simplify the learning process for students, not complicate it. Too often, early innovators worked out convoluted ways to incorporate technology into the classroom which built in resentment if students were required to use it or apathy if they considered it a complex option. Some mini-case studies should clarify this point. Example One: Students in a large, residential research institution were encouraged to use a class home page on the World Wide Web for required peer editing of papers. To do this, most students had to go to a computer lab, sign in, post their papers, use the editing software, and then download the final products. Most students chose to meet in the library or another central location, exchange papers, and conduct their peer editing face-to-face. Example Two: Students enrolled in a first-year composition course at a small, networked four-year college were required for two class sessions in a row to return to their dormitories during regular classroom hours and log on for a "free writing" activity, called a Local Area Network (LAN) session. Ten minutes prior to the beginning of class, the instructor sent a discussion question and the students then wrote frenetically during the next 50 minutes, posting their final products to the class listserv. This approach afforded the instructor the opportunity to prepare a whole-class followup by cutting and pasting from various student papers. Students ideally could read and comment on each other's papers, a requirement on some occasions. However, when electronic peer critiquing was not required, no one opted to do it. Furthermore, the quality of the "forced" comments was uniformly low. The disadvantages far outweighed the one instructor-feedback advantage. Some disadvantages were the result of electronic deficiencies. On two occasions, the instructor's network server crashed prior to the LAN session, necessitating a frantic sprint, disk in hand, to a department with access to a different server. During every session, a significant percentage of students were unable to log on. The greatest disadvantage, however, lay in the "disconnection" between students and the teacher. The LAN sessions required students to write on topics only peripherally related to the upcoming assignment. Thus, students felt that they were wasting their time. Furthermore, students were removed from classroom interactions for a full week, working in isolation on the computer. Example Three: Hawisher and Pemberton (1996) report establishing, for a class linked through an Asynchronous Learning Network (ALN), designated "spaces" where collaborative groups could communicate with one another, set up future meetings, and converse about their projects. Few groups used their separate space on Firstclass, preferring more conventional communication methods, such as the telephone. The authors conclude: "The small-group conference areas became a 'path of **most** resistance' with too many logistical hurdles to overcome for relatively minor benefits. As a consequence, they were largely ignored" (p. 9). Example Four: Although the paired e-mail assignment that will be presented in Appendix A is probably a spoof, it illustrates its point wonderfully. No matter how glitzy our hardware and software, when we design assignments to foster human learning, we are dealing with real humans. Thus, we cannot overlook all the dynamics of cooperative learning, particularly social skills and group processing, that we would monitor with face-to-face group work.

Despite these negative examples, there can be little doubt that a well-constructed assignment, one that contributes to the sequenced learning we have been emphasizing throughout this book, can result in positive student-learning gains. The interactions featured in Figure 10.1 emphasize the major advantage of using electronic approaches such as e-mail, interactive software, or the World Wide Web to extend the classroom walls. As Figure 10.1 suggests, a great deal of independent student learning occurs over a semester if assignments are carefully sequenced to provide outside-of-class reading, writing, and reflecting experiences. Similarly, teachers engage in solitary work as they prepare their lesson plans and respond to student work. In a traditional classroom, the student-student interactions and student-teacher interactions, which foster deep approaches to learning, occur only during scheduled class times. Although some faculty do require students to meet face-to-face outside of class, often—as mentioned in earlier chapters—such requirements are unproductive, due to conflicts of one sort or another. Having a technology option, however, eliminates the logistical barriers and allows productive and meaningful exchanges, thus enhancing the opportunities for active and interactive learning. The choice of media is extremely important, as Creed shows in Tables 10.A and 10.B.

Creed (1997) uses electronic options to enhance his psychology classes. He sequences learning by maximizing the advantages of each type of electronic communication. Table 10.A summarizes the three categories of electronic communication and their possible uses. Creed uses "Private Discourse" in a formal, structured way when his students submit routine writing assignments through e-mail and informally when students need to discuss private course-related topics. A class conference allows a general discussion of course topics through a "Public Forum." Course materials, including the syllabus, writing and reading assignments, and handouts, remain accessible through a "Repository" on the World Wide Web. Thus, sequenced learning is promoted when students have meaningful assignments to complete outside of class which they can then post to the instructor for review. Based on student responses to the course material, the instructor can determine the appropriate level of lecture, can correct any misconceptions, and can build on the knowledge students already possess.

Thus, the learning cycle begins with independent study, which is connected to assignments students find intrinsically motivating. When Creed teaches a unit on Pavlovian conditioning, for example, students read a textbook chapter and some supplementary assignments before completing a writing assignment that engages them in meaningful and personal ways with the theoretical material. The writing assignment consists of three parts:

1. The first part asks them to describe three examples in which they have been Pavlovianly conditioned. I ask them to come up with fairly unique and significant examples, label the components, and explain why they think their examples are Pavlovian conditioning.

TABLE 10.A

THREE CATEGORIES OF ELECTRONIC COMMUNICATION

	Categories		
	Repositories	**Public Forums**	**Private Discourse**
Description	Information stored by a (usually) large entity (schools, museums, government agencies) and retrieved by individuals.	Information from others others is available and can be retrieved; the information is a collective knowledge base.	Two-way communication between individuals. The communicators control what information is available to each other.
Use	Efficient gathering and storage of collected knowledge that an individual or small group would be unable to compile and maintain on their own.	Small groups of individuals with a common purpose come together to share information, create a body of knowledge on a limited topic.	Two (or more) people share information that is of importance to themselves but of little value to others, or needs to be confidential.
Conventional examples	Libraries	Roundtable Discussions, Town Hall meetings	Letters, conversation
Educational examples	Lecture	Cooperative Learning	Tutorial
Electronic forms	World Wide Web	Electronic conferencing	E-Mail
Organization of information	Hierarchical .... Non-hierarchical		
Persistence	Permanent .... Ephemeral		
User input of information	Little .... Considerable		
Modifiability by user	Unmodifiable by users .... Highly modifiable by user		
Audience	Large, Public .... Small, private		
Amount of information	Mass quantities .... Small amounts		
Ease of creating information	Fairly difficult .... Easy		
Intrusiveness	Not... Very		

TABLE 10.B

ADVANTAGES OF ELECTRONIC COMMUNICATION

Advantage	Repository	Public Forum	Private Discourse
Increases accessibility	very high	very high	very high
A pedagogically better technique	—	high	high
More thoughtful communication	—	high	high
Levels the playing field	—	high	high
Enhances student interaction	—	high	high
A unique classroom assessment technique	—	very high	very high
Enhances record keeping and structure	very high	high	very high
Access to diverse sources of information	high	moderate	—

2. The second part asks them to write the one-page text of a speech they would give to a seventh-grade class, explaining what Pavlovian Conditioning is all about.

3. The third part asks them to make up their own question about the chapter and explain why this question is important to them (p. 154).

Creed finds that the first part of the assignment allows "personalization," the second, internal conceptualization, and the third, personal "ownership" of the material as genuine questions are discussed in the "Public Forum" or during class.

Creed carefully structures class time to capitalize on the student interactions needed for deep learning. He allows "processing" of the material prepared outside of class in cooperative groups of three or four students. Students discuss their examples and prepare write-ups with their best samples and additional questions. These write-ups fuel the in-class activities (mini-lectures, group discussions, demonstrations, etc.) which occur during the remaining sessions on this particular unit.

Other educators are equally concerned with the nature of learning with electronic resources. Alexander (1995), for example, puts learning with the World Wide Web in the broader context of deep, not surface learning, citing work by Biggs and Telfer (1987) and Laurillard (1993). With this framework, she states:

> The challenge for educational developers is to use this knowledge of learning, together with an understanding of the features of the WWW, to design learning experiences which promote a deep approach to learning so that 'what' students learn is a deep understanding of the subject content , the ability to analyse and synthesise data and information, and the development of creative thinking and good communication skills (p. 6).

She feels that simply encouraging students to explore hypertext and hypermedia on the WWW does not promote learning because the paths are constructed by someone else, allowing no individual interpretation or construction of knowledge. She agrees with Laurillard (1993) that hypertext is not inherently interactive because there is no feedback on the user's actions and the user does not act upon the media to change the system itself. The Web as a learning tool, however, has potential in two ways: (1) through collaborative authorship, where students construct their own knowledge through collection of data, analysis, and synthesis and (2) through integrated learning experiences, such as the JASON Project initiated by Robert Ballard, the discoverer of the RMS Titanic. In this interdisciplinary project, students on electronic field trips "act on the world (by operating robot mechanisms to take samples from active flowing lava), they receive feedback on those actions, and reflection is encouraged through the use of online journals" (p. 7).

Alexander omits any discussion, however, of the critical dimensions of learning collaboratively. Dillenbourg and Schneider (1995) attempt to address these difficult, but essential aspects of learning through the Internet. As we saw in traditional classrooms, it is simply not sufficient to put students together. They must work on common tasks in a structured, civil environment where they share mutual goals. Dillenbourg and Schneider's research on the conditions for effective collaboration looked at several factors: (1) group composition (small is better; optimal heterogeneity permits the differing viewpoints that trigger productive interaction within the context of "mutual interest and intelligibility"); (2) task features (optimal tasks are challenging enough to require interaction during the reasoning stages and/or are structured, as in Jigsaw, to promote collaboration in an environment which does not "shut down" discussion by providing immediate feedback); and (3) communication media (the medium, which remains largely text-based communication, either synchronous or asynchronous, must be adequate). The authors conclude that collaborative learning through the Internet must be closely monitored to ensure that the mechanisms described above are operative. Because the real nature of learning tasks involves "collaborative problem solving," attention must be focused on why people communicate, so that more effort can be spent on "integrating collaborative features" into current software tools.

SUMMARY

Like it or not, technology is a fact of life. It can be used creatively and cooperatively to enhance student learning. Anytime we consider using technology, we might keep in mind Farrington's (1996) words:

Now the challenge is not just in advancing the technology, but in learning what to do with it; in particular, learning how to harness the power of the new computer technologies to make learning more effective, more humanly interactive, and more widely available (p. 56).

This focus on teaching and learning permeates technology discussions. Interestingly enough, a recent Stanford Forum for Higher Education Futures (1995) concluded two days of deliberations with this admonition:

Undergraduate teaching must emerge from "behind closed doors" to become a collective activity, one which commands the faculty's best attention on both current performance and innovation for future improvements. Only then can the full potential of information technology be realized (p.14).

As we have seen, cooperative learning and technology are natural partners. Creative use of technology, resting on all we know about human learning, involves human dimensions of caring, community, and commitment.

APPENDIX A

The exact source of this story is unknown. It has circulated on the Internet with the following heading: English 44A SMU; Creative Writing; Prof. Miller. It involves a tandem story where one student writes the first paragraph of a short story. The partner reads the first paragraph and then adds another paragraph to the story. The first person then adds a third paragraph, and so on back and forth.

By Rebecca <last name deleted> and Gary <last name deleted>

At first, Laurie couldn't decide which kind of tea she wanted. The camomile, which used to be her favorite for lazy evenings at home, now reminded her too much of Carl, who once said, in happier times, that he liked camomile. But she felt she must now, at all costs, keep her mind off Carl. His possessiveness was suffocating, and if she thought about him too much her asthma started acting up again. So camomile was out of the question.

Meanwhile, Advance Sergeant Carl Harris, leader of the attack squadron now in orbit over Skylon 4, had more important things to think about than the neuroses of an air-headed asthmatic bimbo named Laurie with whom he had spent one sweaty night over a year ago. "A.S. Harris to Geostation 17," he said into his transgalactic communicator. "Polar orbit established. No sign of resistance so far..." But before he could sign off a bluish particle beam flashed out of nowhere and blasted a hole through his ship's cargo bay. The jolt from the direct hit sent him flying out of his seat and across the cockpit.

He bumped his head and died almost immediately, but not before he felt one last pang of regret for psychically brutalizing the one woman who had ever had feelings for him. Soon afterwards, Earth stopped its pointless hostilities towards the peaceful farmers of Skylon 4. "Congress Passes Law Permanently Abolishing War and Space Travel." Laurie read in her newspaper one morning. The news simultaneously excited her and bored her. She stared out the window, dreaming of her youth — when the days had passed unhurriedly and carefree, with no newspapers to read, no television to distract her from her sense of innocent wonder at all the beautiful things around her. "Why must one lose one's innocence to become a woman?" she pondered wistfully.

Little did she know, but she had less than 10 seconds to live. Thousands of miles above the city, the Anu'udrian mothership launched the first of its lithium fusion missiles. The dim-witted wimpy peaceniks who pushed the Unilateral Aerospace Disarmament Treaty through Congress had left Earth a defenseless target for the hostile alien empires who were determined to destroy the human race. Within two hours after the passage of the treaty the Anu'udrian ships were on course for Earth, carrying enough firepower to pulverize the entire planet. With no one to stop them they swiftly initiated their diabolical plan. The lithium fusion missile entered the atmosphere unimpeded. The President, in his top-secret mobile submarine headquarters on the ocean floor off the coast of Guam, felt the inconceivably massive explosion which vaporized Laurie and 85 million other Americans. The President slammed his fist on the conference table. "We can't allow this! I'm going to veto that treaty! Let's blow'em out of the sky!"

This is absurd. I refuse to continue this mockery of literature. My writing partner is a violent, chauvinistic, semi-literate adolescent.

Yeah? Well, you're a self-centered, tedious neurotic whose attempts at writing are the literary equivalent of Valium.

You total #!$*and.

Stupid %and#$!.

REFERENCES

Alexander, S. (1995). *Teaching and Learning on the World Wide Web*. Ausweb95-Education-Learning on the World Wide Web. Online at <http://www.scu.edu.au/authors/education2/alexander/>. Downloaded 22 July 1996. No longer available.

Astin, A.W. (1985). *Achieving Educational Excellence: A Critical Assessment of Priorities and Practices in Higher Education*. San Francisco: Jossey-Bass.

Astin, A.W. (1988, Sept./Oct.). "Competition or Cooperation? Teaching Teamwork as a Basic Skill." *Change: The Magazine of Higher Learning*, 12–19.

Biggs, J.B. and Telfer, R. (1987). *The Process of Learning*. 2d Ed. Sydney: Prentice-Hall.

Collins, A. (1991). "The Role of Computer Technology in Restructuring Schools." *Phi Delta Kappan*, 73(1), 28–36.

Creed, T. (1997). "Extending the Classroom Walls Electronically." In W.E. Campbell and K.A. Smith (Eds.), *New Paradigms for College Teaching* (pp. 149–84). Edina, MN: Interaction Book Company. Online at <http://bingen.cs.csbsju.edu/~creed>. No longer available.

Dalton, D.W., Hannafin, M.J., and Hooper, S. (1989). "Effects of Individual and Cooperative Computer Assisted Instruction on Student Performance and Attitudes." *Educational Technology Research and Development*, 37(2), 15–24.

Degnan, M.J. (1997). "Bringing 'Distant' Guest Speakers into the Classroom." *Wright State Center for Teaching and Learning Jan/Feb 1997 Newsletter*, 5(4), 1–2.

Department of Foreign Languages, U.S. Air Force Academy. (1996, Spring). *Departmental Guidance Statement*. Unpublished Document.

Dillenbourg, P. and Schneider, D. (1995). *Collaborative Learning and the Internet*. Online at <http://tecfa.unige.ch/tecfa/tecfa-research/CMC/colla/iccai95_1.html>. Downloaded 13 Feb. 1997.

Dorwick, K. *Building the Virtual Department: A Case Study of Online Teaching: Three Models for Teachers*. Online at <http://www.uic.edu/~kdorwick/dissertation/models.htm>. Downloaded 13 Feb. 1997.

Ehrmann, S.C. (1995, Mar./Apr.). "Asking the Right Questions: What Does Research Tell us about Technology and Higher Learning?" *Change: The Magazine of Higher Learning*, 27(2), 20–27.

Entwistle, N. (1981). *Styles of Learning and Teaching*. New York: John Wiley and Sons.

Farrington, G.C. (1996, Oct). "Bringing Technology to Education." *ASEE Prism*, 56.

Gilbert, S. (1996, Mar./Apr.). "Double Visions—Paradigms in Balance or Collision?" *Change: The Magazine of Higher Learning*, 28(2), 8–9

Green, K.C. (1996, Mar./Apr.). "The Coming Ubiquity of Information Technology." *Change: The Magazine of Higher Learning*, 28(2), 24–28.

Green, K.C. and Gilbert, S.W. (1995, Mar./Apr.). "Great Expectations: Content, Communications, Productivity, and the Role of Information Technology in Higher Education." *Change: The Magazine of Higher Learning*, 27(2), 8–18.

Hawisher, G.E. and Pemberton, M.A. (1996). *Writing Across the Curriculum Encounters Asynchronous Learning Networks or WAC Meets up with ALN*. Unpublished manuscript.

Hooper, S. (1992). "Cooperative Learning and Computer-based Instruction." *Educational Technology Research and Development*, 40(3), 21–38.

Katzenback, J.R. and Smith, D.K. (1993). *The Wisdom of Teams*. New York: HarperCollins.

Kulik, C.C., Chen-lin, C., and Kulik, J.A. (1991). "Effectiveness of Computer-based Instruction: An Updated Analysis." *Computers in Human Behavior*, 7(1–2), 75–94.

Laurillard, D. (1993). *Rethinking University Teaching: A Framework for the Effective Use of Educational Technology*. London: Routledge.

Light, P.H. and Mevarech, Z.R. (1992). "Cooperative Learning with Computers: An Introduction." *Learning and Instruction*, 2, 155–59.

McMillan, J.H. and Forsyth, D.R. (1991). "What Theories of Motivation Say About Why Students Learn." In R.J. Menges and M.D. Svinicki (Eds.), *College Teaching: From Theory to Practice. New Directions for Teaching and Learning, No. 45* (pp. 39–51). San Francisco: Jossey-Bass.

Menges, R.J. (1994). "Teaching in the Age of Electronic Information." In W.J. McKeachie, *Teaching Tips: Strategies, Research, and Theory for College and University Teachers*. 9th Ed. (pp. 183–93). Lexington, MA: D. C. Heath.

O'Donnell, J.J. (1994, May 18–20). *Where Are We Going and When Did We Get There?* Presentation at the 124th annual meeting of the ARL: The Research Library the Day After Tomorrow. Austin, TX. Online at <http://sunsite.berkeley.edu/ARL/Proceedings/124/ps2going.html> Downloaded 11 Feb. 1997. No longer available.

O'Donnell, J.J. (1995, Mar.) "Teaching with Technology." *Penn Printout: The University of Pennsylvania's Computing Magazine*. Reprinted in *CSS Journal - Computers in the Social*

Studies 5.1(1997). <Online at http://gopher.upenn.edu:80/pennprintout/html/v11/5/ teach.html. Downloaded 11 Feb. 1997. No longer available.

Salomon, G. (1995). *What does the Design of Effective CSCL Require and How do we Study its Effects?* CSCL '95 Conference, Indiana University, Bloomington, IN. October. Online at <http://www_cscl95.indiana.edu/cscl95/outlook/62_Salomon.html>. downloaded 16 Sept. 1997. No longer available.

Schmidt, E. (1996) Keynote address, EDUCOM National Conference. Philadelphia, October, 1996. Reviewed by Glogoff, S. Online at <http://dizzy.library.arizona.edu/users/ sglogoff/educom96.htm#intro>. Downloaded 11 Feb. 1997. No longer available.

Stanford Forum for Higher Education Futures. (1995). *Leveraged Learning: Technology's Role in Restructuring Higher Education.* Technology and Restructuring Roundtable. Palo Alto, CA: Stanford Forum for Higher Education Futures.

Supinski, S. (1996). *A Comparison of Simultaneous versus Sequential Use of Interactive Video Instruction and Cooperative Learning: Effects on Achievement, Amount of Invested Mental Effort, and Attitudes.* Unpublished doctoral dissertation, Florida State University.

Williamson, S.R. (1996). "When Change is the Only Constant: Liberal Education in the Age of Technology." *Educom Review.* 31(6), 31–49.

Woods, D.R. (1994). *Problem-based Learning: How to Gain the Most from PBL.* Waterdown, ON: Donald R. Woods.

PART FOUR

· · · · · · · · ·

Assessing the
Cooperative Classroom

CHAPTER 11

Promoting Learning through
Responsible Assessment

"When you teach well, it always seems as if 75% of the students are above the median."

Jerome Bruner

When teachers are asked what they most dislike about teaching, a majority of them answer, "Grading." It is no wonder; probably no aspect of teaching has a greater impact on student learning than the grading system. Just within a single classroom, grades affect students' motivation to learn, their perceptions about the teacher's integrity, and their relationships with one another. Lowman (1984) calls grades "an unpleasant and unavoidable reality" for both teachers and students (p. 185). Pollio and Humphreys (1990) state:

> Grades, grading, and the uses made of them strongly affect the academic climate within which teaching and learning take place. With the exception of very few institutions, grades and the grading game are the basic facts of academic life for professors and students, and they influence in many and varied ways important interactions between teachers and learners (p. 109).

Grading pressure may be aggravated, ironically, by the cooperative classroom where the instructor assumes a benign, supportive role but still maintains the power to determine an athlete's eligibility to play, a scholarship student's financial status, or a would-be medical student's class ranking. McKeachie (1994) reminds us:

> The students' anxieties about grades are likely to rise if their instructor's procedures make them uncertain about what they must do in order to attain a good grade. For many students, democratic methods seem unorganized and ambiguous. In any ordinary course, students know they can pass by reading assignments and studying lecture notes, but in a student-centered class, they are in a course where the instructor doesn't lecture, doesn't make assignments, and doesn't even say which student comments are right or wrong. The student simply doesn't know what the instructor is trying to do. Thus, if your teaching and grading procedures differ from those your students are used to, you need to be especially careful to specify the procedures and criteria used in grading (p. 112).

Thus, faculty embracing cooperative-learning methods must be particularly explicit about the grading policies they establish and maintain, and, as emphasized in chapter 3, they must be equally careful about how they explain their grading system to students.

Assessment grading should also be carefully linked to the course objectives. Astin, Banta, Cross, El-Khawas, Hutchings, Marchese, McClenny, Mentkowski, Miller, Moran, and Wright (1992) note:

> Assessment is a goal-oriented process. It entails comparing educational performance with educational purposes and expectations—these derived from the institution's mission, from faculty intentions in program and course design, and from knowledge of students' own goals. . . . Clear, shared, implementable goals are the cornerstone for assessment that is focused and useful (p. 2).

Woods (1996) amplifies these thoughts: "The key issue is to assess students so that they learn what we want them to learn; so that they acquire the behaviours [sic] we desire as outcomes of the program" (p. 5-1). In a cooperative classroom, therefore, the grading practices should also encourage and reinforce cooperative practices.

NON-COMPETITIVE GRADING PRACTICES

Most experts agree about the practice of grading on the curve. McKeachie (1986) sums up their thinking: "Don't Do It!" (p. 105). Grading on the curve is essentially a quota system. Regardless of the class composition, instructors announce at the beginning of the term, "Only the top X percent of you will earn A grades. Those in the next X percent will receive B's, and so forth." Hanna and Cashin (1988) offer several compelling reasons why grading on the curve is inherently unfair and can undermine cooperative learning. First of all, unless students are intimately aware of the caliber of their fellow students, such a quota system gives them no indication of how hard they will need to work in order to achieve the grade they seek to earn. Furthermore, because some sections of the same course will often contain stronger students than others, the system penalizes all but the top students in the stronger sections. In small classes (15–20 students) this section-to-section sampling error can result in a one-grade difference for several students. Similarly, in classes composed of 30–50 students, this practice can adversely affect several students. Even in very large sections with several hundred students, where this sampling error is abated, grading on the curve may have other negative consequences. Students are forced to compete with one another even though learning itself is not inherently competitive. Because students are negatively interdependent (one student's success means than another student cannot be as successful), they have no vested reason to help each other learn, thus undercutting a cooperative philosophy. Besides encouraging students to undercut the learning of others, students can feel isolated and excluded. They may feel helpless as well, because their individual efforts are not directly connected with achievement (p. 2).

As an alternative to grading on the curve, teachers can set up a valid criterion referenced system based upon a point accumulation, with various elements of the course (quizzes, exams, homework, etc.) contributing toward the total. To lighten the paper load, homework contributions can be set up on a pass-fail basis, with students receiving the maximum number of points if the submissions are of sufficient quality. As emphasized earlier, such homework assignments will be directly related to course activities in a class predicated on sequenced learning. Thus, the points should be enough to motivate students to come prepared because they know that in-class "processing" activities related to the homework will occur. The points should not be so high, however, that final grades are compromised by a single missed assignment. At any time, students can determine their exact grade in the course by adding the total amount of points and determining the percentage needed for the grade for which they are aiming.

TWO ASSESSMENT ISSUES IN COOPERATIVE LEARNING

Extrinsic Versus Intrinsic Rewards

In the K–12 arena, there have been heavy debates about the efficacy and value of extrinsic versus intrinsic rewards. Chance (1992) makes a research-based plea for the value of extrinsic rewards:

> While intrinsic rewards are important . . . they are insufficient for efficient learning. Nor will encouragement and punishment fill the gap. The teacher must supplement intrinsic rewards with extrinsic rewards. This means not only telling the student when he or she has succeeded, but also praising, complimenting, applauding, and providing other forms of recognition for good work (p. 120).

After providing seven guidelines to follow in using extrinsic rewards, Chance concludes: "Reinforcement is probably the most powerful tool available to teachers, and extrinsic rewards are powerful reinforcers" (p. 121).

Kohn (1993b), the most celebrated advocate of the value of intrinsic motivation and of the debilitating effects of extrinsic awards, responded to Chance's article. The author of *No Contest: The Case against Competition* (1986) and *Punished by Rewards: The Trouble with Gold Stars, Incentive Plans, A's, Praise, and other Bribes* (1993a), Kohn argues that applied behaviorism ("Do this, you'll get that") undermines the incentive to learn. He cites research studies showing that people stop performing desired behaviors when the rewards stop. His article concludes with a plea for "an engaging curriculum that is connected to children's lives and interests: For an approach to pedagogy in which students are given real choices about their studies and for classrooms in which they are allowed and helped to work with one another" (p. 124).

In higher education, grades are the primary extrinsic motivators. No teacher who has heard the dreaded words, "Will this be on the exam?" can doubt their power. However, the research on intrinsic versus extrinsic rewards is clear, as we saw in the literature on deep learning. "An anxiety-provoking assessment system that rewards or tolerates regurgitation of factual material"—material students are not intrinsically motivated to learn—promotes shallow surface learning (Deep learning/Surface learning, 1993, p. 1). Forsyth and McMillan (1991) suggest that students' motivation to learn can be affected by a classroom structure that capitalizes on intrinsic motivation and avoids extrinsic motivators. Many of the extrinsic motivators, not unexpectedly, are grade-related. They recommend that instructors:

1. Use tests and other forms of evaluation to give students' information about their accomplishments, but not to exert control or deny students' autonomy.
2. Exercise care when describing the need for grades, since even subtle nuances can influence motivation.
3. Use the weakest extrinsic motivators possible. If you must use controlling methods—deadlines, pop quizzes, extra readings for poor performance, surveillance, penalties for nonattendance—then make certain that they are minimally sufficient to achieve compliance (Condry, 1987).
4. Minimize competition among students (pp. 54–56).

Creating a mastery orientation can also promote motivation to learn. Students need a sense of control over the final outcome. They should feel that they cause their own grades and can take positive steps to improve them (p. 56).

Like other experts, Forsyth and McMillan advise against norm-referenced grading (grading on the curve) (p. 58).

Group Grading

Assigning undifferentiated group grades is another controversial practice. Kagan (1995) argues that the purpose of grades is to indicate students' mastery of a given subject. "When grading is used for other reasons, " he contends, "to motivate, communicate with, or socialize students—grades lose their meaning" (p. 71). He argues that undifferentiated group grades for group projects are inherently unfair and unwise because: (1) students performing at an equal level may be penalized or rewarded by the performance of other students on their team; (2) group grades that partially reflect the ability of other students undermine the validity of report cards [college transcripts]; (3) students who are evaluated on forces beyond their control (the work of teammates) may be frustrated; (4) group grades undercut a key characteristic of cooperative learning, individual accountability; (5) group grades foster resistance to cooperative learning; and (6) undifferentiated group grades may well be illegal (pp. 69–71). The legality issue has surfaced in lawsuits when the grades of honor students expecting to earn A's were pulled down by less talented teammates.

Despite Kagan's misgivings, a number of instructors do factor final grades on a combination of individual and group results. Team Learning, discussed in chapter 9, follows this practice. Two of the simplest methods to factor in group efforts also build in positive interdependence as well as individual accountability. Both methods are predicated on the concept of recurring quizzes, where each student receives an individual score but can receive additional bonus points, which count toward an accumulated total that is based on the performance of all team members. In the first case, if all members of the class are potentially able to score within a certain range on quizzes, such as 90 percent, and time is allowed for peer coaching, then each team member receives x number of bonus points if all team members reach the desired score. If, however, the class fluctuates widely in ability level and prerequisite preparation, then using this system might create ill-will in teams containing members who cannot meet the stipulated score. In situations such as this, teachers can adopt a second alternative, awarding the bonus points for improvement gains after peer coaching. For example, four teammates who scored 100, 88, 89, and 67 (total 344) on the first quiz understand that each team member will receive one bonus point for each 10 points the team as a whole improves. Time is allowed for peer coaching within the team. The lowest achiever receives a lot of individualized coaching during this session, most of it from the highest achiever, who seeks the additional bonus points. The scores on the second quiz are now 100, 90, 91, and 84 (total 364), allowing each team member their individual score, plus two bonus points. Either of these two systems should be used only after careful thought. Keeler and Steinhorst (1995), for example, report dropping the use of bonus points in an introductory statistics course because they "feel that students see value in the group activity in and of itself without rewards" (p. 3).

Despite the fact that group tests are controversial, instructors who use them find that they alleviate much of the normal test anxiety. Further, the peer discussions that take place as students prepare their answers foster learning. There is evidence that students perform better on group tests than they do individually. (Geiger, 1991; Hendrickson, 1990; Keyworth, 1989; Michaelson, 1996; Toppins, 1989). Faculty use several approaches. The most common method is to have students take an exam individually and then, after submitting their answers, retake the exam as a team. Both grades count toward the final assessment. Creed (1991), a psychology professor at St. John's University and the College of St. Benedict in Minnesota, prefers that his students have their own exams available for reference. He thus distributes purple pens to all students for the individual exam and then collects them so that they cannot change their individual responses during the group discussion. In another variation of group testing, students prepare for an examination jointly, perhaps "jigsawing" possible essay questions, but they take the exam itself individually.

Giving group tests seems to be more justified than giving undifferentiated group grades for group projects. With group tests, individual contributions are reflected in the individual tests; however, they are rarely obvious in group projects. This is particularly true of projects that are done outside of class. Thus, we recommend against undifferentiated group grades for group projects. This is not to say that group tests or projects are not appropriate in a cooperative classroom. This recommendation also does not mean that students cannot be assessed on their individual contributions within a group. They certainly can be. What we argue against is accepting a group project, slapping a B or some other grade on it, and marking in the grade book a B for all team members without making an effort to determine the contributions of each group member. Such contributions can be assessed. The most common methods are individual assessment, peer assessment and self-assessment.

INDIVIDUAL ASSESSMENT

The literature on effective student evaluation is voluminous. Because one of the defining characteristics of cooperative learning is students' individual accountability, faculty may legitimately choose to grade students strictly on their individual achievements under traditional grading practices, including tests, quizzes, homework, individually produced term papers and projects, and student portfolios. Constructing a clear, fair, and functional evaluation system is challenging. Tests, for example, must exhibit both validity and reliability.

Grading students individually for their participation during group activities is problematical at best. The instructor cannot be involved with all groups at all times. In fact, few faculty can accurately monitor the behavior of more than two students at once. Therefore, students should not be assessed for their group contributions for each in-class activity.

Such activities, which constitute a large segment of sequenced learning, help students master the material. The end product, such as a team graphic organizer, can earn points based on the final product, but students should not be rewarded for "business as usual."' An expectation of cooperation and participation should be the class norm. If students raise participation points as an issue for each assignment completed, instructors can simply mention that Professor Graybeard down the hall does not assign participation points based on his students' attentiveness during his lecture.

No matter what system teachers eventually adopt, they should consider consulting some of the excellent resources on student assessment now available. Cashin (1994) has identified some recommended readings:

1. Clearly stating the objectives of the course: Angelo and Cross (1993), chapter 2; Davis (1993), chapters 2–3; Diamond (1989) entire book; Gronlund (1985), chapters 1–5; Lowman (1984), chapter 7; McKeachie (1994), chapter 2; Ryan and Martens (1989), entire book; Hanna and Cashin (1987); Hanna (1993), chapters 2–4.

2. Developing a test plan to be certain you test what you have taught: Jacobs and Chase (1992), chapter 1; Ory and Ryan (1993), chapters 1–2; Hanna (1993), chapters 1–4.

3. Improving essay, oral, and performance items: Davis (1993), chapter 31; Jacobs and Chase (1992), chapters 4–5; McKeachie (1994), chapter 6; Ory and Ryan (1993), chapter 4; Cashin, (1987); Hanna (1993), chapters 7–8.

4. Improving "objective" items: Davis (1993), chapter 30; Jacobs and Chase (1992), chapters 4-5; McKeachie (1994), chapter 6; Ory and Ryan (1993), chapter 3; Clegg and Cashin, 1986), and Hanna (1993), chapters 5–6.

PEER ASSESSMENT

Many faculty members committed to cooperative learning include peer assessment as a component of the final grade. There are many justifications for this practice, even though students, unless properly trained and similarly committed to the practice, may be hesitant about passing judgment on their peers.

Allowing student input into the process of evaluation sends several signals consistent with the cooperative-learning philosophy: (1) Teachers, because they are not the sole abiters of success or failure, play less of a gatekeeper role responsible for weeding out the unfit and the unworthy. The process of evaluation is shared; (2) Students are in a logical position to judge the individual contributions of their peers far more effectively than an instructor can; (3) Peer feedback is usually directed toward an individual within the context of a specific task. Besides being context-specific, it tends to be delivered promptly which is when feedback is most effective; (4) Peer evaluation builds in accountability: students realize that they are held accountable for their academic achievements and group contributions. They may be able to "psyche out" a teacher, but they can rarely hide from their peers. (5) Students benefit from the process of peer review. They learn valuable lessons about the learning process and about teamwork efforts.

Due to accountability and equity issues, teachers should carefully monitor any peer review process. Students must be assessing peers on attainable course objectives based on carefully specified criteria. They must also offer concrete evidence. Woods (1996) advocates training students to do such assessments and providing an environment where peers can give accurate feedback. He suggests: "Create an environment that rewards fair and accurate assessment. We can do this by making assessment a learning objective for the course. That is, students are assessed on their ability to assess others . . . The peer assessment is never considered to be 'Let's say nice things to our friends.' Rather it is a skill under development" (p. 5–9).

Peer assessment becomes even more meaningful when students have input and ownership over the process. For example, in business courses where performance appraisal is a topic of study, teams can develop their own criteria for evaluation and create an instrument which the team will use throughout the semester. Bavaro (1996) describes a process where students in a Health Services Planning and Evaluation course designed and executed their own peer assessment form to award appropriate individual grades for contributions toward a group project. As a first step, the students brainstormed the criteria for evaluation, which they collapsed into five broad areas: attendance, participation, preparation, cooperation, and attitude. The criteria were then defined through supporting standards and finally weighted. After the instrument was accepted by the class, other steps included establishing "ground rules" for its use and giving it a trial run to determine its validity and students' familiarity with it.

Peer review is obviously complex. Woods (1994; 1997) integrates peer review into virtually every aspect of his Problem-based Learning engineering classes. Feedback, whether given by himself or by peers, typically addresses five strengths for every two things that could be worked on. At the end of each group meeting, students complete a feedback form that looks at both their task performance and their group skills. The form reflects clearly thought-out criteria, such as the seven characteristics of valued group members:

1. Attend to both morale and task components.
2. Don't fight for leadership; leadership rotates among members.
3. Help the chairperson be effective.
4. Help the group evolve through the maturing process.
5. Assume the roles the group needs.
6. Reflect on each meeting.
7. Let others know of complications.
8. Clarify the roles of the tutor (pp. 5-8–5-11).

Chairpersons are routinely evaluated according to similarly specified criteria which include agenda-setting, facilitation of meetings, and responding to feedback (pp. 5-11–5-13). Woods (1997) also advocates a unique feedback approach where each student observes another during group processing activities and class discussions. Appendix B contains several sample peer- and self-assessment instruments.

Like Woods, Johnson and Johnson (1996) offer a number of well-constructed feedback forms with clearly specified criteria. They also discuss some unusual group assessment techniques such as group portfolios that can be used for peer and self-assessment.

SELF-ASSESSMENT

Researchers involved in determining ways of promoting deep learning have focused their attention on the students actually engaged in learning by observing, listening, and probing as students study in specific contexts. As Rhem (1995) concludes, "In the end, they [researchers] have focused on metacognition as the heart of learning and view it as a phenomenon more influenced by the demands of particular learning environments than by predispositions of personality" (p. 2). This recognition of the role metacognition plays in learning makes it desirable for teachers to include self-assessment opportunities in courses. Woods (1994) places self-assessment at the heart of learning. Students should learn to evaluate

1. The subject knowledge.
2. The problem solving skills used.
3. The group process used.
4. The chairperson skills displayed.
5. The acquisition of self-directed, interdependent, lifetime learning (p. 8-3).

With assessment comes accountability for both students and teachers. Assessments must be conducted responsibly based on measurable criteria, evidence, and objectivity. Woods (1994) notes:

> Self-assessment is one of the most powerful educational tools available. Being challenged to set personal learning goals motivates and focuses our energies. Having skills in the assessment process puts us at an enviable advantage for life (p. 8-5).

SUMMARY

In sequenced learning, students complete a task independently and then have opportunities to measure their learning, often through in-class activities with peers. Such activities can provide feedback on their learning. Too often, the teacher is thought to be the only one capable of providing viable assessment. In reality, however, when independent work and group work are involved, peer and self-assessment are even more meaningful.

As we will see in other chapters, responsible feedback is an essential part of a cooperative classroom. Faculty members need to clearly think through all assessment activities they design or empower their students to design. They must consider all of the issues, such as intrinsic versus extrinsic motivators and group grades. Assessment should never be considered an "add-on." It is an essential part of the learning process and, like it or not, of faculty work.

APPENDIX A

Cadet Grade Sheet
ENGL 111, US Air Force Academy
Dr. Barbara Millis

Name:

To determine your grade at any time in the course, please add up the total possible points. Then calculate 90% of that total to determine the range for an "A"; 80% for a "B"; 70% for a "C," etc. At the end of the course, you will have completed assignments totaling 400 possible points. The ranges in this total of 400 possible points are as follows:

400-360 points = 100 - 90% = A
359-320 points = 89 - 80% = B
319-280 points = 79 - 70% = C
279-240 points = 69 - 60% = D
Below 239 points = Failing Grade

Please calculate your current grade based on the possible points and continue to add up your scores as the course progresses. Because this is a course predicated on cooperation and peer coaching, all of you can potentially receive the grade for which you aspire.

Note: All homework assignments are intended to prepare you to write your next essay, not simply to add to the possible 50 points. Thus, homework MUST be submitted on time for credit. Doing the activities later in the term will not further your learning nor will it help your teammates who were expecting your contribution.

Here, as you recall from the syllabus, are the possible points in the course:

Essay #1	10% (50 pts)	LAN "idea" sessions	10% (50 pts)
Essay #2	10% (50 pts)	IP Points (Homework, etc.)	10% (50 pts)
Essay #3	15% (75 pts)		
Essay #4	20% (100 pts)		
Essay #5	25% (125 pts)		

Assignment	Poss Pts	My Pts
Critical Incident Writing Assignment	05	
Revision of the "Doolie" Paragraph	03	
Contrast Grid for Friere Essay	02	
Identification of Friere Thesis Statement	01	
Portfolio Reflective Statement # 1	02	
Essay Number One: "Friere as a Frame"	**50**	
Double Entry Journal (Pratt Essay)	02	
Double-Entry Journal (Jacobs Essay)	02	
Essay Two: "Framing the Past To Illuminate"	**50**	
Questions on Gaia, pp. 44-99	02	
Questions on Gaia, pp. 100-146	02	
Article Search Documentation for Essay Three (Gaia)	03	
Essay Three: "The Nature of Scientific Inquiry"	**75**	
Essay Four: "Cultures in Conflict"	**100**	
Thesis Statement for Paper #5	01	
Answering & Asking Questions/Research Proposal	05	
Essay Five: "Your Choice: Bringing It All Together"	**125**	
Revision of First LAN Essay	**25**	
Revision of Second LAN Essay	**25**	
Student Portfolio Reflection #2	20	
TOTAL POINTS FOR COURSE Possible and Earned	400	

Name: _____

Comments _____

APPENDIX B

Cooperative Learning Peer Evaluation Form

The following peer evaluation of your cooperative learning group members is a tool to help enhance your experience with cooperative learning. Its purpose is to determine those who have been active and cooperative members as well as to identify those who did not participate. Be consistent when evaluating each group member's performance by using the guidelines given below.

1-never	2-rarely	3-sometimes	4-usually	5-always

Has the student attended your cooperative
learning group on a regular basis?   1   2   3   4   5

Has the student made an effort at
assigned work?   1   2   3   4   5

Does the student attempt to make
contributions and/or seek help within
the group when he/she needs it?   1   2   3   4   5

Does the student cooperate with
group effort?   1   2   3   4   5

Name of the student being evaluated: _____

Group name (i.e. tens, aces, twos): _____

Source: Cooperative Learning and College Teaching. (Reprinted with permission.)

Feedback Form for Interdependent, Self-Directed Learning

Feedback to: _____ for Unit: _____ Date: _____
Present and on time: ... Present but late by _____ minutes Absent:

Quality of Knowledge: **good intellectual understanding of the topic, the material supplied was complete and appropriate.**

None of these   A few but major omissions   Most of these   All of these

_____
_____
_____

Quality of instruction: **he/she was here on time, the presentation was focused on the new knowledge, and a good choice of material and medium with effective communication and resource material was supplied.**

None of these   A few but major omissions   Most of these   All of these

_____
_____
_____

Follow-up: **As a result of this presentation, I believe the following action is appropriate on my part.**

Must study subject on my own. I learned nothing from your presentation.	Some self-study of the basics needed. I have some starting references from your presentation.	I received all about the basics that I need from your presentation. I do want to reflect about the ideas.

Strengths: Areas to improve on:

_____   _____
_____   _____
_____   _____

Woods, D.R. (1996). *Instructor's Guide for "Problem-based Learning: How to Gain the Most from PBL."*

Group Roles Feedback Form

TASK		♣	♦	♥	♠	W
		Group Members				
Observer—Task Process	Orients group, monitors, summarizes, seeks direction, identifies phases +					
	Ignores phases, pops off, blocks, unaware of contributors -					
Giver—Information Opinion	Assertively gives information, makes suggestions +					
	Withholds information, silent, aggressive or passive -					
Seeker—Information Opinion	Asks questions, asks for opinions, checks comprehension +					
Energizer—Risk Taker	Refuses to ask for information, silent - Enthusiastic, introduces spark, novel ideas +					
	Follower, agrees, silent, unsure -					
MORALE						
Observer—Group Processes	Sensitive to and comments on interpersonal dynamics +					
	Ignores conflicts and tension hoping that they will disappear -					
Giver—Praise, Support	Warm, responsive, gives help, rewards +					
	Puts down peers, aggressive, self-centered, defensive -					
Seeker—Conflict Resolver	Mediates, harmonizes, helps resolve conflicts +					
	Causes problems, seeks personal goals -					
Energizer—Tension	Jokes, laughs, shows satisfaction +					
Relief	Withdraws, causes tension -					

Strengths: Areas to work on:

_____   _____

_____   _____

_____   _____

Woods, D.R. (1996). *Instructor's Guide for "Problem-based Learning: How to Gain the Most from PBL."*

REFERENCES

Angelo, T.A. and Cross, K.P. (1993). *Classroom Assessment Techniques: A Handbook for College Teachers.* 2nd Ed. San Francisco: Jossey-Bass.

Astin, A.W., Banta, T.W., Cross, K.P., El-Khawas, E., Ewell, P.T., Hutchings, P., Marchese, T.J., McClenny, K.M., Mentkowski, M., Miller, M.A., Moran, E.T., and Wright, B.D. (1992). *Principles of Good Practice for Assessing Student Learning.* Washington, DC: American Association of Higher Education.

Bavaro, J.A. (1996). "Exploring One Approach to Evaluating Group Work at the University Level." Unpublished manuscript.

Cashin, W.E. (1987). *Improving Essay Tests.* IDEA Paper No. 17. Manhattan, KS: Center for Faculty Evaluation and Development, Division of Continuing Education, Kansas State University.

Cashin, W.E. (1994). *Readings to Improve Selected Teaching Methods.* IDEA Paper No. 30. Manhattan, KS: Center for Faculty Evaluation and Development, Division of Continuing Education, Kansas State University.

Chance, P. (1992, Nov.). "The Rewards of Learning." *Phi Delta Kappan,* 200–07. Reprinted in *Educational Psychology 97/98 Annual Editions* (pp. 117–21). Guilford, CT: Duskin/ McGraw-Hill.

Clegg, V.L. and Cashin, W.E. (1986). *Improving Multiple Choice Tests.* IDEA Paper No. 16. Manhattan, KS: Center for Faculty Evaluation and Development, Division of Continuing Education, Kansas State University.

Condry, J. (1987). "Enhancing Motivation: A Social Development Perspective. In M.L. Maehr and D.A. Kleiber (Eds.), *Advances in Motivation and Achievement. Vol. 5. Enhancing Motivation.* Greenwich, CT: JAI Press.

Creed, T. (1991). "A Teaching Strategy. In B. Millis (Ed.), *The Bright Idea Network,* 6th Ed. The Professional and Organizational Development Network in Higher Education.

Davis, B.G. (1993). *Tools for Teaching.* San Francisco: Jossey-Bass.

"Deep Learning, Surface Learning." (1993). *AAHE Bulletin,* 45(8), 14–17.

Diamond, R.M. (1989). *Designing and Improving Courses and Curricula in Higher Education: A Systematic Approach.* San Francisco: Jossey-Bass.

Forsyth, D.R. and McMillan, J.H. (1991a). "Practical Proposals for Motivating Students." In R.J. Menges and M.D. Svinicki (Eds.), *College Teaching: From Theory to Practice. New Directions for Teaching and Learning,* No. 45 (pp. 53–65). San Francisco: Jossey-Bass.

Geiger, T. (1991). "Test Partners: A Formula for Success." *Innovation Abstracts: A Newsletter Published by the College of Education, University of Texas at Austin,* 13(11).

Gronlund, N.E. (1985). *Stating Objectives for Classroom Instruction.* 3rd Ed. New York: Macmillan.

Hanna, G.S. (1993). *Better Teaching through Better Testing.* Fort Worth, TX: Harcourt Brace Jovanovich.

Hanna, G.S. and Cashin, W.E. (1987). *Matching Instructional Objectives, Subject Matter, Tests, and Score Interpretation.* IDEA Paper No. 18. Manhattan, KS: Center for Faculty Evaluation and Development, Division of Continuing Education, Kansas State University.

Hanna, G.S. and Cashin, W.E. (1988). *Improving College Grading.* IDEA Paper No. 19. Manhattan, KS: Center for Faculty Evaluation and Development, Division of Continuing Education, Kansas State University.

Hendrickson, A.D. (1990). "Cooperative Group Test-taking." *Focus*, 5(2), 6. (Faculty Newsletter by the Office of Educational Development Programs, University of Minnesota).

Jacobs, L.C. and Chase, C.I. (1992). *Developing and Using Tests Effectively: A Guide for Faculty.* San Francisco: Jossey-Bass.

Johnson, D.W. and Johnson, R.T. (1996). *Meaningful and Manageable Assessment through Cooperative Learning.* Edina, MN: Interaction Book Company.

Kagan, S. (1995). "Group Grades Miss the Mark." *Educational Leadership*, 52(8), 68–71.

Keeler, C.M. and Steinhorst, R. K. (1995). "Using Small Groups to Promote Active Learning in the Introductory Statistics Course: A Report from the Field." *Journal of Statistics Education*, 3(2). On-line, Online at <http://fisher.stat.unipg.it/ncsu/info/jse/v3n2/keeler.html>. Downloaded 27 Feb. 1997. No longer available.

Keyworth, D.R. (1989). "The Group Test." *Teaching Professor*, 3(8), 5.

Kohn, A. (1986). *No Contest: The Case against Competition.* Boston: Houghton Mifflin.

Kohn, A. (1993a). *Punished by Rewards: The Trouble with Gold Stars, Incentive Plans, A's, Praise, and other Bribes.* Boston: Houghton Mifflin.

Kohn, A. (1993b, June). "Rewards versus Learning: A Response to Paul Chance." *Phi Delta Kappan.* (783–87). Reprinted in *Educational Psychology 97/98 Annual Editions.* (122–25). Guilford, CT: Duskin/McGraw-Hill.

Lowman, J. (1984). *Mastering the Techniques of Teaching.* San Francisco: Jossey-Bass.

McKeachie, W.J. (1986). *Teaching Tips: Strategies, Research, and Theory for College and University Teachers.* 8th Ed. Lexington, MA: D. C. Heath.

McKeachie, W.J. (1994). *Teaching Tips: Strategies, Research, and Theory for College and University Teachers.* 9th Ed. Lexington, MA: D. C. Heath.

Michaelsen, L. (1996). *Problems with Learning Groups: An Ounce of Prevention.* Preconference Workshop. Annual Conference of the Professional and Organizational Development Network in Higher Education. Snowbird Resort and Conference Center, Salt Lake City, UT.

Ory, J.C. and Ryan, K.E. (1993). *Tips for Improving Testing and Grading.* Newbury Park, CA: Sage Publications.

Pollio, H.R. and Humphreys, W.L. (1990). "Grading Students." In M. Weimer and R.A. Neff (Eds.), *Teaching College: Collected Readings for the New Instructor.* (109–16) Madison, WI.: Magna Publications.

Rhem, J. (1995). "Deep/surface Approaches to Learning: An Introduction." *The National Teaching and Learning Forum*, 5(1), 1–3.

Ryan, M. P. and Martens, G. G. (1989). *Planning a College Course: A Guidebook for the Graduate Teaching Assistant.* Ann Arbor: University of Michigan, National Center for Research to Improve Postsecondary Teaching and Learning.

Toppins, A.D. (1989). "Teaching by Testing: A Group Consensus Approach." *College Teaching*, 37(3), 96–99.

Woods, D.R. (1994). *Problem-based Learning: How to Gain the Most from PBL.* Waterdown, ON: Donald R. Woods.

Woods, D.R. (1996). *Instructor's Guide for "Problem-based Learning: How to Gain the Most from PBL."* 3rd Ed. Online at <http://chemeng.mcmaster.ca/pbl/pbl.htm>. Downloaded 14 Jan. 1997.

Woods, D.R. (1997). Two-day workshop on Problem-Based Learning, U.S. Air Force Academy, Jan. 12–14.

CHAPTER 12

Using Teacher-Collected Assessment Data to Strengthen Cooperative Courses

"I have come to the conviction that if you cannot translate your thoughts into uneducated prose, then your thoughts are confused."

C. S. Lewis

Faculty who have successfully integrated cooperative-learning structures into their classrooms will, by the nature of the student and pedagogical challenges, keep their teaching skills dynamic. They will continue to grow professionally as they move from the old paradigms of teaching toward views that are more student-centered and that foster an atmosphere of community and cooperation. Dynamic teachers never become complacent, however, which is why assessment is so critical to professional growth. Assessment can occur on many levels.

In this chapter, we will explore assessment practices that can shape instructor decisions about course enhancement. The focus is not just on graded activities, but also on those that offer instructors concrete feedback about all aspects of the course. Such activities are divided into two kinds: (1) those that teachers can conduct and (2) those that require the assistance of an outside colleague. The former activities are based on Classroom Assessment Techniques (CATs), communication tools that enable teachers to test the pulse and climate of the learning communities they create. Such practices augment and enhance cooperative-learning structures and create a better learning environment for college students and instructors alike. Although Classroom Assessment Techniques are often more productive and satisfying when peers are involved, they do not require an outside consultant. Because they are teacher-directed, CATs are integrated into the course curriculum. Like all good assessment practices, they are context-specific.

THE NATURE OF ASSESSMENT

Assessment decisions affect virtually all aspects of learning because they send clear signals to students about what teachers value. Assessment differs from evaluative data in which instructors essentially judge students' levels of performance and their mastery of specified learning outcomes. Evaluation always involves assessment, but not all assessments are evaluative in nature. Assessment can be used at three stages in a learning process. Diagnostic assessment at the beginning of a learning unit helps to discover students' entry-level knowledge, skills, attitudes, or values. Formative assessments are ongoing efforts to measure progress toward learning goals. They offer both students and teachers concrete feedback that can shape the future direction of teaching and learning efforts. Summative assessment, which occurs at the end of a learning unit or semester, provides evidence of the achievement of specified learning goals or objectives.

Johnson and Johnson (1996) recommend that teachers wishing to plan, conduct, and manage meaningful assessments in cooperative classrooms respond to these key questions:

1. What are the student performances that may be assessed?
2. What are the assessment procedures that may be used?
3. What is the purpose of the assessment?
4. What is the focus of the assessment?
5. In what setting will the assessment be conducted?
6. How will these questions be answered so a meaningful assessment results?
7. How will these questions be answered so that assessment is manageable?
8. How will cooperative learning make the assessment more meaningful and manageable (p. 1:2)?

Such questions can affect decisions about what to assess and how to go about it. As Barr and Tagg (1995) point out, "The place to start the assessment of learning outcomes is in the conventional classroom: from there, let the practice grow to the program and institutional levels" (p. 25). Teachers will find that the Classroom Assessment Techniques that follow offer practical, innovative ways to conduct meaningful assessment within their own classrooms.

CLASSROOM ASSESSMENT TECHNIQUES

Classroom Assessment Techniques (Angelo and Cross, 1993) provide instructors with a systematic, student-centered way to find out if and how well students are learning. This type of assessment check is particularly important when instructors adopt new classroom approaches, such as cooperative learning. As Angelo (1994) notes, "As teachers committed to improving student learning, each of us needs ways to find out how well CL [cooperative learning] works for the particular students in our classes" (p. 5). Classroom Assessment Techniques give instructors a particularly useful way to ascertain the effectiveness of new teaching methods, such as cooperative learning, with which they are experimenting.

Using Classroom Assessment Techniques offers at least three benefits to students and teachers. First of all, because students are involved in the CAT activities and receive feedback on their responses, they become actively involved in assessing their own learning. According to Angelo and Cross (1993), faculty report these "four observable, interrelated, positive effects of Classroom Assessment Techniques on their students: more active involvement and participation; greater interest in learning, self-awareness as learners, and metacognitive skill; higher levels of cooperation within the classroom 'learning community'; and greater student satisfaction" (p. 372). These factors also contribute to the group-processing function of cooperative learning.

Second, because these techniques encourage faculty to experiment with and vary their teaching approaches, students tend to enjoy the learning experience more. As Duffy and Jones (1995) point out, instructors must work to stimulate and motivate students, particularly during the interim weeks of a semester, when it may become necessary to beat the doldrums.

Third, teachers receive richer personal rewards by turning teaching into a dynamic and intellectually stimulating activity in its own right. They begin practicing in a systematic, proactive way the Scholarship of Teaching advocated by Boyer (1990) and others.

To use Classroom Assessment Techniques successfully, instructors must keep in mind that these techniques are designed to find out how well students are learning and, based on this information, to make midcourse adjustments in teaching to improve their learning. Cross (1993), for example, distinguishes this kind of interventionist assessment from traditional assessment which seeks only to evaluate after the fact. Angelo and Cross (1993) emphasize that classroom assessment involves an ongoing, formative cycle with planning, implementing, and responding stages.

CATs must be placed in the overall context of the learning environment as outlined in Figure 12.1. Students and professors interact in a dynamic area where goals are established, knowledge and attitudes assessed, and changes made to promote greater learning. Students and professors work together, based on evidence provided by the CATs, to strengthen learning.

Many Classroom Assessment Techniques are particularly useful for the cooperative-learning environment. These include techniques designed to be used at the beginning of the course, techniques designed to assess the group processing function of cooperative learning, and techniques designed to assess student learning of specific material or comprehension of learning objectives.

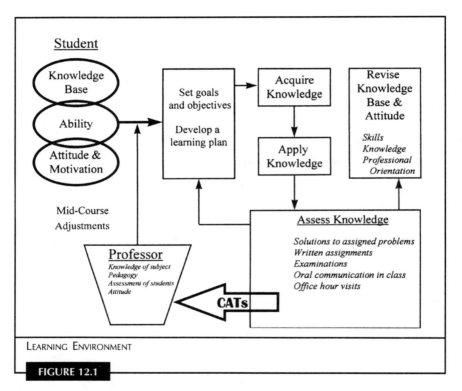

FIGURE 12.1

CATS USEFUL FOR COURSE BEGINNINGS

Seasoned instructors know the importance of a strong start at the opening of a college course. The first day of class is particularly important. Davis (1993), for example, recommends conveying enthusiasm for the material; creating a "relaxed, open classroom environment conducive to inquiry and participation," and laying out clear expectations (p. 20). During the first week or two of class, it is important to build on these first impressions. Several Classroom

Assessment Techniques assist faculty in this regard. The Goal Ranking and Matching Exercise discussed in chapter 3 establishes communication between instructors and students with respect to course expectations. The data help instructors understand student assumptions of which they may have been unaware.

Other techniques, such as the Background Knowledge Probe, Focused Autobiographical Sketches, and Interest/Knowledge/Skills Checklists, can assist faculty with heterogeneous team formation and inform them of the subject knowledge that students bring to the course.

Background Knowledge Probe

According to Angelo and Cross (1993, pp. 121–25), the Background Knowledge Probe serves teachers by helping them determine the most effective point at which to begin instruction. By sampling students' background knowledge before formal instruction on a topic begins, this CAT also provides feedback on the range of preparation among students in the class. This dual feature of the Background Knowledge Probe makes it particularly valuable to the cooperative-learning practitioner because of the appropriate-grouping component of cooperative learning.

The Background Knowledge Probe consists of a short questionnaire to which the students respond on the first day of class. By evaluating these responses, teachers get an idea of the knowledge and experiences students bring to the class at the outset. Teachers should carefully develop the questions with this objective in mind. Before initiating the Background Knowledge Probe, instructors should reflect upon the knowledge they would like students to have at the beginning of the course. Often, we credit students with knowledge they do not possess, especially about a topic familiar to us. If we falsely assume certain background competencies, we may teach at an inappropriate level, overwhelming students with information that they cannot connect to prior knowledge.

It is helpful to include four kinds of questions in a Background Knowledge Probe. The first type of question is a personalized "warm-up," such as asking students in their first accounting course to describe a typical accountant. The second type of question assesses students' preconceptions and misconceptions. For example, students in an American history course might be asked what political factors contributed to the outbreak of the Civil War, or students in an astronomy or physics class could be asked why the days grow colder in winter.

The third type of question probes subject-related knowledge. For example, in a course on *Paradise Lost*, students should have some knowledge of the political climate in England during John Milton's life. The instructor may also wish to ask students some specific questions about the English Restoration. These subject-related questions should be at varying levels of difficulty. One should be of the most elementary nature, a question the instructor expects almost all students to answer correctly. Another should be one to which only a few students will give an accurate response. This question can serve a dual purpose if it is used later in the class period to generate discussion. The instructor rounds out the questionnaire with a couple of questions in-between. It helps to choose questions that will subsequently be addressed in the course material, so that the instructor can refer back to what the students knew on that first day.

The fourth type of question is one that students answer by identifying information they have heard from others and/or telling what they expect from the class. This question provides a nice transition to the course objectives, policies, and other syllabus-related matters.

Questions suitable for an introductory accounting course are:

- What is an accountant?
- How does one determine whether a business is successful?
- What is an asset?
- What is a liability?
- How does cash-flow from operations differ from net income?
- What do you hope to learn in this course?

As with all CATs, Background Knowledge Probes are designed to be formative rather than evaluative. Teachers must therefore take care to design and administer this CAT so that students do not feel as though they are taking a test. Several techniques will accomplish this objective. Perhaps the simplest is to have the students complete the Background Knowledge Probes anonymously. However, anonymous responses turned in to the instructor generally preclude further use of the Background Knowledge Probe in group formation or as a method to document individual student learning.

A second approach is to have the students complete the Background Knowledge Probe individually, but then form temporary groups where they prepare a group response to turn in to the instructor. As with the anonymous submissions, this approach curtails the teacher's ability to use the Background Knowledge Probes for permanent group formation. However, the students can retain their individual responses, thus allowing teachers to demonstrate to them their learning progress throughout the semester.

The preferred approach is to have students complete and turn in individual, signed responses to the Background Knowledge Probe. Usually, a forthright statement about the purpose of the Background Knowledge Probe allays student concerns about being judged on their responses.

Having collected individual responses on the Background Knowledge Probe, the instructor evaluates the student answers and divides them into groups. Angelo and Cross (1993) suggest four piles for Background Knowledge Probes—

[−1] erroneous background knowledge; [0] no relevant background knowledge; [+1] some relevant background knowledge; [+2] significant background knowledge. The instructor can assign students to heterogeneous structured-learning teams by selecting one questionnaire from each pile. At this point, the instructor may wish to use other factors such as student gender, ethnicity, or other background characteristics to increase diversity.

As the semester or quarter ends, teachers have an opportunity to make students aware of their progress. During the class before the final exam, instructors repeat the Background Knowledge Probe, perhaps changing the questions a bit so that students do not recognize them immediately. After the students have completed the instrument, teachers may pass back the original Background Knowledge Probes or ask students to retrieve them from their files. Comparing the before and after instruments gives students the opportunity to reflect on their own learning progress. After such an exercise, many students make remarks like, "I had no idea I had learned so much."

Focused Autobiographical Sketches

A Focused Autobiographical Sketch (Angelo and Cross, 1993) is a short (one or two pages) essay that focuses on a learning episode relevant to the course at hand. If offers specific information about the "students' self-concept and self-awareness within a specified field" (p. 281). As with Background Knowledge Probes, Focused Autobiographical Sketches provide useful data about students' prior knowledge and experiences. More important, this approach also suggests the levels of self-awareness and reflectiveness among students in the class.

An example provided by Angelo and Cross (1993) offers a creative, cooperative use of this technique:

> In a graduate course on leadership skills for mid-career public administrators, the instructor's central goals were to help her students become more explicitly and critically aware of their preconceptions about leadership. In an attempt to determine an appropriate starting point for the class, as well as to collect "pretest" data for later comparison, she asked each student, during the first week of class, to write a one-or-two page Focused Autobiographical Sketch. The specific assignment was:
>
> Write one or two pages—not more—relating and discussing a recent experience in which you exercised leadership in a public context and learned something significant about leadership from your success. Focus not only on what you learned but also on how and why you learned about leadership from that particular experience. What does it suggest about learning how to lead?
>
> During the next class meeting, after she had analyzed and summarized their responses in general terms, the public administration professor divided the large class into prearranged small groups, which she had

structured. Each group of five contained individuals with quite different leadership experiences. The members of each group were to recount their stories very briefly and then extract any common, general principles for learning leadership skills (p. 282).

Other disciplines tailor these sketches accordingly. For example, students in a graduate-level course on College Teaching write an essay similar to the Critical Incident Activity described by Brookfield (1991): Think of two teaching experiences, one that left you feeling good about your teaching and another that left you feeling dissatisfied. Briefly describe each of these experiences. Why was each one satisfying/dissatisfying to you? What contributed to the success of the satisfying experience and the failure of the dissatisfying experience? In another example, students in a public speaking class describe a successful public speaking experience, analyzing those elements that made it successful and reflecting on how they felt before, during, and after it.

Interest/Knowledge/Skills Checklists

Interest/Knowledge/Skills checklists (Angelo and Cross, 1993, pp. 185–289) are modeled after the interest and skills inventories used by guidance and career counselors. They are useful in courses with some flexibility in course construction. The instructor identifies potential topics for her course and the related skills or knowledge students would acquire. The skills or knowledge must then be coded to match the possible topics. Appendix A provides an example of an adaptation of this CAT for a capstone course in accounting.

CATS USEFUL FOR ASSESSING GROUP PROCESSING

Because it is a critical component of cooperative learning, college faculty should judge the effectiveness of the groups in the cooperative classroom. The most effective way to keep track of these vital leadership, decision-making, communication, and conflict-resolution skills is through vigilant group monitoring. However, often this technique alone is not enough, since students may behave differently in the presence of the instructor. Instructors will therefore want to gather from the students their perceptions of how well the groups are progressing and how well the instructor is accomplishing teaching through groups. Two CATs can assist with these goals.

Group Instructional Feedback Technique (GIFT)

Angelo (1994) suggests three simple questions for this CAT: (1) "What specific things do I do that really help you learn from group work? (2) What specific things do I do that make it more difficult for you to learn from group work? and (3) What are one or two specific, practical changes that we could make to help you learn better in your group?" Properly administered, the GIFT not only can provide feedback when there are problems in a class, it also gives students a chance to take more responsibility for suggesting solutions. If students are given timely feedback, they can compare their responses to those of their classmates, particularly those in their structured-learning teams. In an even simpler variation, teachers ask students to identify things they should "stop," "start," and "continue."

Group Processing Form

This CAT is designed to collect feedback from students about the interactions, individual responsibilities, and positive interdependence they perceive in their cooperative-learning groups. This information shows teachers what is going well in the groups and what is not, so that potentially destructive conflicts can be discovered and defused. Both faculty and students gain insights into the group process. A sample form used by one instructor is shown in Appendix B. The form can easily be adapted to include questions on any skills the instructor wants students to develop.

CATS DESIGNED TO ASSESS STUDENT LEARNING

The primary purpose of classroom assessment is to provide faculty and students with the information and insights needed to improve teaching effectiveness and learning quality. Faculty analyze feedback gleaned from Classroom Assessment Techniques and use it to make adjustments in their teaching. They also share that feedback with the students in order to help them improve their learning strategies, learning skills, and study habits.

While classroom assessment is appropriate for all faculty, regardless of the pedagogy used, it meshes particularly well with cooperative learning. In this section, we will focus on CATs that have been particularly successful in cooperative-learning classrooms.

Minute Paper

Instructors use the Minute Paper (Angelo and Cross, 1993, pp. 148–53) to get written feedback on two or three questions about a specific class session. Instructors typically ask variants to two questions: "What was the most important thing you learned today?" and "What questions still remain unanswered?" In reality, the Minute Paper usually takes three to five minutes, depending on the difficulty of the learning to be assessed. For example, after assigning a complex chapter as advance reading, the teacher of an art history course asks students as a Structured Problem-Solving activity to produce paragraphs discussing three defining characteristics of Impressionism, followed in each case by two specific examples. She then uses a Three-Stay, One-Stray report-out method, with the reporter from each group rotating to another to share their team's responses. Although the instructor has been monitoring the working groups to avoid misinformation, she wants to ascertain exactly how each student feels about mastery of the material. For this reason, she decides to use a Minute Paper. Toward the end of class, she distributes index cards and asks students to provide three pieces of information: (1) Select a number from one to five, with five being the most confident, to describe your level of understanding about Impressionism. (2) What was the most important thing about Impressionism you learned today? (3) What questions about Impressionism still remain unanswered? She tells students that they have five minutes to complete their cards, responding with phrases or short sentences. "I'll share the feedback with you during our next class period," she says with a smile.

Instructors should give students the option of responding anonymously on the Minute Papers. Responses are usually divided about evenly between those signed and those unsigned. As a result, instructors may want to use two methods of communicating feedback to students. For those students who are unclear about material and provide their names, teachers can write brief responses to their queries on the backs of the cards. These responses may consist of references to the appropriate textbook pages, short explanations, or invitations to discuss the questions during an appointment.

Instructors must respond indirectly to those students who choose not to divulge their names. They can search for commonalities among the questions and concerns expressed on the cards, preparing a whole-class response when three or four cards raise essentially the same question. For example, after reviewing the index cards, the art history teacher discovered that most students felt reasonably confident that they understood the characteristics of Impressionism (the mean on that question was 4.2). However, 60 percent of the class raised questions about the Impressionists' use of light as the source of color. The teacher therefore decided to deliver a 15-minute mini-lecture, with illustrative slides, on this topic at the beginning of the next period.

As students grow accustomed to the idea that they must identify and express concepts and pinpoint things that remain unclear, they focus more upon their own learning processes. This metacognitive awareness helps them become better learners. Moreover, because they are constantly assessing their own progress, they are less likely to flounder unknowingly. Students who respond to questions about learning in structured-learning teams also acquire a greater appreciation for community and the value of learning from peers.

Instructors find that Minute Papers keep them close to the pulse of the classroom. They become aware of academic and, sometimes, group dynamic problems. Their concern and their responsiveness help build student rapport and trust.

Muddiest Point

This CAT (Angelo, 1993, pp. 154–58) is a variation of the Minute Paper. As its name suggests, it provides information to the instructor about what students find least clear about a particular lesson or topic. Faculty use this feedback to discover which points are most difficult for students to learn and to guide decisions about what topics to emphasize and how much time to spend on each. In response to this CAT, learners quickly identify what they do not understand and articulate those "muddy points." Consequently, student responses require some higher-order thinking even though, like the Minute Paper, the technique is easy to administer. It is also remarkably efficient, providing a high information return for a very low investment of time and energy.

Instructors distribute index cards or half-sheets of paper (or place them in the team folders) and ask the students a single question. For example, a teacher might pose the following question after a short lecture: "What was the most confusing point in the lecture you just heard?" The focus of the muddiest point could be a lecture, a discussion, a film, a homework assignment, or a topic explored in cooperative-learning groups.

Feedback/Participation Form

A more elaborate adaptation of the Minute Paper, a Feedback/Participation Form, sometimes called a Teacher-Designed Feedback Form (Angelo, 1993, pp. 330–33), is particularly well-suited to the cooperative-learning environment. On this form, faculty ask students specific questions that explore the students' understanding of course content. The form may also be used by students to ask questions that have arisen in their studies, in a lecture, or in group work.

The Feedback/Participation Forms offer faculty the flexibility to probe student understanding of the course content while assessing group processing. Instructors will find an example of the form at Appendix C. The form may be easily modified to fit any classroom situation and/or instructor question. Changing the form from time to time discourages students from simply checking the boxes rather than carefully considering the questions.

Directed Paraphrasing

Instructors use Directed Paraphrasing (Angelo and Cross, 1993, pp. 232–35) to determine the degree to which students have understood and internalized the main point of a learning objective. From the students' attempts to concisely paraphrase a concept, instructors learn how well they have understood it. Directed Paraphrases are particularly useful for assessing students' understanding of important topics that they will later explain to others, making this

CAT an exercise in "authentic learning." Many professions involve the communication of complex ideas to lay persons.

To initiate this assessment technique, instructors select a point in the course after the completion of a major reading assignment, an important lecture, or a complex cooperative-learning activity. Instructors identify a realistic, yet challenging audience and also give students time and space limits for the paraphrase. For example, nursing students may be asked to paraphrase a definition of *lupus vulgaris* as though they were explaining the nature of this disease to a teenage girl and her mother. Special education students might be asked to offer a Directed Paraphrase of the meaning of an Individualized Education Program (IEP) to third grade teachers at a local elementary school.

The Directed Paraphrase usually takes the form of a short written exercise that students turn in to the instructor. After the paraphrases are complete, the instructors must provide feedback, so that students will know how well they are mastering the material. Angelo and Cross (1993) recommend that responses be sorted into four categories, "confused," "minimal," "adequate," and "excellent," with a focus on the accuracy of the paraphrase, its appropriateness for the target audience, and its efficacy.

To extend the value of a Directed Paraphrase, faculty can combine it with a Think-Pair-Share activity, enabling students to receive feedback from one another as well. Directed Paraphrasing allows teachers to find out quickly, and in some detail, how well students have understood a given learning objective. These responses force both teachers and students to consider the wider relevance of the topic being studied and the necessity of weighing the needs and interests of the intended audience.

Focused Listing

As the name implies, this CAT (Angelo and Cross, pp. 126–31) directs students to list several ideas or major points concerning a key concept in the course. The feedback collected allows faculty to quickly determine what students recall as the most important points related to a particular topic. Repeated use of Focused Listing activities can help students learn to center their attention and strive to improve their retrieval of important course information. Faculty may use a cooperative-learning structure, such as Think-Pair-Square, to strengthen student learning outcomes while gathering important assessment feedback. Teachers can employ Focused Listing to gauge starting points, to make midpoint corrections, and to measure the class's progress in learning specific aspects of the course content. Topics are virtually unlimited: "Osmosis," "Sampling Strategies," "Situational Leadership," "Parody," "Correlational Research," "Truss," "Anorexia."

To initiate Focused Listing, the instructor selects an important topic or concept that the class has just studied, or is about to study. The instructor describes this concept in a brief word or phrase which the students write as the heading of their focused list. Having been given a time constraint or a limit as to the number of items, the students list important words or phrases related to the main point on their individual paper. Alternatively, a cooperative-learning structure, such as Roundtable, may be used to help students glean group understanding of the most important concept. While the students are working on their lists, instructors may make wish to complete a list under the same time constraints as the students. They can then structure a comparison of their "expert" list with those generated by individual students or student groups. Such comparisons often reinforce the students' sense of competence. If there are key discrepancies, however, between the students' lists and the teacher's list, these deficiencies can serve as a "wake-up call" to both parties.

Pro and Con Grid

Most disciplines contain content areas where a particular course of action has benefits and drawbacks. In such cases, students' understanding of a topic may depend on their awareness of more than one side of an issue. As virtually every student development model suggests, this awareness is a difficult but valuable step in students' intellectual development. The Pro and Con Grid (Angelo and Cross, 1993, pp. 168–71) gives faculty a quick overview of the class's analysis of an issue while providing important information on the depth and breadth of the students' analyses and their capacities for objectivity.

To use this CAT, instructors focus on a decision, a judgment, a dilemma, or an issue which has learning implications in the course. The instructor writes a prompt that asks students to list the two sides of the issue. This CAT is usually more effective if instructors tell students how many pros and cons they expect. Some examples might be:

- The U.S. decision to invade Grenada involved a number of complex factors. List three arguments in favor of the invasion and three in favor of non-intervention.
- Nora in Ibsen's *Doll House* decides to leave her husband. Give three reasons justifying her action and three reasons, given the societal context of the time, why she should have remained.
- Read this detailed case study of a third grader who continually causes problems at school. List two reasons to prescribe Ritalin and two reasons to adopt more conservative treatment.
- Study the given scenario from South America where economic needs conflict with ecological ones. Give three reasons for and three reasons against the continued harvesting of rain forests in the area.
- Psychoanalysis as a form of therapy has been a controversial practice. Give three reasons to support the use of psychoanalysis and three reasons to argue against it.

- A client firm is considering adopting LIFO inventory. Give three reasons in favor of this decision and three arguments against it.
- Certain books, such as *The Adventures of Huckleberry Finn* and *I Know Why the Caged Bird Sings* have caused controversy in public school systems. Give reasons for and against requiring students to read books to which their parents may object.

Self-Diagnostic Learning Logs

Instructors may view Self-Diagnostic Learning Logs (Angelo and Cross, 1993, pp. 311–15) as limited, tightly focused versions of academic journals. Although Angelo and Cross recommend ongoing logs, instructors can use them for specific assignments, such as a complex problem or case from the course text. Instructors explain to students that the purpose of their learning log is to enhance their ability to learn course concepts and principles and to assist them in becoming reflective, self-directed learners. On the day the problems or cases are due, students hand in a one-page learning log report that answers the following questions: (1) Which course concept or principle that you learned from lectures, from your work in your structured-learning team, or from studying the current chapter, did you find useful in working the current case or problem? (2) Which course concept or principle that you previously learned did this new concept or principle build upon? (3) If you experienced difficulty or were unable to work the problem or case, what information or knowledge would have enhanced your ability to work it?

Students writing learning logs are forced to identify and communicate the course concepts they are applying. They therefore learn these concepts and principles to a much fuller extent than they would by simply focusing on the end solution to a problem or case. Their learning is further reinforced if the students spend a few minutes discussing their learning logs in their teams. This discussion aids in the group-processing element of cooperative learning, but it also helps students identify and support team members who are struggling. Because of the focus questions, teammates can more readily diagnose difficulties.

Instructors also benefit from these added insights because they identify specific course concepts that confuse many students and then respond with carefully focused instruction. Moreover, the learning logs cause students to practice and improve their writing skills, particularly in quantitative disciplines, thus enhancing their marketability in a world that relies more and more heavily on rapid and effective communication.

What Did I Learn from the Exam?

This exam-oriented adaptation of the Self-Diagnostic Learning Log serves two useful purposes. First, students are prompted to view a course examination in a fuller context than the typical "What grade did I get?" response. The process of completing this CAT helps them analyze their own successes and failures while reinforcing the value of productive study habits and learning skills. Sharing appropriate portions of the log in cooperative-learning groups gives students access to the successful learning strategies of their peers. Second, instructors who study the feedback from students can learn whether their exams accomplish their desired objectives. They can also pinpoint trouble spots for students if many of them make the same errors for the same reasons. Instructors also gain a greater understanding of students' awareness of their own learning strategies.

The following questions, which can be modified appropriately, prove useful for this CAT: (1) Briefly describe the exam. What was it about? (2) What was your most successful response to an exam question? What made it so successful? (3) What was your least successful response to an exam question? What did you do wrong or fail to do in that case? (4) The next time you confront a similar situation, what, if anything, could you do to increase your performance and/or your learning? Students may need coaching and examples to become sophisticated at this type of analysis, thus making it useful to employ this technique repeatedly during a series of exams or quizzes.

Quality Circles

The Classroom Assessment Quality Circle (Angelo and Cross, 1993, pp. 339–42) is a CAT originally adapted from industrial quality-control circles where production-line employers work closely with managers to identify and solve production problems. To establish a Classroom Assessment Quality Circle, instructors conduct an election in each section of a course they teach: students vote for one or two class representatives from a group of volunteers. Once the Classroom Assessment Quality Circle has been established, instructors encourage all students to take any course-related suggestions, complaints, or compliments they wish to express to their representative. To elicit as frank an assessment as possible, instructors must assure the students that they will not request, and that the class representatives will not reveal, any names of those providing feedback to the circle.

Instructors meet frequently with the Classroom Assessment Quality Circle throughout the term. To communicate symbolically to the students the importance of the circle, meetings should be held, when possible, in a formal, high-prestige setting, such as a dean's conference room. Instructors can arrange this room to resemble one that would be suitable for a business meeting.

Instructors will quickly gain the trust of their Classroom Assessment Quality Circle if they avoid reacting negatively to comments or suggestions brought by representatives of the circle, no matter how trivial or immature these comments might seem. A working guideline for this, and all other CATs, is "Never ask a student a question you don't want to hear the answer to." Instructors should also resist the temptation to probe for the source of student comments, no matter how their curiosity is piqued. Once trust is established, instructors will glean helpful information from the students in the circle. In particular, they will receive valuable feedback about student perceptions (both positive and negative) and about cooperative-learning structures and their effectiveness. Instructors will also learn about those rare instances when a team becomes dysfunctional because of personality conflicts, student apathy, conflicting demands on team members' time, or other reasons. With this information, instructors will be able to adjust their teaching to ensure that the class has a positive learning environment and that students are assimilating the course material. In the case of negative team-related experiences, instructors may want to work with the circle to seek a resolution. It is far better for the elected students to intervene in any class-related problems (either team or whole-class) than for the instructor to take unilateral draconian measures. Students are more likely to respect and to respond positively to changes suggested by their peers, particularly if they are aware of the serious deliberations behind them.

STUDENT MANAGEMENT TEAMS

Student Management Teams, developed by Nuhfer (1990; 1997), are based on participatory management models by Deming (1986), Glasser (1990), and Peters and Waterman (1982). The teams, typically composed of three or four students plus the teacher, are formed within a single class to help improve teaching. The students, who are charged with the managerial role of facilitating the class's success, meet weekly in a neutral setting removed from the classroom. The teacher usually attends only every other week. The students are responsible for functioning as a quality circle that monitors the course, conducts research that typically involves input from other students, and makes recommendations to the instructor for course enhancements. Such teams empower students by enabling them to make meaningful contributions to their own academic success. By working with the faculty to strengthen their own class, they nurture the entire academic community. Teachers also benefit, since they are perceived as caring, committed educators, and because they have the opportunity to receive broad-based, constructive feedback about their course while it is ongoing. Such feedback proves useful for the immediate course, but it also helps the instructor reshape upcoming courses.

Nuhfer (1997) has identified several reasons why Student Management Teams have a less than two-percent failure rate. They are successful because

1. The members meet regularly over a sustained period of time rather than for the customary single consultation with the expert;
2. The team members are committed to improvement and quality;
3. Teams may acquire data through formative evaluations . . . and classroom assessment techniques (Angelo and Cross, 1993), which are the same data available to expert consultants, and
4. The synergy of regular, purposeful group discussion produces insights that an individual would not likely achieve alone. (p. 112)

SUMMARY

Classroom Assessment Techniques ideally become part of the learning process itself. Faculty who ask students, for example, to complete a Pro and Con Grid, and to then share their results with fellow students, are building critical-thinking skills by helping students to reflect on both sides of an issue and then compare their thinking with that of others. These CATs offer faculty members quick, meaningful ways to discover the nature and extent of student learning. They offer substantive classroom activities involving the active learning and feedback that lead to deep, not surface learning.

APPENDIX A

A Sample Interest/Knowledge/Skills Checklist

Part I: Interest in Possible Course Topics

Directions: Please circle the number after each item below that best represents your level of interest in that topic. The numbers stand for the following responses:

0 = No interest in the topic
1 = Interest in an overview of the topic
2 = Interest in reading about and discussing the topic
3 = Interest in learning how to apply ideas about the topic this semester

Possible Course Topics

1. Theories/research on financial accounting	0	1	2	3
2. History/process of standard setting	0	1	2	3
3. Financial accounting research skills	0	1	2	3
4. Tax accounting research skills	0	1	2	3
5. Current practice in managerial accounting	0	1	2	3
6. Current practice in auditing	0	1	2	3
7. Design of accounting systems	0	1	2	3
8. Accountants as consultants	0	1	2	3

Part II: Self-assessment of Related Skills and Knowledge

Directions: Please circle the letter after each item below that best represents your level of skill or knowledge in relation to that topic. The letters stand for the following responses:

N = No skills, no knowledge
B = Basic skills and knowledge
F = Functionally adequate skills and knowledge
A = Advanced skills and knowledge

Areas of Skills and/or Knowledge (numbers in parentheses refer to course topics listed in Part I)

The role of the APB and the FASB (1)	N	B	F	A
Content of current FASB pronouncements (2)	N	B	F	A
Library research skills (3 & 4)	N	B	F	A
Database research skills (3 & 4)	N	B	F	A
Decision-making in organizations (4, 5, & 8)	N	B	F	A
Internal auditing (5, 6, & 8)	N	B	F	A
Content of current auditing standards (6)	N	B	F	A
Computer programming/systems design (6, 7, & 8)	N	B	F	A

APPENDIX B
Group Processing Form*

Group Name: _____

1. Overall, how effectively did your group work together in learning the course subject matter? (circle the appropriate response)

not at all	poorly	adequately	well	extremely well
1	2	3	4	5

2. How many of the group members participated actively most of the time? (circle the appropriate number)

    1   2   3   4   5

3. How may of the group members were fully prepared for group work most of the time? (circle the appropriate number)

    1   2   3   4   5

4. Give one specific example of something you have learned from the group that you probably would not have learned on your own.

5. Give one specific example of something the other group members learned from you that they probably would not have learned without you.

6. Suggest one specific, practical change the group could make that would help improve everyone's learning.

* This form is adapted from a form developed by T.A. Angelo, as found in "Using Assessment to Improve Cooperative Learning." *Cooperative Learning and College Teaching,* 4(3) 5–7.

APPENDIX C
Feedback/Participation Form*

If you prefer, you may omit your name, section, and team.
Name:_____ Section: _____ Team:_____

1. _____ I have the following question relating to:

    _____ Text Material (page/section _____)

    _____ Lecture Material and/or Class Discussion

    _____ Problem Material (Which One? _____)

    My question is:

    _____ I don't have a question today—I'm all set.

2. How well do you understand the material you covered in your
   team today?
        _____ I understand all of it!
        _____ I understand most of it.
        _____ I'm so confused!

    Comments:

* This form is adapted from a form developed by Professor Elaine Harwood, as found in her working paper "The Effectiveness of Classroom Assessment Techniques (CATs) in Introductory Accounting Courses: An Empirical Examination of Minute Papers." (Used with permission.)

REFERENCES

Angelo, T.A. (1994, Spring). "Using Assessment to Improve Cooperative Learning." *Cooperative Learning and College Teaching,* 4(3), 5–7.

Angelo, T.A. and Cross, K.P. (1993). *Classroom Assessment Techniques: A Handbook for College Teachers,* 2nd Ed. San Francisco: Jossey-Bass.

Barr, R.B. and Tagg, J. (1995, Nov./Dec.). *Change: The Magazine of Higher Learning,* 13–25.

Boyer, E.L. (1990). *Scholarship Reconsidered: Priorities of the Professoriate.* Princeton, NJ: Carnegie Foundation for the Advancement of Teaching.

Brookfield, S.D. (1991). *The Skillful Teacher: On Technique, Trust, and Responsiveness in the Classroom.* San Francisco: Jossey-Bass.

Cross, K.P. (1993, Mar.). *The Student Side of Classroom Research.* Presentation, National Conference on Higher Education, American Association for Higher Education, Washington, DC.

Davis, B.G. (1993). *Tools for Teaching.* San Francisco: Jossey-Bass.

Deming, E. (1986). *Out of Crises.* Massachusetts Institute of Technology Center for Advanced Engineering Study.

Duffy, D.K. and Jones, J.W. (1995). *Teaching within the Rhythms of the Semester.* San Francisco: Jossey-Bass.

Glasser, W. (1990). *The Quality School.* New York: Harper & Row .

Johnson, D.W. and Johnson, R.T. (1996). *Meaningful and Manageable Assessment through Cooperative Learning.* Edina, MN: Interaction Book Company.

Nuhfer, E.B. (1990). *A Handbook for Student Management Teams.* Denver, CO: The Office of Teaching Effectiveness.

Peters, T. and Waterman, R.H., Jr. (1982). *In Search of Excellence: Lessons from America's Best Run Companies.* New York: Harper & Row.

CHAPTER 13

Colleague-Assisted
Assessment Procedures

"All for one and one for all."

Alexandre Dumas

Besides using assessment techniques to gather data from their students, teachers may also invite colleagues or faculty development specialists to observe their classes or to interview students. The first three approaches—classroom observations, Small Group Instructional Diagnosis (SGID), and student focus groups—each involve a three-step process: (1) an initial interview, where teachers discuss such issues as the overall course objectives; the nature of the course; their teaching philosophy; the teaching methodologies they most often employ; their perceptions of the students and the course; their specific concerns or expectations; the "logistics" behind the visit or interview, and so forth; (2) the observation or interview itself; and (3) the debriefing, where teachers and colleagues discuss and interpret the data collected and plan for future changes.

CLASSROOM OBSERVATIONS

Class observations are most effective when they are conducted as an ongoing series rather than a single visit which results in a quick, but isolated "snapshot." Minimally, the initial observation is followed by a second one to determine if the proposed changes have had the desired effect. Observing cooperative classrooms requires special skills because the teacher is not always the proper focus of attention. For example, observers may want to note whether students in structured small groups are on- or off-task; they may want to assess depth of student knowledge by listening to "thinking-out-loud" activities; they may want to comment on the students' mastery of interpersonal and group skills. Some basic guidelines, such as those offered by Millis (1992), can maximize the value of these focused observations.

Framed within the context of the three-step cycle listed above, classroom observations should be conducted in a positive atmosphere. Several researchers (Weimer, 1990; Wilkerson, 1988) recommend a collaborative, reciprocal approach where the professional status of both parties is respected and celebrated. This positive atmosphere also involves the students, who should be key players in the process. Teachers inform them of the nature and purpose of the visit, introduce them to the visitors, and encourage them to welcome those visitors into the classroom. The visitors should attempt to capture holistically what is occurring in the classroom, keeping in mind the particular aspects of teaching and learning identified by the instructor during the pre-observation conference. Many observers find that using a yellow tablet works well because it enables them to record a virtual transcript of what unfolds and make detailed notes about the dynamics of the small groups they observe. At the same time, they can record notes in the margins to be shared later with the instructor.

The feedback is critically important. In the case of a voluntary visit, often the feedback is oral, not written. Either way, however, the feedback should be accurate, providing an objective record of the behaviors and activities recorded. It should be honest, offering information that may at times be painful for the instructor. Although honest, the feedback should be positively phrased, with an emphasis on behaviors rather than judgmental interpretations. Often a questioning technique can accompany the data: "As you can see by the notes I took, three of the four groups I observed seemed to be engaged in off-task behaviors, such as wagering on this weekend's football game or speculating about the natural hair color of your colleague next door. Have you ever tried monitoring the groups, much as I did? Or assigning student roles, such as Group Leader and Timekeeper, to help students become more responsible for the activities within the groups? I noticed that two of the four groups moved to irrelevant discussions only after they had completed the task you gave them. Have you thought about designating extension activities—extra assignments that groups must turn to when they have completed the initial task?"

The feedback should be context-specific and concrete so that the instructor knows exactly when given behaviors occurred. For example, an observer in a beginning German class might note, "Following your explanation of the subjunctive case, the six students seated near me seemed puzzled: they flipped through their textbooks, looked quizzically at one another, and several shrugged their shoulders." The discussion should also be action-oriented with an emphasis on: "Here are the data. Here is how we can interpret them. Now, what can we do to strengthen the learning in this class?" The observer might say, for instance, "I could not read your diagrams on the board from my seat at the back of the class. Students seemed to have the same problem because they continually squinted, peered at each others' notes, and whispered among themselves. Next time, could you draw larger figures, distribute the critical information in a handout, or use an overhead projector?"

Successful classroom observations should accomplish at least two goals: (1) they should reinforce positive behaviors (things that the instructor is doing right) and (2) they should lead to changes in behaviors to strengthen teaching (things the instructor could improve). Thus, a skilled observer will both offer information and provide inspiration. Based on the observation, the instructor should know what to change and be motivated to extend the effort needed to change. It is helpful to record the teaching improvement activities that emerge from the post-visit discussion. This activity might also be considered a "teaching action plan." Followup visits to determine the effectiveness of the changes are extremely important because they place the visit within the context of a continuous improvement process.

SMALL-GROUP INSTRUCTIONAL DIAGNOSIS

A whole-class interviewing technique called Small-Group Instructional Diagnosis can gather consensus-based student data that enable instructors to make informed decisions about teaching/learning changes. This technique is based on research conducted by Joseph Clark (1982) when he served as a project director for FIPSE (Fund for the Improvement of Postsecondary Education) at the University of Washington, Seattle. Because the in-class data collection is based on information gleaned from structured small-group work, the technique uses cooperative-learning methods to gather data that may be useful in strengthening classes predicated on cooperative learning. Practitioners such as Diamond (1988) and Nyquist and Wulff (1988) agree on the basic steps involved.

During the pre-interview meeting, the SGID facilitator collects course-specific information from the instructor. A checklist similar to one designed by Wulff (1996), helps ensure systematic data collection. The two parties discuss important course information and the SGID data-collection process; the instructor selects his or her preferred SGID Feedback Form (generic form appears as Figure 13.1).

During the thirty-minute in-class interview, usually conducted at the mid-term point, the facilitator introduces herself, explains the SGID process, and asks students to form groups of six to eight and to select a recorder. The students

(Course)

No. of Participants in Group_____

1. List the major strengths in the course. (What is helping you learn?) Please explain briefly or give an example for each strength.

        Strengths   Explanation/Example

2. List changes that you would make in the course to assist you in learning. Please explain how these suggested changes could be made.

        Changes   Ways To Make Changes

3. Optional Question

SGID Feedback Form

FIGURE 13.1

students then discuss the questions on the SGID Feedback Form and the recorder writes down the points on which they reach consensus. After this process, which takes only 8–12 minutes, the facilitator or a student records the comments of each group on a central chalkboard. Another recorder copies everything from the board for later analysis. The facilitator has several major tasks. She asks students for clarification or amplification on ambiguous points, and she seeks to determine whether there is whole-class consensus on the issues raised. This can be accomplished by asking for a show of hands indicating agreement or disagreement with particular comments.

In the next phase of SGID, the facilitator analyzes and organizes the material to make it meaningful to the instructor. The comments can be arranged, for example, in order of frequency under the central headings of "Things to Continue;" "Things to Consider Changing;" and "Additional Suggestions." The facilitator should try to "chunk" data under common themes to be shared with the instructor. Not all comments are included verbatim, particularly ones with potentially hurtful phrasing, but representative ones can give the flavor of the interview.

The facilitator and the instructor then meet for a "debriefing" at which the interview process is described, the data are analyzed and discussed, and further action is planned. White (1991) describes the process as follows:

> Soon after the SGID, the facilitator meets with the instructor and summarizes the information, answering questions, explaining comments, and offering alternative interpretations of apparent contradictions. During this phase, the tasks are to support the instructor and faithfully represent student perspectives. Though the intent is not to persuade faculty to agree with the students, it is to highlight themes and explanations that integrate student and instructor perceptions. In this manner, the facilitator promotes reflection on the issues, not just on the words. The conversation then moves to strategies for change, and what the instructor can say when he or she returns to the class (pp. 7; 10).

Diamond (1988) suggests that these questions should guide the action plan:

1. "What happened in class to elicit this comment?"
2. "Is x within my control?"
3. "Is x important to student learning?"
4. "Can I reasonably change in regard to x?"
5. "Do I want to change in regard to x?"
6. "What action can I take now?—the next time I teach the class?" (p. 92).

During the final phase, the instructor must discuss the results of the SGID with the students. As with the Classroom Assessment Techniques advocated by Angelo and Cross (1993), the SGID process raises student expectations for positive changes. Thus, it is essential that faculty members offer explanations of those course elements they are willing and able to address. Wulff (1994) describes, for example, an instructor who reduced the workload in response to student input from an SGID. During the followup with students, she thanked them for their honest comments and announced that she would try to make the workload more manageable by previewing assigned readings, eliminating overlapping readings, and assigning only two major readings in the week that papers were due.

STUDENT FOCUS GROUPS

Focus groups are a common marketing tool used by corporations to gather data about new products, customer satisfaction, and a host of other issues. They tend to be action-oriented in that clients will typically base decisions on data they feel are representative and reliable. Such groups involve highly paid professional moderators; expensive facilities, including one-way mirrors and sophisticated recording equipment; and complex data analysis that takes into account both nonverbal and verbal responses. Focus groups conducted by professionals in higher education have frequently targeted recruiting and fundraising issues (Topor, 1996).

However, focus groups can also be conducted effectively and efficiently by skilled nonprofessionals trained to gather data about individual classes or new courses or programs of study. Like other forms of assessment that use an outside facilitator, focus groups involve a three-step process featuring a pre-interview conference, the interview itself, and the post-interview "debriefing." Course focus groups are similar to SGIDs in that they involve facilitators conducting structured student interviews. However, there are some major differences. For one thing, the SGIDs are conducted in the classroom during regular classroom hours, so it is likely that many students will participate. Focus groups rely on volunteers, so the sample is more likely to be biased, attracting students who particularly like or dislike a course. However, since focus groups are often drawn from heterogeneous samples from different classes, there is greater opportunity for candid interactions outside the familiar peer relationships in ongoing classes. Wright and Hendershott (1992), for example, discovered focus groups to be an invaluable means of tapping student perceptions within a university setting. They found that interactions among students, particularly when the facilitators were able to probe responses, yielded rich data that could not have been obtained from traditional surveys.

It is useful to have two facilitators: one to conduct the questioning session and another to record the responses. Tape recording the sessions maximizes the data capture, but, even if the session is recorded, it is helpful for the second facilitator to record at least the opening words of each comment and any directives given by the processing facilitator. They may also note any visual clues provided by students (frowning, shrugging, etc.) that might help with the transcription. Having students number off and then proceed each comment by their number helps the transcriber, but more important, this anonymous "coding" assures students that their names will not be associated with any comments. To begin the session, it is important that the facilitator who will conduct the session establish the ground rules for the discussion. Student respondents have specific rights which should be clarified: they need to know the purpose and scope of the focus-group interview; they must be informed of any audio- or videotaping; they must be assured of confidentiality; and they must be assured that they will be treated with dignity, courtesy, and respect. It is therefore important that the group agree to some norms, such as attentive listening, on-task participation, and constructive disagreements. The structure of the session can include guarantees for equal participation.

Effective focus-group facilitators will structure sessions with great care. After discussing the objectives and possible questions with the instructor, they will design activities to maximize the data collection in the allotted time. Thus, they will use a variety of techniques. For example, some questions—those which may be idiosyncratic— could be compiled in a mini-survey which students complete when they first arrive. A good opening activity is to ask each student to record two things on an index card: A single word that describes their perceptions of the course (e.g., "boring," "stimulating," "confusing," etc.) and a number from 1–5 which describes their satisfaction in the course, with 1 being the lowest and 5 the highest. The facilitator can get a quick feel for the students' overall response to the class by having them quickly read off, "round robin style," their answers to the two questions posed. The latter question might also be answered on a sticky note, with students then posting their responses on a blackboard for a quick tally.

Cooperative-learning techniques can be used effectively during the session. For example, students in small groups use a Roundtable technique to generate ideas for positive changes in the class (e.g., the instructor needs to provide more structure; the other students need to pull their share of the weight in cooperative groups, etc.). Then the students are asked—using a Structured Problem-Solving format—to reach consensus and rank-order the most important changes that should be made within the class. The group spokespersons then share the results. It is important to use discussion methods that discourage domination by a few vocal students. Some questions can be given out to the entire group with only a few responses solicited (e.g., "Do you think all students understand the grading system used in the course?") In other cases, it might be useful to pose the question and then ask each student for a quick response (e.g., "Do you think the grading system is fair?").

After the interview is over, the second facilitator prepares a transcript based on the audio- or videotape, and his notes. One or both of the facilitators should then sit down with the faculty member to discuss and interpret the findings and to plan future changes.

VIDEOTAPING

Videotaping involves having an outside colleague run the camera, and it is also helpful to have a supportive colleague or a faculty development consultant to help analyze and interpret the results. Some colleges and universities have campus media centers that will offer such services. Because the students will be working in groups, teachers will want to be certain that the camera person recognizes the need to film the students. If sophisticated equipment is available, it may be possible for the camera person to capture the activities of single groups by filtering out the background noise.

Instructors should select a typical course, preferably one that combines both lecture and discussion (Davis, 1993). The students need to be informed of the videotaping process, so that they can begin to get comfortable with the idea of having a camera focused both on themselves and on the teacher. Usually, everyone is initially self-conscious, but then the disruptions are minimized as class time unfolds normally.

After the taping is complete, some instructors prefer to view by themselves, remembering that it typically takes twice as long to complete a serious analysis as it does to conduct a class. It is probably best to initially view the tape as a whole, trying not to be overly critical of presentation-type concerns, such as a missing earring or too many "Uhs." Faculty tend to be overly critical of themselves, focusing on minor details that in the classroom context are rarely noticeable. Krupnick (1987) has dubbed this "video-induced despair." Fuhrmann and Grasha (1983) suggest these questions:

1. What are the specific things I did well?
2. What are the specific things I could have done better?
3. What do students seem to enjoy most?
4. What do students seem to enjoy least?
5. If I could do this session over again, what three things would I change?
6. How could I go about making those three changes?

The second time around, it is best to focus on areas of specific concern, using a self-designed checklist if that seems appropriate. In a cooperative classroom, for example, teachers might be interested in their monitoring practices. Are they getting to each group or are they getting "stuck"? Does their presence disrupt students from their assigned tasks? Are groups asking them questions only after all members concede that they do not know the proper response?

THE REFLECTIVE JUDGMENT MODEL

Few faculty are aware of the value of the Reflective Judgment Model (King and Kitchener, 1994) as an assessment tool. The model comes from the developmental psychology literature which recognizes that the demands placed on students must be developmentally appropriate (Sanford, 1966). Too often, as Kurfiss (1988) notes, well-meaning instructors, intending to challenge their students, assign tasks that require critical-thinking skills, but expect students to acquire these skills based on their "ingenuity, good fortune, and native ability" (p. 4).

Evaluators, including faculty colleagues trained to use Reflective Judgment approaches, can help faculty measure the value of essay questions that pinpoint the developmental level of their students. Specifically, the model can be used to ascertain how well students respond to ill-defined problems. Once this is determined, as Kronholm's (1993) recent research indicates, faculty can deliberately design appropriate course-related activities to foster critical-thinking skills.

Using manuals and materials (Lynch, 1995; Lynch, Kitchener, and King, 1994), trained faculty can help colleagues assess their students' progress through carefully evaluated essays and interviews. To rate an essay, the evaluator looks for student statements consistent with views of knowledge and approaches to unstructured problem solving (Wolcott and Lynch, 1997). Although the evaluative essays are typically more complex, here are some examples of briefly stated ill-defined problems from several disciplines that have been used to assess reflective thinking of adolescents and adults:

> **Psychology:** Some researchers contend that alcoholism is due, at least, in part, to genetic factors. They often refer to results from a number of family studies to support this contention. Other researchers, however, do not think that alcoholism is in any way inherited; rather, that it is psychologically determined. They claim that the reason that several members of the same family often suffer from alcoholism is because they share common family experiences, socioeconomic status, or employment.
>
> **History:** Most historians claim that the pyramids were built as tombs for kings by the ancient Egyptians, using human labor, aided by ropes, pulleys, and rollers. Others have suggested that the Egyptians could not have built such huge structures by themselves, for they had neither the mathematical knowledge, and necessary tools, nor an adequate source of power.
>
> **Science:** The safety of nuclear energy is currently being debated by scientists in many fields. Some scientists believe that nuclear energy is safe and that it can substantially alleviate our dependence on nonrenewable resources. Others argue that nuclear energy is inherently unsafe and that nuclear power plants will lead to widespread and longterm environmental pollution.
>
> **Chemistry:** Some scientists believe that explanations for chemical phenomena, such as atomic theory, are accurate and true descriptions of atomic structure. Others say we cannot know whether this is true, but that scientists can only use such theories as working models to explain what is observed (Lynch, Kitchener, and King, 1995, pp. 14–16).

SUMMARY

Because cooperative learning techniques may be new to students—if not to faculty!—it is important to assess ongoing classes. Using faculty colleagues to collect data offers instructors an objective look at the classroom that student input may not provide. Faculty development professionals or committed peers offer insights through activities such as classroom observations, SGIDs, student focus groups, videotaping, and Reflective Judgment Model assessment. Colleagues that help one another also help expand the model of community beyond the immediate classroom and forge broader connections. Levine and

Tompkins' (1996) comments about Temple University apply to all institutions where classroom doors are opening in the spirit of improved teaching:

> Learning communities are helping to change the culture of the university, furnishing a forum where faculty can reflect together on their roles as teachers and members of teams—that is, members of groups seeking to improve student learning. That teaching is the most private aspect of academic work is now a truism; but in learning communities faculty come together to share their teaching, considering syllabus preparation, class presentations, and student problems (p. 5).

REFERENCES

Angelo, T.A. and Cross, K.P. (1993). *Classroom Assessment Techniques: A Handbook for College Teachers.* 2nd Ed. San Francisco: Jossey-Bass.

Davis, B.G. (1993). *Tools for Teaching.* San Francisco: Jossey-Bass.

Diamond, N.A. (1988). "S.G.I.D. (Small Group Instructional Diagnosis): Tapping Student Perceptions of Teaching." In E. C. Wadsworth (Ed.), *POD: A Handbook for New Practitioners* (pp. 89–93). Stillwater, OK: New Forums Press, Inc.

Fuhrmann, B.S. and Grasha, A.F. (1983). *A Practical Handbook for College Teachers.* Boston: Little, Brown.

King, P.M. and Kitchener, K.S. (1994). *Developing Reflective Judgment: Understanding and Promoting Intellectual Growth and Critical Thinking in Adolescents and Adults.* San Francisco: Jossey-Bass.

Kronholm, M.M. (1993). *The Impact of a Developmental Instruction Approach to Environmental Education at the Undergraduate Level on Development of Reflective Judgment.* Doctoral dissertation, Southern Illinois University.

Krupnick, C.G. (1987). "The Uses of Videotape Replay." In C. R. Christensen with A.J. Hansen (Eds.), *Teaching and the Case Method.* Boston: Harvard Business School.

Kurfiss, J.G. (1988). *Critical Thinking: Theory, Research, Practice, and Possibilities.* ASHE-ERIC Higher Education Report No. 2. Washington, DC: Association for the Study of Higher Education.

Levine, J.H. and Tompkins, D.P. (1996, June). "Making Learning Communities Work: Seven Lessons from Temple." *AAHE Bulletin,* 48(10), 2–6.

Lynch, C.L. (1995). *Reflective Developmental Markers.* Unpublished manuscript available through Reflective Judgment Associates, New Concord, KY 42076, (502) 436-5839, 74671.2342@compuserve.com.

Lynch, C.L., Kitchener, K.S., and King, P.M. (1994). *Developing Reflective Judgment in the Classroom: A Manual for Faculty.* New Concord, KY: Reflective Judgment Associates.

Millis, B.J. (1992). "Conducting Effective Peer Classroom Observations." In D.H. Wulff, and J. D. Nyquist (Eds.), *To Improve the Academy: Resources for Faculty, Instructional, and Organizational Development* (pp. 189–201). Stillwater, OK: New Forums Press, Inc.

Nyquist, J.D. and Wulff, D.H. (1988). "Consultation Using a Research Perspective." In E.C. Wadsworth (Ed.), *POD: A Handbook for New Practitioners.* (pp. 81–88). Stillwater, OK: New Forums Press, Inc.

Sanford, N. (1966). *Self and Society: Societal Change and Individual Development.* New York: Atherton.

Topor, R. (1996). "How to Run a Focus Group for Higher Education." Sample article from *Marketing Higher Education*. Online at <http://www.marketing.com/news/focus.html>. Downloaded 23 Dec. 1996.

Weimer, M. (1990). *Improving College Teaching*. San Francisco: Jossey-Bass.

White, K. (1991). "Small Group Instructional Diagnosis: Alternate Adult Assessment." *Adult Assessment Forum*, 1(3), 6–7;10.

Wilkerson, L. (1988). "Classroom Observation: The Observer as Collaborator." In E.C. Wadsworth (Ed.), *POD: A Handbook for New Practitioners*. (95–98). Stillwater, OK: New Forums Press, Inc.

Wolcott, S.K. and Lynch, C.L. (1997). *Critical Thinking in the Accounting Classroom: A Reflective Judgment Model*. Unpublished manuscript.

Wright, S.P. and Hendershott, A. (1992). In D.H. Wulff and J.D. Nyquist (Eds.), *To Improve the Academy: Resources for Faculty, Instructional, and Organizational Development* (87–104). Stillwater, OK: New Forums Press, Inc.

Wulff, D.H. (1994). "The Case of the Worrisome Workload." In W.C. Rando and L.F. Lenze, *Learning from Students: Early Term Feedback in Higher Education* (29–32). University Park, PA: National Center on Postsecondary Teaching, Learning, and Assessment.

Wulff, D.H. (1996, Fall). Small Group Instructional Diagnosis (SGID) Training workshops conducted at the U.S. Air Force Academy.

PART
FIVE

• • • • • • • • •

Supporting Cooperative Efforts

CHAPTER 14

Supporting Faculty's Cooperative Efforts

"Teaching is a lifelong art, that . . . involves continuous learning not just for the student but for the teachers as well."

Joseph Katz and Mildred Henry

Bonwell and Eison (1991), like many others, have identified a noticeable gap in the practice of higher education between "How faculty typically teach (i.e., relying largely on the lecture method) and how they should teach (i.e., employing active learning to facilitate students' mastery of subject matter, develop intellectual skills, and form personal attitudes and values)" (p. 4). Astin (1991) attributed this gap to a failure, in part, to apply educational research:

> Some of the most important findings from higher education research have not yet been translated into practice. For example, despite the considerable body of evidence suggesting that undergraduate programs could be strengthened through greater use of cooperative learning and other "active learning" strategies, faculty members continue to rely heavily on the traditional lecture (p. A36).

It is not difficult to understand why changes come slowly. It is far easier to maintain the status quo. Calvin, the well-known cartoon character, exclaims to Hobbes: " I hate change. It's too disruptive. When things are different, you have to think about the change and deal with it! I like things to stay the same, so I can take everything for granted." Even if faculty are willing to consider new cooperative approaches, they are often at a loss as to how to proceed, Thus, support for faculty is essential.

SUPPORTING COOPERATIVE FACULTY

Faculty need to be supported in their efforts to transform their classrooms. Fortunately, faculty development efforts, which gained wide acceptance in the 1960s, continue to be prevalent today. A survey by Erickson (1986) found that half of all baccalaureate institutions have faculty development programs of some kind. Thus, faculty development efforts are widespread, and their effectiveness, particularly in enhancing teaching, has been increasingly documented (Cuseo, 1989).

Furthermore, faculty seem more receptive to faculty development efforts than in past years. Issues of quality and accountability and the subsequent close scrutiny of faculty roles and rewards—how and why professors spend their time—have prompted faculty to reexamine some of their basic academic premises. This reflection has been stimulated by additional forces such as the assessment movement; the necessity for lifelong learning in a technologically driven, multicultural workplace; the influx of nontraditional students into classrooms, and an increasing awareness that timeworn methods of delivery are ineffective for a majority of students.

As a result, many faculty seem more open to teaching/learning innovations, and faculty developers who once suffered from the "Maytag syndrome" now find faculty eager for their services. Davis (1993) attributes this, in part, to a growing awareness that teaching is being seen now, primarily because of the assessment movement, as a "we" thing: "The days are gone when we can go to class, teach our subject, and hope that some of our students will 'get it.' It is no longer possible to avoid probing questions about the amount and quality of student learning" (p. 367). Thus, faculty developers who wish to support faculty in their efforts to introduce innovative classroom approaches, such as cooperative learning, must be aware of the complexities involved; specifically, of the variables in different higher education institutions. In addition, the developers must motivate faculty to overcome barriers and guide them toward carefully thought-out implementation efforts.

Campus and Individual Variables

Any efforts to support faculty must take into account the individuals delivering classes and the institutional mission. Community colleges, small liberal arts colleges, state and private institutions, and large research institutions vary widely in the types of teachers they typically hire. For example, courses are delivered on large research campuses by a variety of individuals with differing expertise, needs, and commitments. Beginning Teaching Assistants (TAs) responsible for small-group discussions to support large introductory lecture courses will differ in the creative teaching expertise they bring to their assignments, in the amount of guidance they receive, and in the amount of time—given their own graduate workloads—that they are willing to commit to their responsibilities. TAs obviously differ from junior faculty members who are often stretched and stressed to further their academic careers: the challenge of introducing new, perhaps labor-intensive approaches, such as cooperative-learning, may not be the top priority for them in a "publish-or-perish" environment. Junior faculty differ, in turn, from tenured full professors, who may or may not be motivated to teach conscientiously and creatively. The picture is further compounded by the adjunct lecturers common on many campuses, who often receive little support or encouragement.

The climate and expectation for faculty development in higher education differs as much as the teaching population. Cooperative-learning advocates face even more challenges if they hope to build cadres of dedicated "groupies" on a campus. Getting faculty to agree readily on a new textbook, let alone a concerted course of instruction such as cooperative learning, is virtually unheard of. One faculty developer describes organizing faculty as akin to herding cats. For one thing, faculty loyalties usually lie with their disciplines more than to particular institutions. Bondeson (1992) expresses it eloquently:

> Simply put, we profess our disciplines. We stand up and display an existential commitment to those disciplines; and, by our act of teaching them, we show that those disciplines are embodied in our own lives. Our commitment to our discipline is our way of saying to our students, as we profess, that it is worthy of their consideration and their time. . . . At the moment we teach, we are the only connection between the rich tradition of our disciplines and the students before whom we stand. That is awesome and humbling, but any attempt to improve teaching must begin with the realization that true teaching is professing (p. 5).

It is not surprising that McKeachie (1994) reports that faculty acquire new ideas about teaching more frequently from colleagues than they do from readings or workshops. Conversations with colleagues within one's own discipline can be context-specific, dealing with both content and strategy. A biologist who might tune out a workshop presenter's exhortations to use "Think-Pair-Share" activities, for example, might well accept the word of a colleague that students grasped the concept of osmosis more cogently when she followed up her lecture by having pairs of students jointly develop both a clear definition and an analogy.

Svinicki (1996) also reminds us that "faculty are no more alike in their learning styles than are their students" (p. 1). Thus, faculty must be offered a variety of ways to learn: workshops, reading lists, one-on-one consultations, even technologically delivered instruction.

Faculty development efforts to introduce cooperative learning in higher education must take into account all of these variables. They must be carefully targeted to the individual teachers and to their institutions. Furthermore, faculty, with so many conflicting demands on their time and efforts, are pulled in many directions. They must therefore be convinced that a given plan of action, such as developing a cooperative classroom, is worthwhile.

The Importance of Faculty Motivation

Faculty, like students, must have positive incentives to adopt new strategies. Fortunately, most faculty are by nature intellectually curious. As Boyer (1990) and others have indicated, teaching brings its own set of intellectual challenges. Thus, teachers may be motivated to enact changes by the recognition that traditional ways of teaching no longer work for all students. No one wants to teach poorly. If faculty members can be convinced that adopting cooperative-learning techniques will have a "payoff" in terms of increased student achievement and satisfaction, then they may be willing to make the investment. Svinicki (1996) suggests a model based on "task value" and "expectancy for success." A skill that is needed immediately, such as syllabus construction guidelines prior to the start of a term, is more likely to be learned. Faculty also need practical examples, and, as suggested above, peer examples are particularly compelling: "When we see peers using new information or skills successfully, our expectation of personal success increases. And this increased sense of self-efficacy increases our motivation" (p. 3).

Often, teachers cannot even consider the incentives until they have gotten past mental barriers that block further action. Faculty developers, eager to help faculty adopt cooperative-learning techniques, should address the concern that cooperative learning is merely a K-12 fad enjoying a brief emergence in the higher education arena. Many faculty members, especially those in large research institutions, may be skeptical of what they regard as pedagogical fads or, further, they may be nettled by what Rhem (1992) characterizes as the style of cooperative learning: the unfamiliar, immature-sounding jargon, such as "think-pair-share," or the nontraditional classroom activities where student voices replace the lecture. This concern is valid, since much effective material on cooperative learning is targeted toward elementary and secondary school teachers.

As McKeachie (1994) points out, sensitivity to social norms can also be a motivating factor. In institutions where teaching is valued and considered a legitimate form of scholarship, then faculty will quickly realize that they must adopt student-centered approaches. Experimentation thus becomes more acceptable.

Faculty may also be motivated by the realization that cooperative-learning strategies can be adopted incrementally. Faculty willing to take risks with their teaching methods should not become so ambitious that they set themselves—and their students—up for failure by attempting too much too soon. "Start small" is a good credo. As Cooper, Prescott, Cook, Smith, Mueck, and Cuseo (1990) point out, "Because it is a teaching strategy rather than a style, cooperative learning can be included easily in existing modes of teaching . . . [and] incorporated into classes which use more traditional formats" (p. 21). Svinicki (1996) reminds us that faculty, like all learners, must start with the fundamentals. Even though they will reach a level of sophistication far more quickly than students might, they are essentially learning a new content area. Thus, they must first learn the "basics"—practical strategies and implementation techniques—before we can expect them to reach higher levels of understanding.

McKeachie (1994) encourages faculty wishing to change to set clear and measurable goals. They should also think in terms of identifying criteria that will indicate success. It is easier, for example, to resolve to use a Think-Pair-Share strategy twice over the next two weeks than it is to decide to "motivate students." After determining the desired course of action, the cooperative game plan, it is helpful to rehearse the new strategies before trying them out in the classroom. Before initiating any change, he suggests that faculty ask themselves these four questions based on the theory of reasoned action (Ajzen and Madden, 1986): Question your beliefs to determine that you are truly committed to a given goal; Ask yourself how much control you actually have to effect the proposed changes; Consider the consequences of your actions by theorizing how likely they are to occur and how positive they will be; finally, examine seriously the views that others hold about the change (p. 311).

Probably the most important motivating factor in any professional change is the faculty's sense of "ownership." Wood and Thompson (1993) consider this to be a major assumption in faculty development: "Those who are changing their professional behavior must make an individual and collective commitment to and feel ownership for the new programs and practices before they will want to participate in staff development activities" (p. 54).

The turning point in a cooperative classroom lies in the formation of permanent or semi-permanent learning teams. Johnson, Johnson, and Smith (1991a, 1991b) call these "formal" groups and distinguish them from short-term "informal" groups used for brief activities. Until faculty are ready to make the major commitment toward permanent or semi-permanent learning teams, they can begin with a few low-risk structures, such as Think-Pair-Share. As they experience success, they can move toward the more complex structures, such as Jigsaw, that require learning teams.

STRATEGIES TO ENGAGE FACULTY

Cooperative-learning advocates who wish to involve higher education faculty must overcome barriers, emphasize the benefits of cooperative learning, and adopt proactive, genuine strategies to help faculty accept or refine an innovative teaching strategy. This can be done through four approaches: (1) dissemination of broad-based literature on cooperative learning which becomes discipline-specific whenever possible; (2) institutional support; (3) workshops to introduce faculty to cooperative learning and to encourage more experienced practitioners to share teaching ideas; and (4) networking, within a specific institution and across campus and discipline lines.

Literature Dissemination

Weimer (1988) suggests that self-directed reading about teaching strategies can be both instructional and inspirational. Faculty find it a private, discreet endeavor, one that involves little or no risk. They need opportunities to read and reflect. Many books and articles are available now on cooperative-learning techniques in higher education, and more are coming every day. Cooperative-learning strategies should be placed in the broader context of good practice in teaching and learning with connections to other trends and initiatives, such as Cross and Angelo's classroom assessment techniques, the "Seven Principles for Good Practice in Undergraduate Education," and even the writing-across-the-curriculum movement. Many teaching centers maintain resource libraries, drawing from a wide variety of sources. These libraries should contain the cooperative-learning resources that enable faculty to read about, reflect on, and implement cooperative-learning strategies. A key newsletter is *Cooperative Learning and College Teaching* (New Forums Press, Inc., 1722 Cimarron Plaza, Stillwater, OK 74075). Faculty developers interested in promoting cooperative learning often make available to faculty specific articles or even "how-to" packets designed to increase their familiarity with and confidence in cooperative learning. Discipline-specific teaching journals may also prove useful. A list is currently available on the World Wide Web at <http://www.byu.edu/tmcbucs/fc/period.htm econ>. The secret, of course, lies in the faculty member's willingness to move from the ideas on pages, or computer screens, to actions within a classroom.

Institutional Support

Many campuses now have faculty development offices or committees where trained professionals can assist faculty through a variety of services, including consultations, classroom observations, and resource identification. Many campuses now also offer teaching-related grants that allow faculty the resources and time to experiment with innovations. Sometimes such grants offer opportunities to attend teaching conferences.

"Learning is a risky business and takes courage and support," Svinicki (1996) asserts. Thus, faculty developers must establish trusting relationships with faculty before expecting them to launch into new initiatives:

> They need to feel that we know what we're doing and are willing to support them while they take those first new steps. They need to feel safe that they will not be embarrassed or tricked into displaying a lack of skill. Their overall expertise and intelligence must be acknowledged, while at the same time we take into account the background and experience they may lack. For faculty, as for students, trust necessarily precedes the risk of learning something new (p. 4).

Workshops and Seminars

Workshops are an effective means of helping faculty enhance their teaching proficiency. They are widely used because they are easy to organize; they provide practical, interactive, hands-on experiences, prepare faculty to try new techniques in their classrooms, and are normally fairly cost-effective. Cooperative-learning workshops must be of high quality. Usually they tap two resources: inhouse cooperative-learning practitioners and outside consultants. Campus practitioners who testify to the value of cooperative learning and who model effective practices can be extremely effective. Besides having credibility with their peers, they are also readily available for further consultation. Carefully chosen presenters from outside the institution can be extremely effective, and their workshops often create interest and stimulate enthusiasm for follow-up activities. In addition, outsiders with national reputations will sometimes catch the attention of skeptical faculty members and they can provide important connections to other campuses and practitioners. To identify external consultants, faculty developers may seek advice from outside sources, such as the Professional and Organizational Development Network in Higher Education (POD:US), the Society for Teaching and Learning in Higher Education (STLHE:Canada), the Staff and Educational Development Association (SEDA:UK), and the Higher Education Research and Development Society of Australia (HERDSA:Aus).

In both cases, the workshop presenters effectively present and model cooperative-learning practices. They also provide action-oriented, experiential activities, since no one can lecture effectively about cooperative learning. Faculty actually have to experience the structured activities before they understand the principles and the classroom applications. Effective presenters often build in time for reflection and for the opportunity to develop specific classroom applications.

Workshop presenters must model positive cooperative-learning classroom behaviors. They should, for example, actively monitor groups, commenting, paraphrasing, and reinforcing positive behavior. Comments such as "Tom very effectively asked Mary probing questions" or "Alice did a fine job of summarizing Richard's cooperative-learning efforts when he taught a large lecture class" also build rapport between the presenter and the participants. Such faculty developers often assume an eclectic approach, drawing the best ideas from all schools of cooperative learning and from what is known about effective teaching and learning in general.

Handouts for later reading are a good followup for workshops. Such handouts also conserve workshop time. Presenters will not need to lecture, for example, on cooperative learning's extensive research base if the handout packet provides relevant articles by credible resources such as Astin (1993). Handouts distributed later to faculty can reinforce the interest and enthusiasm generated by the workshops. These expand upon information gleaned from workshops and also offer renewed inspiration and incentives. Appendix A contains a memo Prescott (1996) distributed to participants several months after a workshop. Presenters might also ask faculty to write themselves a letter in which they record impressions from a workshop and/or their "action plans." By specifying the time the presenter will mail them, faculty members can optimize the point at which they need self-generated inspiration.

Karre (1996) has developed a 40-minute videotape and handbook that can be used for faculty development workshops. The length of these workshops can vary from one to three hours, depending on how facilitators use the video segments in conjunction with individual and interactive team applications and discussions. Some faculty may be dissatisfied by what they perceive as lack of depth and unfamiliar terminology (structures, for example, are designated as "tools"). One advantage, however, is seeing footage of actual cooperative classrooms.

While general workshops are effective, discipline-specific cooperative-learning sessions are more so, due to immediate faculty interest and opportunities for application.

Networking

Networking can occur on a number of levels. For example, faculty can join national and regional organizations and networks. Even though it is primarily a K-12 organization, faculty should consider joining the International Society for the Study of Cooperation in Education (IASCE, Box 1582, Santa Cruz, CA 95061-1582) and its local chapters, such as the MidAtlantic Society for the Study of Cooperation in Education (MAACIE). Most importantly, they should join the Cooperative-learning in Higher Education Network (HFA-B316, California State University Dominguez Hills, 1000 E. Victoria Street, Carson,

CA 90747). All of these organizations produce newsletters or journals filled with solid cooperative-learning teaching ideas.

Organized opportunities for faculty to share cooperative-learning ideas, such as campus support groups, are highly effective. The Cooperative Learning Users Group (CLUG) at California State University, Dominguez Hills, encourages faculty to share experiences and provide support for one another's efforts in the cooperative classroom. This model has been replicated on other campuses. Problems can be solved, successes celebrated, and new ideas generated through faculty collaboration that extends between the classrooms. Such support groups typically are interdisciplinary, allowing faculty to experience the stimulating cross-fertilization of ideas that occurs beyond departmental boundaries. Smith, Johnson, and Johnson (1992) observe that "Change is hard and typically does not occur without a group of colleagues who care and provide support and encouragement for one another. The research support for cooperation among faculty is just as strong as that for cooperation among students" (p. 36).

The K-12 literature on staff development strongly advocates on-the-job coaching to reinforce principles learned through a theoretical understanding of the new innovation, through demonstrations, and through supervised trials (Joyce, Showers, and Weil, 1993). The coach, who encourages experimentation, can be a faculty development expert or a more experienced peer (Sparks, 1983). Prescott (1996) suggests that faculty identify a "cooperative buddy" (p. 10). Pairs working together can provide a sounding board for new ideas, and they can help troubleshoot potential problems. Psychologically, too, there is more commitment to a given plan of action when it is shared with someone else. Roy (1996) finds peer coaching programs "particularly powerful for supporting continuous improvement of cooperative learning" The coach should visit classes to serve as "another set of eyes and ears for the teacher" (p. 8).

Observing the classes of experienced cooperative faculty can be as useful as having peers visit a class. Faculty, especially "buddies," should consider reciprocal classroom observations. Skinner and Welch (1996), in fact, find reciprocal coaching, where the two faculty members "become both learners and teachers," more effective than the one-sided coaching that can occur when an expert is paired with a novice (p. 154). Few faculty members experienced positive group work during their undergraduate days. Many, in fact, may have been burned by loosely structured, ineffective group work where overachievers completed ill-defined tasks. Thus, role models for effective classroom implements are essential. As Ekroth (1990) notes, "Observing classes taught effectively in alternate ways or talking with instructors who approach teaching differently can stimulate creative changes in one's teaching. Modeling provides one of the most effective means of learning new behavior styles" (p. 2).

Faculty who make sustained changes in their teaching approaches understand that theory and research informs practice. They do not have unrealistic assumptions about overnight success. In fact, Weimer (1992) feels that genuine faculty development efforts can be undermined by the quick fix or the bag of tricks:

> Teaching is a highly complex, idiosyncratic, dynamic process. To convey the impression that it is nothing more than a bag of tricks, that getting students involved in a class is no more than knowing 22 participation strategies, belies the inherent complexity of the teaching phenomenon. . . . To improve instruction by technique alone is to oversimplify and underestimate the complexity of teaching and the process of improving it. And when we oversimplify, we devalue (pp. 18–19).

Weimer's concerns are echoed by Palmer (1997): "Good teaching cannot be reduced to technique. Good teaching comes out of the identity and integrity of the teacher, as that identity and integrity find ways to create the capacity for connectedness . . . " (p. 12). Cooperative learning is certainly not a quick fix. Its solid theoretical and research base can be shared with faculty, as needed. Murray (1994) makes the case, in fact, that teachers need this global perspective if they are to be knowledgeable, versatile practitioners.

Moving to a cooperative classroom approach should not be considered radical. Rather, such a move can be placed within the context of professionalism, of what it means to be a teacher. McKeachie (1994) states, for example, "With each success, even a small success, there are great benefits—increased confidence, a sense of learning, and a feeling of growth—all of which help to renew professional vitality" (p. 307). Such a move should be placed in the context of what it means to be a professor in a complex, changing world headed for the 21st century. Nevin, Smith, and Udvari-Solner (1994) clearly articulate this new professionalism:

> Professors who practice cooperative learning often find themselves collecting rich data sources: student anecdotes, increased class averages, and changes in the quality as well as the quantity of student products. If this data is published, professors integrate two of the four forms of scholarship promoted by Boyer (1990)—the scholarship of teaching and the scholarship of integration. This type of balanced academic life may be the hallmark of professors who actualize the new paradigm of college teaching (p. 126).

APPENDIX*

School of Education
Department of Teacher Education
California State University, Dominguez Hills

3/6/96

To: FACULTY
From: Susan Prescott
Re: Using cooperative learning with your students

I want to thank you for your enthusiastic participation during our workshop on January 19th. Because of time constraints, we weren't able to cover in-depth details regarding starting steps. I am writing a memo to highlight some ideas that might provide support to those faculty members who are just starting to experiment with active learning strategies.

ESTABLISH PURPOSE AND CLIMATE FOR COOPERATION

We cannot assume that students unfamiliar with the strategy will automatically appreciate and support our initial attempts to use cooperative learning. It is absolutely necessary to take the time to explain what you are doing and why:

- explain that the research on college teaching shows that students learn more and earn higher grades when given the opportunity to work on course content together in class
- discuss the relationship of cooperative skills to their future or current employment setting
- tell them that the content in the group tasks is directly related to the content that will be on exams, papers, and projects
- lead a discussion on specific skills that will help facilitate pair or group work
- make sure partners or group members have a chance to get acquainted and learn a little about each other so that they feel more connected

CREATE CLEAR COOPERATIVE TASKS

Be sure that the activities you ask students to do together are clear, tightly structured, and related to essential course content:

- start with one course and use only pairs for several weeks or months
- each weekend, decide what will be the most essential content for each class meeting during the following week, and record it in your planning book

---

*Source: Cooperative Learning and College Teaching. (Reprinted with permission.)

- decide how cooperative learning could enhance each class session [to motivate, give a concrete experience, check for understanding during lecture, provide practice, etc.]
- use your text to help you think of an activity that matches both the priority content and the teacher need [listing interpretations of a diagram, writing a caption for a photo, answering a question at the end of a section, etc.] or use an original activity of your own
- make sure that the task is very specific ["list three possible explanations for the character's self-destructive behavior"] vs. vague ["discuss your homework reading"]

PROVIDE CLEAR EXPECTATIONS FOR BEHAVIOR

Some instructors become discouraged when students appear to engage in unproductive behaviors or do not complete the task as intended by the teacher. This usually occurs because the students aren't clear on what is expected. It is crucial to take time to clearly spell out exactly what is required in the cooperative activity and how they can work together to accomplish the task:

- anticipate misunderstandings and/or errors with the task and discuss them
- walk over to one pair or group and demonstrate the procedure for the whole class
- directly and assertively [with good feeling—humor helps] tell the class the specific behaviors that will increase their learning and which behaviors to avoid because they will adversely affect learning
- observe students as they work in order to provide encouragement and redirection as necessary

MAINTAIN A SUPPORT SYSTEM

- be sure to find a buddy to meet with on an ongoing basis; it really helps to have someone with whom to share your experiences, ideas, and questions
- reread the articles in our workshop packet; they can be useful resources
- seek out colleagues who have been trying cooperative-learning for some time
- stay positive, have fun, and give yourself encouragement for trying to increase students' learning

REFERENCES

Ajzen, I. and Madden, T.J. (1986). "Prediction of Goal-directed Behavior: Attitudes, Intentions, and Perceived Behavioral Control." *Journal of Experimental Social Psychology*, 22, 453–74.

Astin, A.W. (1991, July). "VMI Case Dramatizes Basic Issues in the Use of Educational Research." *Chronicle of Higher Education*, "Point of View," 37(44), A36.

Astin, A.W. (1993). *What Matters in College: Four Critical Years Revisited.* San Francisco: Jossey-Bass.

Bondeson, W.B. (1992). "Faculty Development and the New American Scholar." In D.H. Wulff, and J.D. Nyquist (Eds.), *To Improve the Academy: Resources for Faculty, Instructional, and Organizational Development,* 11 (pp. 3–12). The Professional and Organizational Development Network in Higher Education. Stillwater, OK: New Forums Press, Inc.

Bonwell, C.C. and Eison, J.A. (1991). *Active Learning: Creating Excitement in the Classroom.* ASHE-ERIC Higher Education Report No. 1. Washington, DC: The George Washington University, School of Education and Human Development.

Boyer, E.L. (1990). *Scholarship Reconsidered: Priorities of the Professoriate.* Princeton, NJ: The Carnegie Foundation for the Advancement of Teaching.

Cooper, J., Prescott, S., Cook, L., Smith, L. Mueck, R., and Cuseo, J. (1990). *Cooperative Learning and College Instruction: Effective Use of Student Learning Teams.* Long Beach, CA: The California State University Foundation.

Cuseo, J.B. (1989). "Faculty Development: The Why and How of It." In S. Kahn (Ed.). *To Improve the Academy: Resources for Faculty, Instructional, and Organizational Development,* 8 (13–36). The Professional and Organizational Development Network in Higher Education. Stillwater, OK: New Forums Press, Inc.

Davis, J.R. (1993). *Better Teaching, More Learning: Strategies for Success in Postsecondary Settings.* Phoenix, AZ: Oryx Press.

Ekroth, L. (1990). "Why Professors Don't Change." In L. Ekroth (Ed.). *Teaching Excellence: Toward the Best in the Academy,* (Winter-Spring). The Professional and Organizational Development Network in Higher Education. Stillwater, OK: New Forums Press, Inc.

Erickson, G. (1986). "A Survey of Faculty Development Practices." In M.D. Svinicki (Ed.), *To Improve the Academy: Resources for Student, Faculty, and Institutional Development.* (pp. 182–196).The Professional and Organizational Development Network in Higher Education and National Council for Staff, Program, and Organizational Development. Stillwater, OK: New Forums Press, Inc.

Johnson, D.W., Johnson, R.T., and Smith, K.A. (1991). *Active Learning: Cooperation in the College Classroom.* Edina, MN: Interaction Book Company.

Johnson, D.W., Johnson, R.T., and Smith, K.A. (1991). *Cooperative Learning: Increasing College Faculty Instructional Productivity.* ASHE-ERIC Higher Education Report No. 4. Washington, DC: The George Washington University, School of Education and Human Development.

Joyce, B., Showers, B., and Weil, M. (1993). *Model of Teaching.* Englewood Cliffs, NJ: Prentice-Hall.

Karre, I. (1996). *Busy, Noisy, and Powerfully Effective: Cooperative Learning in the College Classroom,* Videotape and Faculty Handbook. Greeley, CO: University of Northern Colorado.

McKeachie, W.J. (1994). *Teaching Tips: Strategies, Research, and Theory for College and University Teachers.* 9th Ed. Lexington, MA: D. C . Heath.

Murray, F.B. (1994). "Why Understanding the Theoretical Basis of Cooperative Learning Enhances Teaching Success." In J.S. Thousand, R.A. Villa, and A.I. Nevin (Eds.), *Creativity and Collaborative Learning: A Practical Guide to Empowering Students and Teachers* (pp. 3–11). Baltimore: Paul H. Brookes Publishing Co.

Nevin, A.I., Smith, K., and Udvari-Solner. (1994). "Cooperative Group Learning and Higher Education." In J.S. Thousand, R.A. Villa, and A.I. Nevin (Eds.), *Creativity and Collaborative Learning: A Practical Guide to Empowering Students and Teachers* (pp. 115–27). Baltimore: Paul H. Brookes Publishing Co.

Palmer, P. J. (1997). "The Renewal of Community in Higher Education." In W.E. Campbell and K.A. Smith, *New Paradigms for College Teaching.* (pp. 1–18). Edina. MN: Interaction Book Company.

Prescott, S. (1996, Spring). "Troubleshooting Cooperative Learning." *Cooperative Learning and College Teaching,* 6(3), 10–11.

Rhem, J. (1992). "Getting Past the Doorman." *The National Teaching and Learning Forum,* 2(1), 4.

Roy, P. (1996). "Staff Development that Makes a Difference." *Cooperative Learning: Publications for Cooperative in Education.* 16(2), 3–12.

Skinner, M.E. and Welch, F.C. (1996). "Peer Coaching for Better Teaching." *College Teaching,* 44(4), 153–56.

Smith, K.A., Johnson, D.W., and Johnson, R.T. (1992). "Cooperative Learning and Positive Change in Higher Education." In A. Goodsell, M. Mahler, V. Tinto, B.L. Smith, and J. MacGregor (Eds.). *Collaborative Learning: A Sourcebook for Higher Education.* (pp. 34–36). University Park, PA: National Center on Postsecondary Teaching, Learning, and Assessment.

Sparks, G. (1983). "Synthesis on Research on Staff Development for Effective Teaching." *Educational Leadership,* 42(6), 65–72.

Svinicki, M. D. (1996). "When Teachers Become Learners." *The National Teaching and Learning Forum,* 5(3), 1-5.

Weimer, M. G. (1988). "Reading Your Way to Better Teaching." *College Teaching,* 36(2), 48–53.

Weimer, M. G. (1992). "Improving Higher Education: Issues and Perspectives on Teaching and Learning." In D.W. Wulff and J.D. Nyquist (Eds.), *To Improve the Academy: Resources for Faculty, Instructional and Organizational Development* (pp. 13–23). The Professional and Organizational Development Network in Higher Education. Stillwater, OK: New Forums Press, Inc.

Wood, F.H. and Thompson, S.R. (1993). "Assumptions about Staff Development based on Research and Best Practice." *Journal of Staff Development,* 14(4), 52–57.

BIBLIOGRAPHY

Abrami, P., Chambers, P.C., B., Poulsen, C., Howden, J., d'Apollonia, S., De Simone, C., Kastelorizios, K., Wagner, D., and Glashan, A. (1993). *Using Cooperative Learning*. Montreal: Concordia University: Centre for the Study of Classroom Processes.

Accounting Education Change Commission. (1990, August). *AECC Urges Priority for Teaching in Higher Education*. Issues Statement No. 1, Torrance, CA: Accounting Education Change Commission.

Adams, M. (1992). "Cultural Inclusion in the American College Classroom." In N. V. N. Chism, and L. L. B. Border (Eds.), *Teaching for Diversity: New Directions for Teaching and Learning, No. 49*. San Francisco: Jossey-Bass.

Ajzen, I. and Madden, T. J. (1986). "Prediction of Goal-directed Behavior: Attitudes, Intentions, and Perceived Behavioral Control." *Journal of Experimental Social Psychology, 22*, 453–74.

Alexander, S. (1995). *Teaching and Learning on the World Wide Web*. Ausweb95-Education-Learning on the World Wide Web. Online at <http://www.scu.edu.au/authors/education2/alexander/> Downloaded 22 July 1996. No longer available.

Angelo, T.A. (1994, Spring). "Using Assessment to Improve Cooperative Learning." *Cooperative Learning and College Teaching, 4*(3), 5–7.

Angelo, T.A. (1996). "Seven Shifts and Seven Levers: Developing More Productive Learning Communities." *The National Teaching and Learning Forum. 6*(1), pp. 1–4.

Angelo, T.A. and Cross, K.P. (1993). *Classroom Assessment Techniques: A Handbook for College Teachers*. 2nd Ed. San Francisco: Jossey-Bass.

Arambula-Greenfield, T. (1996). "Implementing Problem-based Learning in a College Science Class." *Journal of College Science Teaching, 26*(1), 26–30.

Aronson, E., Stephan, C., Sikes, J., and Snapp, M. (1978). *The Jigsaw Classroom.* Beverly Hills, CA: Sage.

Astin, A.W. (1985). *Achieving Educational Excellence: A Critical Assessment of Priorities and Practices in Higher Education.* San Francisco: Jossey-Bass.

Astin, A.W. (1988, Sept./Oct.). "Competition or Cooperation? Teaching Teamwork as a Basic Skill." *Change: The Magazine of Higher Learning,* 12–19.

Astin, A.W. (1991, July 24). "VMI Case Dramatizes Basic Issues in the Use of Educational Research." *Chronicle of Higher Education, "Point of View,"* 37(44), A36.

Astin, A.W. (1993). *What Matters in College: Four Critical Years Revisited.* San Francisco: Jossey-Bass.

Astin, A.W., Banta, T.W., Cross, K.P., El-Khawas, E., Ewell, P.T. , Hutchings, P., Marchese, T.J., McClenny, K.M., Mentkowski, M., Miller, M.A., Moran, E.T., and Wright, B.D. (1992). *Principles of Good Practice for Assessing Student Learning.* Washington, DC: American Association of Higher Education.

Baird, J. (Ed.), (1992). *Shared Adventure: A View of Quality Teaching and Learning. Second Report of the Teaching and Learning Science in Schools Project.* School of Graduate Studies, Monash University.

Barell, J. 1988, cited (p. 59) in Costa and O'Leary, "Co-cognition: The Cooperative Development of the Intellect." In Davidson, J. and Worsham, T (Eds.), *Enhancing Thinking through Cooperative Learning.* (1988, April). *Cogitare: A Newsletter of the ASCD Network on Teaching Thinking,* 3(1).

Barr, R.B. and Tagg, J. (1995, Nov./Dec.). *Change: The Magazine of Higher Learning,* 13–25.

Barrows, H.S. and Myers, A.C. (1993). *Problem Based Learning in Secondary Schools.* Unpublished monograph, Springfield, IL: Problem Based Learning Institute, Lanphier High School, and Southern Illinois University Medical School.

Bavaro, J.A. (1996). "Exploring One Approach to Evaluating Group Work at the University Level."Unpublished manuscript.

Bean, J.C. (1996). *Engaging Ideas: The Professor's Guide to Integrating Writing, Critical Thinking, and Active Learning in the Classroom.* San Francisco: Jossey-Bass.

Belenky, M.F., Clinchy, B.M., Goldberger, N.R., and Tarule, J.M. (1986). *Women's Ways of Knowing: The Development of Self, Voice, and Mind.* New York: Basic Books, Inc.

Bellanca, J. (1990). *The Cooperative Think Tank: Graphic Organizers to Teach Thinking in the Cooperative Classroom.* Palatine, IL: Skylight Publishing.

Bellanca, J. (1992). *The Cooperative Think Tank II: Graphic Organizers to Teach Thinking in the Cooperative Classroom.* Palatine, IL: II/Skylight.

Bender, T.A. (1986). "Monitoring and the Transfer of Individual Problem Solving." *Contemporary Educational Psychology,* 11, 161–69.

Berry, D.C. (1983). "Metacognitive Experience and Transfer of Logical Reasoning." *The Quarterly Journal of Experimental Psychology,* 35A, 39–49.

Biggs, J.B. and Telfer, R. (1987). *The Process of Learning.* 2nd Ed. Sydney: Prentice-Hall.

Bloom, B.S. (1956). *Taxonomy of Educational Objectives (Cognitive Domain).* New York: Longman.

Boehm, L. (1992). "In Wake of Crisis: Reclaiming the Heart of Teaching and Learning." In T. J. Frecka (Ed.), *Critical Thinking, Interactive Learning and Technology: Reaching for Excellence in Business Education* (pp. 24–40). Arthur Andersen Foundation.

Boehrer, John. (1990–1991). "Spectators and Gladiators: Reconnecting the Students with the Problem." *Teaching Excellence,* 2(7), The Professional and Organizational Development Network in Higher Education. Stillwater, OK: New Forums Press, Inc.

Bondeson, W.B. (1992). "Faculty Development and the New American Scholar." In D.H. Wulff and J.D. Nyquist (Eds.), *To Improve the Academy: Resources for Faculty, Instructional, and Organizational Development,* 11 (pp. 3–12). The Professional and Organizational Development Network in Higher Education, Stillwater, OK: New Forums Press, Inc

Bonwell, C. (1996). "Building a Supportive Climate for Active Learning." *The National Teaching and Learning Forum.* 6(1), pp. 4–7.

Bonwell, C.C., and Eison, J.A. (1991). *Active Learning: Creating Excitement in the Classroom.* ASHE-ERIC Higher Education Report No. 1. Washington, DC: The George Washington University School of Education and Human Development.

Bossert, S.T. (1988). "Cooperative Activities in the Classroom." *Review of Educational Research,* 15, 225–50.

Boud, D. and Feletti, G. (Eds.), (1991). *The Challenge of Problem Based Learning.* New York: St. Martin's Press.

Boyce, L.A. (1996, Spring). "Brain Bingo: Using an Old Game to Help Students Learn New Material." *Cooperative Learning and College Teaching,* 6(3), pp. 11–12.

Boyer, E.L. (1987). *College: The Undergraduate Experience in America.* New York: Harper and Row.

Boyer, E.L. (1990). *Scholarship Reconsidered: Priorities of the Professoriate.* Princeton, NJ: The Carnegie Foundation for the Advancement of Teaching.

BradyLink, A. (1996) *Cooperative Learning in Computer Science: Assignment for General Education or CSO Course.* Online at <http://bingen.cs.csbsju....egler/CSO.hypercard.html> Downloaded 25 June 1996. No longer available.

Bredehoft, D.J. (1991). "Cooperative Controversies in the Classroom." *College Teaching,* 39(3), 122–25.

Bridges, E. and Hallinger, P. (1992). *Problem Based Learning for Administrators.* ERIC Clearinghouse on Educational Management, University of Oregon.

Brookfield, S.D. (1987). *Developing Critical Thinkers: Challenging Adults to Explore Alternative Ways of Thinking and Acting.* San Francisco: Jossey-Bass.

Brookfield, S.D. (1991). *The Skillful Teacher: On Technique, Trust, and Responsiveness in the Classroom.* San Francisco: Jossey-Bass.

Bruffee, K.A. (1993). *Collaborative Learning: Higher Education, Interdependence, and the Authority of Knowledge.* Baltimore, MD: The Johns Hopkins University Press.

Bruffee, K.A. (1995, January/February). "Sharing Our Toys: Cooperative versus Collaborative Learning." *Change: The Magazine of Higher Learning,* 27(1), 12–18.

Burch, K. (1995). "PBL and the Lively Classroom." *About Teaching,* 47, University of Delaware: A Newsletter of the Center for Teaching Effectiveness. Online at <http://www.physics.udel.edu/~pbl/cte/jan95-posc.html> Downloaded 18 Feb. 1997.

Buscaglia, L. (1982). *Living, Loving and Learning.* Troy, MI: Holt, Rinehart, and Winston.

Cashin, W.E. (1987). *Improving Essay Tests.* IDEA Paper No. 17. Manhattan, KS: Center for Faculty Evaluation and Development, Division of Continuing Education, Kansas State University.

Cashin, W.E. (1994). *Readings to Improve Selected Teaching Methods.* IDEA Paper No. 30. Manhattan, KS: Center for Faculty Evaluation and Development, Division of Continuing Education, Kansas State University.

Chance, P. (1992, Nov). "The Rewards of Learning." *Phi Delta Kappan,* pp. 200–207. Reprinted in *Educational Psychology 97/98 Annual Editions* (117–21). Guilford, CT: Duskin/McGraw-Hill.

Charrier, G.C. (1965). *Cog's Ladder: A Model of Group Growth.* Unpublished paper at Proctor and Gamble Co.

Chickering, A.W., and Gamson, A.F., (1987). *Seven Principles for Good Practice in Undergraduate Education.* Racine, WI: The Johnson Foundation, Inc./Wingspread. [Available by contacting the Seven Principles Resources Center, P.O. Box 5838, Winona State University, Winona, MN 55987-5838; (507) 457-5020]

Christensen, C.R. and Hansen, A.J. (1987). *Teaching and the Case Method.* Boston: Harvard Business School.

The Chronicle of Higher Education Almanac. (1996, September 2). "College Enrollment by Age of Students, Fall 1993." 43(1), p. 17.

Clark, D. and Redmond, M. (1982). *Small Group Instructional Diagnosis: Final Report.* ERIC Document Reproduction Service No. ED 217954.

Clarke, J. (1994). "Pieces of the Puzzle: The Jigsaw Method." In S. Sharan (Ed.), *Handbook of Cooperative Learning Methods* (pp. 34–50). Westport, CT: Greenwood Press.

Clegg, V.L. and Cashin, W.E. (1986). *Improving Multiple Choice Tests.* IDEA Paper No. 16. Manhattan, KS: Center for Faculty Evaluation and Development, Division of Continuing Education, Kansas State University.

Cohen, E.G. (1994). "Restructuring the Classroom: Conditions for Productive Small Groups." *Review of Educational Research,* 64, 1–35.

Collins, A. (1991) "The Role of Computer Technology in Restructuring Schools." *Phi Delta Kappan*, 73(1), 28–36.

Combs, A.W. (1979). *Myths in Education: Beliefs that Hinder Progress and their Alternatives*. Boston: Allyn and Bacon.

Condry, J. (1987). "Enhancing Motivation: A Social Development Perspective." In M.L. Maehr and D.A. Kleiber (Eds.), *Advances in Motivation and Achievement, Vol. 5: Enhancing Motivation*. Greenwich, CT: JAI Press.

Cooper, J. (1990, May). "Cooperative Learning and College Teaching: Tips from the Trenches." *The Teaching Professor*, 4(5), 1–2.

Cooper, J. (1993). "Review of the Harvard Assessment Seminars." *Cooperative Learning: The Magazine for Cooperation in Higher Education*, 13(30), 46–47.

Cooper, J, Prescott, S., Cook, L., Smith, L., Mueck, R., and Cuseo, J. (1990). *Cooperative Learning and College Instruction: Effective Use of Student Learning Teams*. Long Beach, CA: The California State University Foundation.

Cooper, J. and Mueck, R. (1990). "Student Involvement in Learning: Cooperative Learning and College Instruction." *Journal on Excellence in College Teaching*, 1, 68–76. [Article is reprinted in Goodsell, A., Mayer, M., Tinto, V., Smith, B.L., and J. MacGregor (Eds.), (1992). *Collaborative Learning: A Sourcebook for Higher Education*, pp. 68–74). University Park, PA: National Center on Postsecondary Teaching, Learning, and Assessment.]

Cooperative Learning Center, University of Minnesota, College of Education and Human Development. Online at <http://134.84.183.54/pages/conflict.html>. Downloaded 10 Feb. 1997. No longer available.

Cottell, P.G. and Millis, B.J. (1992). "Cooperative Learning in Accounting." *The Journal of Accounting Education*, 10, 95–111.

Cottell, P.G. and Millis, B.J. (1993). "Cooperative Learning Structures in the Instruction of Accounting." *Issues in Accounting Education*. 8(1), 40–59.

Covey, S.R. (1989). *The Seven Habits of Highly Successful People: Restoring the Character Ethic*. New York: Simon and Schuster.

Creed, T. (1991). "A Teaching Strategy." In B. Millis (Ed.), *The Bright Idea Network*, 6th Ed. The Professional Organizational and Development Network in Higher Education.

Creed, T. (1996). *Empowering Learners: Transforming Faculty and Student Roles* (with Millis). Presentations at 1996 Faculty Regional Workshops, Council of Independent Colleges, Raleigh, SC (May 29-31) and Cleveland, OH (June 6-8).

Creed, T. (1997). "Extending the Classroom Walls Electronically." In W.E. Campbell and K.A. Smith (Eds.), *New Paradigms for College Teaching*. (pp. 149–84). Edina, MN: Interaction Book Company. Online at <http://bingen.cs.csbsju.edu/~creed>. No longer available.

Cross, K. P. (1986, March). *Taking Teaching Seriously*. Paper presented at the national conference of the American Association for Higher Education, Washington, DC.

Cross, K.P. (1991, October). "Effective College Teaching." *ASEE Prism*, 27–29.

Cross, K.P. (1993, March). *The Student Side of Classroom Research*. Presentation, National Conference on Higher Education, American Association for Higher Education, Washington, DC.

Culross, R. (1996, November/December). "Remediation: Real Students, Real Standards." *Change: The Magazine of Higher Learning*, 28(6), pp. 50–52.

Cuseo, J. (1992, Winter). "Collaborative and Cooperative Learning in Higher Education: A Proposed Taxonomy," *Cooperative Learning and College Teaching*, 2(2), 2–4.

Cuseo, J.B. (1989). "Faculty Development: The Why and How of It." In S. Kahn (Ed.), *To Improve the Academy: Resources for Faculty, Instructional, and Organizational Development*, 8 (13–36). The Professional and Organizational Development Network in Higher Education. Stillwater, OK: New Forums Press, Inc.

Cuseo, J.B. (1994). "Critical Thinking and Cooperative Learning: A Natural Marriage." *Cooperative Learning and College Teaching*, 4(2), 2–5.

Dalton, D.W., Hannafin, M. J., and Hooper, S. (1989). "Effects of Individual and Cooperative Computer Assisted Instruction on Student Performance and Attitudes." *Educational Technology Research and Development*, 37(2), 15–24.

Dansereau, D.F. (1983). *Cooperative Learning: Impact on Acquisition of Knowledge and Skills* [Report No. 341]. Abilene, TX: U.S. Army Research Institute for the Behavioral and Social Sciences. [ERIC Document Reproduction Service No. ED 243 088]

Dansereau, D.F. (1986). *Dyadic and Cooperative Learning and Performance Strategies*. Paper presented at the annual meeting of the American Educational Research Association, San Francisco.

Davidson, N. (1990). "The Small-group Discovery Method in Secondary- and College-level Mathematics." In N. Davidson (Ed.), *Cooperative Learning in Mathematics: A Handbook for Teachers* (pp. 335–61). Menlo Park, CA: Addison-Wesley.

Davidson, N. (Ed.), (1990). *Cooperative Learning in Mathematics: A Handbook for Teachers*. Reading, MA: Addison-Wesley.

Davidson, N. (1994). "Cooperative and Collaborative Learning: An Integrative Perspective." In J.S. Thousand, R.A. Villa, and A.I. Nevin (Eds.), *Creativity and Collaborative Learning: A Practical Guide to Empowering Students and Teachers*. Baltimore, MD: Paul H. Brookes Publishing Co.

Davis, B.G. (1993). *Tools for Teaching*. San Francisco: Jossey-Bass.

Davis, J.R. (1993). *Better Teaching, More Learning: Strategies for Success in Postsecondary Settings*. Phoenix, AZ: Oryx Press.

Davis, S.S. (1994). *Problem Based Learning in Medical Education: A Qualitative Study of Curriculum Design and Students' Experience in an Experimental Program*. Unpublished dissertation. The Ohio State University.

"Deep Learning, Surface Learning." (1993). *AAHE Bulletin*, 45(8), pp. 14–17.

Degnan, M.J. (1997). "Bringing 'Distant' Guest Speakers into the Classroom." *Wright State Center for Teaching and Learning Jan/Feb 1997 Newsletter*, 5(4), 1–2.

Deming, E. (1986) *Out of Crises*. Massachusetts Institute of Technology Center for Advanced Engineering Study.

Dentler, D. (1994). "Cooperative Learning and American History." *Cooperative Learning and College Teaching*, 4(3), 9–12.

Department of Foreign Languages, U. S. Air Force Academy. (1996, Spring). *Departmental Guidance Statement*. Unpublished Document.

Diamond, N.A. (1988). "S. G. I. D. (Small Group Instructional Diagnosis): Tapping Student Perceptions of Teaching." In E. C. Wadsworth (Ed.), *POD: A Handbook for New Practitioners* (pp. 89–93). Stillwater, OK: New Forums Press, Inc.

Diamond, R.M. (1989). *Designing and Improving Courses and Curricula in Higher Education: A Systematic Approach*. San Francisco: Jossey-Bass.

Dillenbourg, P. and Schneider, D. (1995). *Collaborative Learning and the Internet*. Online at <http://tecfa.unige.ch/tecfa/tecfa-research/CMC/colla/iccai95_1.html> Downloaded 13 Feb. 1997.

Dorwick, K. *Building the Virtual Department: A Case Study of Online Teaching: Three Models for Teachers*. Online at <http://www.uic.edu/~kdorwick/dissertation/models.htm> Downloaded 13 Feb. 1997.

Drohan, T. (Nov. 1994). *Teaching with Cases at the Academy*, Workshop at the United States Air Force Academy.

Duch, B.J. (1996). "Problems: A Key Factor in PBL." *About Teaching: A Newsletter of the Center for Teaching Effectiveness*, 50, 7–8. University of Delaware.

Duffy, D.K. and Jones, J.W. (1995). *Teaching within the Rhythms of the Semester*. San Francisco: Jossey-Bass.

Duffy, T.M. (1994). *Corporate and Community Education: Achieving Success in the Information Society*. Unpublished paper. Bloomington, IN: Indiana University.

Ehrmann, S.C. (1995, Mar./Apr.). "Asking the Right Questions: What Does Research Tell us about Technology and Higher Learning?" *Change: The Magazine of Higher Learning*, 27(2), 20–27.

Eison, J. and Bonwell, C. (1988, March). *Making Real the Promise of Active Learning*. Paper presented at the national conference of the American Association for Higher Education, Washington, DC.

Ekroth, L. (1990). "Why Professors Don't Change." In L. Ekroth (Ed.), *Teaching Excellence: Toward the Best in the Academy*. (Winter-Spring). The Professional and Organizational Development Network in Higher Education. Stillwater, OK: New Forums Press, Inc.

Entwistle, N. (1981). *Styles of Learning and Teaching*. New York: John Wiley and Sons.

Erickson, G. (1986). "A Survey of Faculty Development Practices." In M. D. Svinicki (Ed.), *To Improve the Academy: Resources for Student, Faculty, and Institutional Development* (pp. 182–96). Stillwater, OK: The Professional and Organizational Development Network in Higher Education and National Council for Staff, Program, and Organizational Development.

Fantuzzo, J.W., Dimeff, L.A., and Fox, S.L. (1989). "Reciprocal Peer Tutoring: A Multimodal Assessment of Effectiveness with College Students." *Teaching of Psychology*, 16(3), 133–35.

Fantuzzo, J.W., Riggio, R.E., Connelly, S., and Dimeff, L.A. (1989). "Effects of Reciprocal Peer Tutoring on Academic Achievement and Psychological Adjustment: A Component Analysis." *Journal of Educational Psychology*, 81(2), 173–77.

Farrington, G.C. (1996). Oct. "Bringing Technology to Education." *ASEE Prism*, 56.

Fassinger, P.A. (1995). "Understanding Classroom Interaction: Students' and Professors' Contributions to Students' Silence." *Journal of Higher Education*. 66, 82–96.

Felder, R.M. and Brent, R. (1994) *Cooperative Learning in Technical Courses: Procedures, Pitfalls, and Payoffs*. Eric Document Reproduction Service Report ED 377038. Online at <http://www2.ncsu.edu/unity/lockers/user/f/felder/public/Papers/Coopreport.html>.

Fiechtner, S.B. and Davis, E,A. (1985). "Why Groups Fail: A Survey of Student Experiences with Learning Groups." *The Organizational Behavior Teaching Review*, 9(4), 58–73.

Finkle, D.L. and Monk, G.S. (1983). "Teachers and Learning Groups: Dissolution of the Atlas Complex." In C. Bouton and R.Y. Garth (Eds.), *Learning in Groups. New Directions for Teaching and Learning, No. 14* (pp. 83–97). San Francisco: Jossey-Bass.

Forsyth, D.R. and McMillan, J.H. (1991a). "Practical Proposals for Motivating Students." In R.J. Menges and M. D. Svinicki (Eds.), *College Teaching: From Theory to Practice. New Directions for Teaching and Learning, No. 45* (pp. 53–65). San Francisco: Jossey-Bass.

Forsyth, D.R. and McMillan, J.H. (1991b). "What Theories of Motivation Say about Why Students Learn." In R.J. Menges and M. D. Svinicki, *College teaching: From Theory to Practice. New Directions for Teaching and Learning, No. 45* (pp. 39–51). San Francisco: Jossey-Bass.

Frierson, H. (1986). "Two Intervention Methods: Effects on Groups of Predominantly Black Nursing Students' Board Scores." *Journal of Research and Development in Education*, 19, 18–23.

Fuhrmann, B.S. and Grasha, A.F. (1983). *A Practical Handbook for College Teachers*. Boston: Little, Brown.

Gabennesch, H. (1992). "The Enriched Syllabus: To Convey a Larger Vision." *The National Teaching and Learning Forum*, 1(4), 4.

Gaff, Jerry G. (1992) "Beyond Politics: The Educational Issues Inherent in Multicultural education," *Change: The Magazine of Higher Learning*, 24(1), 1992, 31–35.

Gagne, R.M. and Smith, E.C. (1962). "A Study of the Effects of Verbalization on Problem Solving." *Journal of Experimental Psychology*, 63(1), 12–18.

Garfield, J. (1993). "Teaching Statistics Using Small-Group Cooperative Learning." *Journal of Statistics Education, 1*(1) Online at <http://fisher.stat.unipg.it/ncsu/info/jse/v1n1/garfield.html> Downloaded 1 Mar. 1997. No longer available.

Gartner, A., Kohler, M., and Riessmann, F. (1971). *Children Teach Children: Learning by Teaching.* New York: Harper and Row.

Geiger, T. (1991). "Test Partners: A Formula for Success." *Innovation Abstracts: A Newsletter Published by the College of Education, University of Texas at Austin,* 13(11).

Gere, A.R. (1987). *Writing Groups: History, Theory, and Implications.* Carbondale and Edwardsville: Southern Illinois University Press.

Gibsen, J. (1995). "Protein Model Lab ala Rand." In Nurrenbern, S. C. (Ed.), *Experiences in Cooperative Learning: A Collection for Chemistry Teachers* (p. 62). Madison, WI: Institute for Chemical Education.

Gibson, B. (1991). "Research Methods Jeopardy: A Tool for Involving Students and Organizing the Study Session." *Teaching of Psychology,* 18(3), 176–177.

Giezkowski, W. (1992). "The Influx of Older Students Can Revitalize College Teaching." *The Chronicle of Higher Education,* 38(29), 133–134.

Gilbert, S. (1996, March/April). "Double Visions—Paradigms in Balance or Collision?" *Change: The Magazine of Higher Learning,* 28(2), 8–9

Glasser, W. (1990). *The Quality School.* New York: Harper and Row.

Graves, L. N. (1994). "Creating a Community Context for Cooperative Learning." In S. Sharan (Ed.), *Handbook of Cooperative Learning Methods* (pp. 283–99) (pp. 34–50). Westport, CT: Greenwood Press.

Gray-Shellberg, L. (1994). "Jeopardy 305: A Cooperative Learning Method for Teaching History and Systems of Psychology." *Cooperative Learning and College Teaching,* 5(1), pp. 12–14.

Green, K.C. and Gilbert, S.W. (1995, Mar./Apr.). "Great Expectations: Content, Communications, Productivity, and the Role of Information Technology in Higher Education." *Change: The Magazine of Higher Learning,* 27(2), 8–18.

Green, K.C. (1996, March/April). "The Coming Ubiquity of Information Technology." *Change: The Magazine of Higher Learning,* 28(2), 24–28.

Groner, R., Groner, M., and Bischof, W. F., eds. (1983). *Methods of Heuristics.* Hillsdale, NJ: Lawrence Eribaum Associates.

Gronlund, N.E. (1985). *Stating Objectives for Classroom Instruction.* 3rd Ed. New York: Macmillan.

Hanna, G.S. and Cashin, W.E. (1987). *Matching Instructional Objectives, Subject Matter, Tests, and Score Interpretation.* IDEA Paper No. 18. Manhattan, KS: Center for Faculty Evaluation and Development, Division of Continuing Education, Kansas State University.

Hanna, G.S. and Cashin, W.E. (1988). *Improving College Grading.* IDEA Paper No. 19. Manhattan, KS: Center for Faculty Evaluation and Development, Division of Continuing Education, Kansas State University.

Hanna, G.S. (1993). *Better Teaching through Better Testing*. Fort Worth, TX: Harcourt Brace Jovanovich.

Harris, M.M. (1993). "Motivating with the Course Syllabus." *The National Teaching and Learning Forum.* 3(1), pp. 1–3.

Hawisher, G.E. and Pemberton, M.A. (1996). *Writing Across the Curriculum Encounters Asynchronous Learning Networks or WAC Meets up with ALN.* Unpublished manuscript.

Hendrickson, A.D. (1990). "Cooperative Group Test-taking." *Focus*, 5(2), 6. (Faculty Newsletter by the Office of Educational Development Programs, University of Minnesota).

Hirsch, E,D. (1996). *The Schools We Need: And Why We Don't Have Them.* New York: Doubleday.

Hooper, S. (1992). "Cooperative Learning and Computer-based Instruction." *Educational Technology Research and Development*, 40(3), 21–38.

Howe, A. (1988). *Expanding Horizons: Teaching through Whole Class Discussion.* Sheffield, England: National Association for Teachers of English

Hughes, C. (Spring 1996). "The Dynamics of Group Formation: An Applied Method for Selecting Team Membership." *USAFA Educator*, 4(3), pp. 8;10. Reprinted in *Cooperative Learning and College Teaching*, 6(3), 13–14.

Jacobs, L.C. and Chase, C.I. (1992). *Developing and Using Tests Effectively: A Guide for Faculty.* San Francisco: Jossey-Bass.

Johnson, D.W. and Johnson, R.T. (1993, Spring). "What We Know about Cooperative Learning at the College Level." *Cooperative Learning: The Magazine for Cooperation in Higher Education*, 13(3), 17–18.

Johnson, D.W. and Johnson, R.T. (1995) *Creative Conflict: Intellectual Challenges in the Classroom.* Edina, MN: Interaction Book Company.

Johnson, D.W. and Johnson, R.T. (1996). *Meaningful and Manageable Assessment through Cooperative Learning.* Edina, MN: Interaction Book Company.

Johnson, D.W. and Johnson, R.T. (1997). "Academic Controversy: Increase Intellectual Conflict and Increase the Quality of Learning." In W. E. Campbell and K. A. Smith (Eds.), *New Paradigms for College Teaching.* Edina, MN: Interaction Book Company.

Johnson, D.W., Johnson, R.T., and Smith, K. (1991). *Active Learning: Cooperation in the College Classroom.* Edina, MN: Interaction Book Company.

Johnson, D.W., Johnson, R.T., and Smith, K.A. (1991) *Cooperative Learning: Increasing College Faculty Instructional Productivity.* ASHE-ERIC Higher Education Report No. 4. Washington, DC: The George Washington University, School of Education and Human Development.

Johnson, R.T. and Johnson, D.W. (1994). "An Overview of Cooperative Learning." In J.S. Thousand, R.A. Villa, and A.I. Nevin (Eds.), *Creativity and Collaborative Learning: A Practical Guide to Empowering Students and Teachers* (pp. 31–44). Baltimore, MD: Paul H. Brookes Publishing Co.

Johnston, C. (1995). *Fostering Deeper Learning.* Economics Department, University of Melbourne. Online at <http://www.econ.unimelb.edu.au/ecowww/

fost.html> Last modified 19 Sept. 1995. Downloaded, July 30, 1996. No longer available.

Jones, P. (1991, Apr.). *You Be the Judge: A Series of Cooperative Learning Activities based on Three Fairy Tales.* Unpublished manuscript, Modern Languages, Donevan Collegiate, Oshawa.

Joyce, B., Showers, B., and Weil, M. (1993). *Model of Teaching.* Englewood Cliffs, NJ: Prentice-Hall.

Kagan, S. (1989). *Cooperative Learning Resources for Teachers.* San Juan Capistrano, CA: Resources for Teachers, Inc.

Kagan, S. (1992). *Cooperative Learning.* San Juan Capistrano, CA: Resources for Teachers, Inc.

Kagan, S. (1994). "The Structural Approach." In S. Sharan (Ed.), *Handbook of Cooperative Learning Methods* (pp. 114–133). Westport, CT: Greenwood Press.

Kagan, S. (1995). "Group Grades Miss the Mark." *Educational Leadership, 52*(8), 68–71.

Karre, I. (1996). *Busy, Noisy, and Powerfully Effective: Cooperative Learning in the College Classroom.* Videotape and Faculty Handbook. Greeley, CO: University of Northern Colorado.

Katzenback, J.R. and Smith, D.K. (1993). *The Wisdom of Teams.* New York: HarperCollins.

Keeler, C.M. and Steinhorst, R.K. (1995). "Using Small Groups to Promote Active Learning in the Introductory Statistics Course: A Report from the Field." *Journal of Statistics Education, 3*(2). Online at <http://fisher.stat.unipg.it/ncsu/info/jse/v3n2/keeler.html> Downloaded 27 Feb. 1997. No longer available.

Keenan, D. and Maier, M.H. (1995). *Economics Live! Learning Economics the Collaborative Way.* 2nd Ed. New York: McGraw-Hill.

Keyworth, D.R. (1989). "The Group Test." *Teaching Professor* 3(8), 5.

King, A. (1990). "Enhancing Peer Interaction and Learning in the Classroom through Reciprocal Questioning." *American Educational Research Journal,* 27(4), 664–687.

King, A. (1992). "Promoting Active Learning and Collaborative Learning in Business Administration Classes." In T. J. Frecka (Ed.), *Critical Thinking, Interactive Learning and Technology: Reaching for Excellence in Business Education* (pp. 158–173). Arthur Andersen Foundation.

King, A. (1995, Winter). "Guided Peer Questioning: A Cooperative Learning Approach to Critical Thinking." *Cooperative Learning and College Teaching,* 5(2), pp. 15–19.

King, P.M. and Kitchener, K.S. (1994). *Developing Reflective Judgment: Understanding and Promoting Intellectual Growth and Critical Thinking in Adolescents and Adults.* San Francisco: Jossey-Bass.

Kinlaw, D. (1990). *Developing Superior Work Teams.* New York: Free Press.

Kohn, A. (1986). *No Contest: The Case Against Competition.* Boston: Houghton Mifflin.

Kohn, A. (1993). *Punished by Rewards: The Trouble with Gold Stars, Incentive Plans, A's, Praise, and Other Bribes.* Boston: Houghton Mifflin.

Kohn, A. (1993b, June). "Rewards versus Learning: A Response to Paul Chance." *Phi Delta Kappan.* (783–87). Reprinted in *Educational Psychology 97/98 Annual Editions.* (122–25) Guilford, CT: Duskin/McGraw-Hill.

Kronholm, M.M. (1993). *The Impact of a Developmental Instruction Approach to Environmental Education at the Undergraduate Level on Development of Reflective Judgment.* Doctoral dissertation, Southern Illinois University.

Krupnick, C.G. (1987). "The Uses of Videotape Replay." In C.R. Christensen with A.J. Hansen (Eds.), *Teaching and the Case Method.* Boston: Harvard Business School.

Kuhn, T. (1962). *The Structure of Scientific Revolutions.* Chicago: University of Chicago Press.

Kulik, C.C., Chen-lin, C., and Kulik, J.A. (1991). "Effectiveness of Computer-based Instruction: An Updated Analysis." *Computers in Human Behavior, 7*(1–2), 75–94.

Kurfiss, J.G. (1988). *Critical Thinking: Theory, Research, Practice and Possibilities.* ASHE-ERIC Higher Education Report No. 2. Washington, DC: Association for the Study of Higher Education.

Larkin, J.H. and Chabay, R.W. (1989). "Research on Teaching Scientific Thinking: Implications for Computer-based Instruction." In L.B. Resnick and L.E. Klopfer (Eds.), *Toward the Thinking Curriculum: Current Cognitive Research* (pp. 150–72). Alexandria, VA: Association for Supervision and Curriculum Development.

Larson, C.O. and Dansereau D.F. (1986). "Cooperative Learning in Dyads." *Journal of Reading, 29,* 516–20.

Larson, C.O. Dansereau, D.F., O'Donnell, A.M., Hythecker, V.I., Lambiotte, J.G., and Rocklin, T.R. (1985). *Effects of Metacognitive and Elaborative Activity on Cooperative Learning and Transfer, 10,* 342–48.

Laurillard, D. (1993). *Rethinking University Teaching: A Framework for the Effective Use of Educational Technology.* London: Routledge.

Lawlor, E.J. (1997). *Small Group 'Research' on Biocultural Evolution of the Genus Homo.* Presentation at the 1997 Regional Conference on College Teaching: Using Cooperative Learning in Discipline-Specific Settings. February 21-22, 1997, Occidental College, Los Angeles.

Lepper, M.R. and Malone, T.W. (1985). "Intrinsic Motivation and Instructional Effectiveness in Computer-based Education." In R. E. Snow and M. J. Farr (Eds.), *Aptitude, Learning, and Instruction: III. Conatative and Affective Process Analysis.* Hillsdale, NJ: Erlbaum. 1985.

Levine, J.H. and Tompkins, D.P. (1996, June). "Making Learning Communities Work: Seven Lessons from Temple." *AAHE Bulletin,* 48(10), 2–6.

Lewis, R.B. (1995). *Practical Applications of Critical Thinking in the Engineering Classroom.* Booklet to accompany workshop given at the United States Air Force Academy.

Light, P.H. and Mevarech, Z.R. (1992). "Cooperative Learning with Computers: An Introduction." *Learning and Instruction, 2,* pp. 155–159.

Light, R.J. (1990). *The Harvard Assessment Seminars: First Report*. Cambridge, MA: Harvard University Press.

Light, R.J. (1992). *The Harvard Assessment Seminars: Second Report*. Cambridge, MA: Harvard University Press.

Lochhead, J. and Whimbey, A. (1987). "Teaching Analytical Reasoning through Think-aloud Pair Problem Solving." In J. E. Stice (Ed.), *Developing Critical Thinking and Problem-solving Abilities (72–93). New Directions for Teaching and Learning No. 30*. San Francisco: Jossey-Bass.

Lowman, J. (1984). *Mastering the Techniques of Teaching*. San Francisco: Jossey-Bass.

Lyman, F. (1981). "The Responsive Class Discussion." In A. S. Anderson (Ed.), *Mainstreaming Digest*. College Park, MD: University of Maryland College of Education.

Lynch, C.L. (1995). *Reflective Developmental Markers*. Unpublished manuscript available through Reflective Judgment Associates, New Concord, KY 42076, (502) 436–5839, 74671.2342@compuserve.com.

Lynch, C.L., Kitchener, K.S., and King, P.M. (1994). *Developing Reflective Judgment in the Classroom: A Manual for Faculty*. New Concord, KY: Reflective Judgment Associates.

Macaulay, B.A. and Gonzales, V.G. (1996, March). *Enhancing the Collaborative/ Cooperative Learning Experience: A Guide for Faculty Development*. Workshop presented at the AAHE National Conference on Higher Education.

Magner, D.K. (1996, 13 Sept). "Fewer Professors Believe Western Culture should be the Cornerstone of the College Curriculum: A Survey Finds Growing Commitment to Diversity and Multiculturalism." *The Chronicle of Higher Education*, 43(3), A12–A15.

Massey, W. (1996). *From Handicraft to Systems Thinking*. Presentation at the AAHE Summer Quality Academy, Breckenridge, CO, July 27-31.

Matthews, R.S., Cooper, J.L., Davidson, N., and Hawkes, P. (1995, July/August). "Building Bridges between Cooperative and Collaborative Learning." *Change: The Magazine of Higher Learning*, 35–39.

McKeachie, W.J. (1986) *Teaching Tips: Strategies, Research, and Theory for College and University Teachers*. 8th Ed. Lexington, MA: D. C. Heath.

McKeachie, W.J. (1994). *Teaching Tips: Strategies, Research, and Theory for College and University Teachers*. 9th Ed. Lexington, MA: D. C. Heath.

McKeachie, W.J., Pintrich, P.R., Lin, Y., and Smith, D.A. (1986). *Teaching and Learning in the College Classroom: A Review of the Research Literature*. Ann Arbor, MI: the University of Michigan.

McMillan, J.H. and Forsyth, D.R.(1991). "What Theories of Motivation Say About Why Students Learn." In R. J. Menges and M. D. Svinicki, *College Teaching: From Theory to Practice. New Directions for Teaching and Learning*, No. 45 (pp. 39–51). San Francisco: Jossey-Bass.

McTighe, J. (1992) "Graphic Organizers: Collaborative Links to Better Thinking." In N. Davidson and T. Worsham, (Eds.), *Enhancing Thinking through Cooperative Learning*. (pp. 182–97) New York: Teachers College Press.

Menges, R.J. (1994). "Teaching in the Age of Electronic Information." In W. J. McKeachie, *Teaching Tips: Strategies, Research, and Theory for College and University Teachers.* 9th Ed. (pp. 183–93). Lexington, MA: D. C. Heath.

Meyers, C. (1993). *Teaching Students to Think Critically: A Guide for Faculty in All Disciplines.* San Francisco: Jossey-Bass.

Meyers, G.D. (1988). "A Lesson in Rhetoric: Writing and Performing TV Commercials." In J. Golob (Ed.), *Focus on Collaborative Learning: Classroom Practices in Teaching English, 1988* (pp. 133–37). Urbana, IL: National Council of Teachers of English.

Michaelsen, L. (1996). *Problems with Learning Groups: An Ounce of Prevention.* Preconference Workshop, Annual Conference of the Professional and Organizational Development Network in Higher Education. Snowbird Resort and Conference Center, Salt Lake City, UT.

Michaelsen, L.K. (1992). "Team Learning: A Comprehensive Approach for Harnessing the Power of Small Groups in Higher Education." In D.H. Wulff and J.D. Nyquist (Eds.), *To Improve the Academy: Resources for Faculty, Instructional, and Organizational Development,* Vol. 11 (pp. 107–22). The Professional and Organizational Development Network in Higher Education. Stillwater, OK: New Forums Press, Inc.

Michaelsen, L.K., Fink, D.L., and Black, R.H. (1996). "What Every Faculty Developer Needs to Know about Learning Groups." In L. Richlin (Ed.), *To Improve the Academy: Resources for Faculty, Instructional, and Organizational Development,* Vol. 15 (pp. 31–57). The Professional and Organizational Development Network in Higher Education. Stillwater, OK: New Forums Press, Inc.

Miller, J.E. (1995, Oct. 10). Syllabus sent with private correspondence.

Miller, J.E. (1996). "Cognitive Styles and their Relevance in Improving Cooperative Learning Courses." *Cooperative Learning and College Teaching,* 7(1), pp. 11–14.

Miller, M.P. (1996). "Introducing Art History through Problem-based Learning." *About Teaching: A Newsletter of the Center for Teaching Effectiveness,* 50, University of Delaware, 3.

Millis, B.J. (1992). "Conducting Effective Peer Classroom Observations." In D. H. Wulff and J. D. Nyquist (Eds.), *To Improve the Academy: Resources for Faculty, Instructional, and Organizational Development* (pp. 189–201). Stillwater, OK: New Forums Press, Inc.

Millis, B.J. (1994, Spring). "Increasing Thinking through Cooperative Writing." *Cooperative Learning and College Teaching,* 4(3), pp. 7–9.

Millis, B.J. Lyman, F.T., and Davidson, N. (1995). "Cooperative Structures for Higher Education Classrooms." In Harvey C. Foyle (Ed.), *Interactive Learning in the Higher Education Classroom: Cooperative, Collaborative, and Active Learning Strategies* (pp. 204–225). Washington, DC: National Education Association.

Millis, B.J., Cottell, P., and Sherman, L. (1993, Spring). "Stacking the DEC to Promote Critical Thinking: Applications in Three Disciplines." *Cooperative Learning and College Teaching,* 3(3), 12–14.

Milter, R.G. and Stinson, J.E. (1994). "Educating Leaders for the New Competitive Environment." In G. Gijselaers, S. Tempelaar, and S. Keizer (Eds.), *Education Innovation in Economics and Business Administration: The Case of Problem-based Learning*. London: Kluwer Academic Publishers.

Murray, D. (1978). "Internal Revision: A Process of Discovery." In C.R. Cooper and L. O'Dell (Eds.), *Research on Composing: Points of Departure*. (pp. 85–104) Urbana, IL: National Council of Teachers of English.

Murray, F.B. (1994). "Why Understanding the Theoretical Basis of Cooperative Learning Enhances Teaching Success." In J.S. Thousand, R.A. Villa, and A.I. Nevin (Eds.), *Creativity and Collaborative Learning: A Practical Guide to Empowering Students and Teachers* (pp. 3–11). Baltimore, MD: Paul H. Brookes Publishing Co.

Myers, C. and Jones, T.B. (1993). *Promoting Active Learning: Strategies for the College Classroom*. San Francisco: Jossey-Bass.

Natasi, B.K. and Clements D.H. (1991). "Research on Cooperative Learning: Implications for Practice." *School Psychology Review*. 20(1), 110–31.

National Center for Research To Improve Postsecondary Teaching and Learning. (1990). "Teaching Thinking in College." *Accent on Improving College Teaching and Learning*, No. 7. Ann Arbor, Michigan: NCRIPTAL.

Nelson, C.E. (1996). "Student Diversity Requires Different Approaches to College Teaching, Even in Math and Science." *American Behavioral Scientist*. 40(2), 165–175.

Nelson, C.E. (1997). "Tools for Tampering with Teaching's Taboos." In W.E. Campbell and K.A. Smith (Eds.), *New Paradigms for College Teaching*. (pp. 51–77). Edina. MN: Interaction Book Company.

Nevin, A.I., Smith, K., and Udvari-Solner. (1994). "Cooperative Group Learning and Higher Education." In J.S. Thousand, R.A. Villa, and A.I. Nevin (Eds.), *Creativity and Collaborative Learning: A Practical Guide to Empowering Students and Teachers* (pp. 115–27). Baltimore, MD: Paul H. Brookes Publishing Co.

Newmann, F.M. and Wehlage, G.G. (April 1993). "Five Standards for Authentic Instruction." *Educational Leadership*, 50(7), 8–12.

Nuhfer, E.B. (1990). *A Handbook for Student Management Teams*. Denver, CO: The Office of Teaching Effectiveness.

Nuhfer, E.B. (1997). "Student Management Teams—the Heretic's Path to Teaching Success." In W.E. Campbell and K.A. Smith (Eds.), *New Paradigms for College Teaching* (pp. 103–25). Edina, MN: Interaction Book Company.

Nurrenbern, S.C. (Ed.), (1995). *Experiences in Cooperative Learning: A Collection for Chemistry Teachers*. University of Wisconsin-Madison: Institute of Chemical Education.

Nyquist, J.D. and Wulff, D.H. (1988). "Consultation Using a Research Perspective." In E.C. Wadsworth (Ed.), *POD: A Handbook for New Practitioners* (pp. 81–88). Stillwater, OK: New Forums Press, Inc.

O'Donnell, J.J. (1994). *Where Are We Going and When Did We Get There?* Presentation at the 124th annual meeting of the ARL: The Research Library the Day

After Tomorrow. Austin, TX, May 18-20, 1994. Online at <http://sunsite.berkeley.edu/ARL/Proceedings/124/ps2going.html> Downloaded 11 Feb. 1997. No longer available.

O'Donnell, J.J. (1995, March) "Teaching with Technology." *Penn Printout: The University of Pennsylvania's Computing Magazine*. Reprinted in CSS Journal - Computers in the Social Studies. 5.1(1997). Online at <http://ccat.sas.upenn.edu/teachdemo> Downloaded 11 Feb. 1997. No longer available.

Ory, J.C. and Ryan, K.E. (1993). *Tips for Improving Testing and Grading*. Newbury Park, CA: Sage Publications.

Palmer, P.J. (1983). *To Know As We Are Known: A Spirituality of Education*. San Francisco: Harper Collins.

Palmer, P.J. (1997). "The Renewal of Community in Higher Education. In W.E. Campbell and K.A. Smith (Eds.), *New Paradigms for College Teaching* (pp. 1–18). Edina, MN: Interaction Book Company.

Perry, W. (1970). *Forms of Intellectual and Ethical Development in the College Years: A Scheme*. New York: Holt, Rinehart and Winston.

Peters, T. and Waterman, R.H. Jr. (1982). *In Search of Excellence: Lessons from America's Best Run Companies*. New York: Harper and Row.

Pollio, H.R. and Humphreys, W. L. (1990). "Grading Students." In M. Weimer and R.A. Neff (Eds.), *Teaching College: Collected Readings for the New Instructor*. (pp. 109–116) Madison, WI.: Magna Publications.

Prescott, S. (1993, Fall). "Troubleshooting Cooperative Learning." *Cooperative Learning and College Teaching*, 4(1), 6–9.

Prescott, S. (1996, Spring). "Troubleshooting Cooperative Learning." *Cooperative Learning and College Teaching*, 6(3), 10–11.

Presselsen, B.Z. (1992). "A Perspective on the Evolution of Cooperative Thinking." In N. Davidson, and T. Worsham (Eds.), *Enhancing Thinking through Cooperative Learning*, (pp. 1–6) New York: Teachers College Press.

Redding, N. (1990). "The Empowering Learners Project." *Educational Leadership*, 47(5), 46–48.

Rhem, J. (1992). "Getting Past the Doorman." *The National Teaching and Learning Forum*, 2(1), 4.

Rhem, J. (1994). "Conference Report: Emerging Trends in College Teaching for the 21st Century." *The National Teaching and Learning Forum*, 3(4), 12.

Rhem, J. (1995). "Deep/surface Approaches to Learning: An Introduction." *The National Teaching and Learning Forum*, 5(1), 1–3.

Rhem, J. (1995b). "Close-Up: Going Deep." *The National Teaching and Learning Forum*, 5(1), 4.

Rhem, J. (1996). "Urgings and Cautions in Student-centered Teaching." *The National Teaching and Learning Forum*, 5(4), 1–5.

Rhoades, J. and McCabe, M. (1991). "Practice Activities and Your Textbooks." *Cooperative Learning and College Teaching*, 2(1), pp. 6;8.

Rivkin, M.S. (1994). "Using Jigsaw for Perspective-taking." In S. Kadel and J.A. Keehner (Eds.), *Collaborative Learning: A Sourcebook for Higher Education*, Vol.

II (p. 143). University Park, PA: National Center on Postsecondary Teaching, Learning, and Assessment.

Robertson, L., Davidson, N., and Dees, R.L. (1994). "Cooperative Learning to Support Thinking, Reasoning, and Communicating in Mathematics. In S. Sharan (Ed.), *Handbook of Cooperative Learning Methods* (pp, 245–266). Westport, CT: Greenwood Press.

Rowe, M.B. (1974). "Wait-time and Rewards as Instructional Variables: Their Influence on Language, Logic, and Fate Control. *Journal of Research on Science Teaching*, 2, 81–94.

Rowe, M.B. (1978). "Wait, Wait, Wait . . .." *School Science and Mathematics*, 78, 207–16.

Roy, P. (1996). "Staff Development that Makes a Difference." *Cooperative Learning: Publications for Cooperative in Education*. 16(2), 3–12.

Ryan, A. (1993, February 11). "Invasion of the Mind Snatchers." *New York Review of Books*, 15(4), 13–15.

Ryan, M.P. and Martens, G.G. (1989). *Planning a College Course: A Guidebook for the Graduate Teaching Assistant*. Ann Arbor: University of Michigan, National Center for Research to Improve Postsecondary Teaching and Learning.

Salomon, G. (1995). *What does the Design of Effective CSCL Require and How do we Study its Effects?* CSCL '95 Conference, Indiana University, Bloomington, IN. October. Online at <http://www_cscl95.indiana.edu/cscl95/outlook/62_Salomon.html>. downloaded 16 Sept. 1997. No longer available.

Sanford, N. (1966). *Self and Society: Societal Change and Individual Development*. New York: Atherton.

Sapon-Shevin, M., Ayres, B.J., and Duncan, J. (1994). "Cooperative Learning and Inclusion." In J.S. Thousand, R.A. Villa, and A.I. Nevin (Eds.), *Creativity and Collaborative Learning: A Practical Guide to Empowering Students and Teachers* (pp. 45–58). Baltimore, MD: Paul H. Brookes Publishing Co.

Savery, J.R. and Duffy, T.M. (1995, Sept./Oct.). "Problem-based Learning: An Instructional Model and its Constructivist Framework." *Educational Technology*. (pp. 31–38.) Reprinted in *Educational Psychology 97/98 Annual Editions* (pp. 143–51). Guilford, CT: Duskin/McGraw-Hill.

Schmidt, E. (1996) Keynote address, EDUCOM National Conference. Philadelphia, PA, October, 1996. Reviewed by Glogoff, S. Online at <http://dizzy.library.arizona.edu/users/sglogoff/educom96.htm#intro> Downloaded, 11 Feb. 1997. No longer available.

Schon, D.A. (1986). *Educating the Reflective Practitioner: Toward a New Design for Teaching and Learning in the Professions*. San Francisco: Jossey-Bass.

Semb, G.B. and Ellis, J.A. (Summer 1994). "Knowledge Taught in School: What is Remembered?" *Review of Educational Research*, 64(2), 253–86.

Sharan, Y. and Sharan, S. (1992). *Expanding Cooperative Learning through Group Investigation*. New York: Teachers College Press.

Sharon, Y. and Sharan, S. (1994). "Group Investigation in the Cooperative Classroom." In Sharon, S. (Ed.), *Handbook of Cooperative Learning Methods* (pp. 97–114). Westport, CT: Greenwood Press.

Sherman, L.W. (1991). *Cooperative Learning in Postsecondary Education: Implications from Social Psychology for Active Learning.* Paper presented at the annual meeting of the American Educational Research Association, Chicago.

Sherman, S.J. (1994). "Cooperative Learning and Science." In S. Sharan (Ed.), *Handbook of Cooperative Learning Methods* (pp. 226–44). Westport, CT: Greenwood Press.

Silverman, R. and Welty, W. (Winter 1994). "Case Studies to Promote Active Learning in the Classroom," *Chalkboard*, No. 9. University of Missouri-Columbia, pp. 1–2. Adapted with permission from "Case Studies in Diversity for University Faculty Development," Rita Silverman and William Welty, 1993, Center for Case Studies in Education, Pace University.

Skinner, M.E. and Welch, F.C. (1996). "Peer Coaching for Better Teaching" *College Teaching*, 44(4), 153–56.

Slavin, R. E. (1986). *Using Student Team Learning: The Johns Hopkins Team Learning Project.* Baltimore, MD: The Johns Hopkins University Press.

Slavin, R.E. (1989-1990). "Research in Cooperative Learning: Consensus and Controversy." *Educational Leadership*, 47(4), 52–55.

Slavin, R.E. (1993). "What Can Post-secondary Cooperative Learning Learn from Elementary and Secondary Research?" *Cooperative Learning and College Teaching*, 4(1), 2–3.

Smith, B.L. and MacGregor, J.T. (1992). "What is Collaborative Learning?" In A. Goodsell, M. Mahler, V. Tinto., B.L. Smith, and J. MacGregor (Eds.), *Collaborative Learning: A Sourcebook for Higher Education.* (pp. 9–22). University Park, PA: National Center on Postsecondary Teaching, Learning, and Assessment.

Smith, K.A. (1993, Winter). "Cooperative Learning and Problem Solving." *Cooperative Learning and College Teaching*, 3(2), pp. 10–12.

Smith, K.A. and Waller, A.A. (1997). "Cooperative Learning for New College Teachers." In W.E. Campbell and K.A. Smith (Eds.), *New Paradigms for College Teaching* (pp. 183–09). Edina, MN: Interaction Book Company.

Smith, K.A., Johnson, D.W., and Johnson, R.T. (1992). "Cooperative Learning and Positive Change in Higher Education." In A. Goodsell, M. Mahler, V. Tinto, B.L. Smith, and J. MacGregor (Eds.), *Collaborative Learning: A Sourcebook for Higher Education* (pp. 34–36). University Park, PA: National Center on Postsecondary Teaching, Learning, and Assessment.

Smith, P. (1996). *An Exercise in Designing Software from Specifications.* Online at <http://bingen.cs.csbsju….SoftwareEngineering.html> Downloaded 25 June 1996. No longer available.

Soloman, R., Davidson, N., and Soloman, E. (1993). *The Handbook for the Fourth R: Relationship Activities for Cooperative and Collegial Learning,* Vol. III. Columbia, MD: National Institute for Relationship Training.

Sousa, D.A. (1995). *How the Brain Learns: A Classroom Teacher's Guide.* Reston, VA: The National Association of Secondary School Principals.

Sparks, G. (1983). "Synthesis on Research on Staff Development for Effective Teaching." *Educational Leadership*, 42(6), 65–72.

Stanford Forum for Higher Education Futures (1995). *Leveraged Learning: Technology's Role in Restructuring Higher Education.* Technology and Restructuring Roundtable. Palo Alto, CA: Stanford Forum for Higher Education Futures.

Supinski, S. (1996). *A Comparison of Simultaneous versus Sequential Use of Interactive Video Instruction and Cooperative Learning: Effects on Achievement, Amount of Invested Mental Effort, and Attitudes.* Unpublished doctoral dissertation, Florida State University.

Sugar, S. (1994). Workshop at the University of Maryland. College Park, MD.

Svensson, L. and Hogfors, C. (1988). "Conceptions as the Content of Teaching: Improving Education in Mechanics. In P. Ramsden (Ed.), *Improving Learning: New Perspectives* (pp. 255–72). London: Kogan.

Svinicki, M.D. (1991). "Practical Implications of Cognitive Theories." In R.J. Menges and M.D. Svinicki (Eds.), *College Teaching: From Theory to Practice. New Directions for Teaching and Learning,* No. 45 (pp. 27–37). San Francisco: Jossey-Bass.

Svinicki, M.D. (1991). "Theories and Metaphors We Teach By." In R.J. Menges and M.D. Svinicki (Eds.), *College Teaching: From Theory to Practice. New Directions for Teaching and Learning,* No. 45 (pp. 111–19). San Francisco: Jossey-Bass.

Svinicki, M.D. (1996). "When Teachers Become Learners." *The National Teaching and Learning Forum,* 5(3), 1–5.

Tenenberg, J.D. (1995). *Using Cooperative Learning in the Undergraduate Computer Science Classroom.* Paper to appear in the Proceedings of the Midwest Small College Computing Conference, 1995. Online at <http://phoenix.iusb.edu/ ...coop/papers/mwscc95.html> Downloaded 25 June 1996. No longer available.

Topor, R. (1996). "How to Run a Focus Group for Higher Education." Sample article from *Marketing Higher Education.* Online at <http://www.marketing.com/ news/focus.html> Downloaded 23 Dec. 1996.

Toppins, A.D. (1989). "Teaching by Testing: A Group Consensus Approach." *College Teaching,* 37(3), 96–99.

Tower, P. (1995). "Teaching with Cases: The Tao of the Classroom." *USAFA Educator,* 4(1), pp. 1; 4–6.

Treisman, U. (1985). "A Study of the Mathematics Performance of Black Students at the University of California, Berkeley [Doctoral Dissertation, University of California, Berkeley, 1986]." *Dissertation Abstracts International,* 47, 1641A.

Ventimiglia, L.M. (1994, Winter). "Cooperative Learning at the College Level." *Thought and Action: The NEA Almanac of Higher Education,* 9(2), 5–30.

Watson, W.E., Kumar, K., and Michaelsen, L.K. (1993). ""Cultural Diversity's Impact on Group Process and Performance: Comparing Culturally Homogeneous and Culturally Diverse Task Groups." *The Academy of Management Journal.* 36(3), 590–602.

Watson, W.E., Michaelsen, L.K. and Sharp, W. (1991). "Member Competence, Group Interaction, and Group Decision-making: A Longitudinal Study." *Journal of Applied Psychology,* 76, 801–809.

Weaver, M. (1997). *The First Amendment and the Howard Stern Show*. Presentation at the 1997 Regional Conference on College Teaching: Using Cooperative Learning in Discipline-Specific Settings. February 21–22, 1997, Occidental College, Los Angeles.

Webb, N. (1983). "Predicting Learning from Student Interaction: Defining the Interaction Variable." *Educational Psychologist*, 18, 33–41.

Webb, N. (1991). "Task-related Verbal Interaction and Mathematics Learning in Small Groups." *Journal of Research in Mathematics Education*, 22, 366–389.

Weimer, M. (1990). *Improving College Teaching*. San Francisco: Jossey-Bass.

Weimer, M.G. (1988). "Reading Your Way to Better Teaching." *College Teaching*, 36(2), 48–53.

Weimer, M.G. (1992). "Improving Higher Education: Issues and Perspectives on Teaching and Learning." In D.W. Wulff, and J.D. Nyquist (Eds.), *To Improve the Academy: Resources for Faculty, Instructional and Organizational Development* (pp. 13–23). The Professional and Organizational Development Network in Higher Education. Stillwater, OK: New Forums Press, Inc.

Wellins, R.S, Byham, W.C., and Wilson, J.M. (1991). *Empowered Teams: Creating Self-directed Work Groups that Improve Quality, Productivity, and Participation*. San Francisco: Jossey-Bass.

Whimbey, A. and Whimbey, L. (1975). *Intelligence Can be Taught*. New York: Innovative Science.

Whimbey, A. (1984). "The Key to Higher Order Thinking is Precise Processing." *Educational Leadership*, 42(1), 66–70.

White, K. (1991). "Small Group Instructional Diagnosis: Alternate Adult Assessment." *Adult Assessment Forum*, 1(3), pp. 6–7;10.

Whitman, N.A. (1988). *Peer Teaching: To Teach Is To Learn Twice*. ASHE-ERIC Higher Education Report No. 4. Washington, DC: Association for the Study of Higher Education.

Widick, C., Knelfelkamp, L., and Parker, C. (1975). "The Counselor as Developmental Instructor." *Counselor Education and Supervision*, 14, 286–296.

Wilkerson, L. and Boehrer, J. (1992). "Using Cases about Teaching for Faculty Development." In D. H. Wulff and J. D. Nyquist (Eds.), *To Improve the Academy: Resources for Faculty, Instructional, and Organizational Development*, 11 (pp. 253–262). The Professional and Organizational Development Network in Higher Education, Stillwater, OK: New Forums Press, Inc.

Wilkerson, L. (1988). "Classroom Observation: The Observer as Collaborator. In E. C. Wadsworth (Ed.), *POD: A Handbook for New Practitioners* (pp. 95–98). Stillwater, OK: New Forums Press, Inc.

Williamson, S.R. (1996). "When Change is the Only Constant: Liberal Education in the Age of Technology." *EDUCOM Review*. 31(6), 31–49.

Wolcott, S.K. and Lynch, C.L. (1997). *Critical Thinking in the Accounting Classroom: A Reflective Judgment Model*. Unpublished manuscript.

Wood, F.H. and Thompson, S.R. (1993). "Assumptions about Staff Development based on Research and Best Practice." *Journal of Staff Development*, 14(4), 52–57.

Woods, D.R. (1994). *Problem-based Learning: How to Gain the Most from PBL*. Waterdown, ON: Donald R. Woods.

Woods, D.R. (1996). *Instructor's Guide for "Problem-based Learning: How to Gain the Most from PBL."* 3rd Ed. Online at <http://chemeng.mcmaster.ca/pbl/pbl.htm> Downloaded 14 January 1997.

Woods, D.R. (1997) Two-day workshop on Problem-Based Learning, US Air Force Academy.

Wright, S.P. and Hendershott, A. (1992). In D.H. Wulff and J.D. Nyquist (Eds.), *To Improve the Academy: Resources for Faculty, Instructional, and Organizational Development* (pp.87–104). Stillwater, OK: New Forums Press, Inc.

Wulff, D.H. (1994). "The Case of the Worrisome Workload." In W.C. Rando and L.F. Lenze, *Learning from Students: Early Term Feedback in Higher Education* (pp. 29–32). University Park, PA: National Center on Postsecondary Teaching, Learning, and Assessment.

Wulff, D.H. (1996, Fall). Small Group Instructional Diagnosis (SGID) Training workshops conducted at the US Air Force Academy.

Ziegler, L. (1996). *Cooperative Learning: A Normal Class Day*. Online at <http://bingen.cs.csbsju.edu/~lziegler/normal.html> Downloaded 25 June 1996.

INDEX

by Cynthia D. Bertelsen

FACULTY
DEVELOPMENT
COLLECTION